MW00444249

The Grace of God,
the Bondage of the Will

MR|234.9/sch|v.02

The Grace of God, the Bondage of the Will

Volume 2

Historical and Theological Perspectives on Calvinism

Edited by Thomas R. Schreiner and
Bruce A. Ware

RMR- 1531

Baker Books

A Division of Baker Book House Co
Grand Rapids, Michigan 49516

© 1995 by Thomas R. Schreiner and Bruce A. Ware

Published by Baker Books
a division of Baker Book House Company
P.O. Box 6287, Grand Rapids, MI 49516-6287

Printed in the United States of America

All rights reserved. No part of this publication may be reproduced, stored in a retrieval system, or transmitted in any form or by any means—for example, electronic, photocopy, recording—without the prior written permission of the publisher. The only exception is brief quotations in printed reviews.

Library of Congress Cataloging-in-Publication Data

The grace of God, the bondage of the will / edited by Thomas R. Schreiner and Bruce A. Ware.
    p.   cm.
    Includes bibliographical references.
    Contents: v. 1. Biblical and practical perspectives on Calvinism.—v. 2. Theological and historical perspectives on Calvinism.
    ISBN 0-8010-2002-6 (v. 1 : pbk.).—ISBN 0-8010-2003-4 (v. 2 : pbk.).
    1. Grace (Theology). 2. Calvinism. 3. Arminianism. 4. Predestination—Biblical teaching. I. Schreiner, Thomas R. II. Ware, Bruce A.
BT761.2.G694   1995
234'.9—dc20   95-6821

Unless otherwise indicated, Scripture taken from the HOLY BIBLE, NEW INTERNATIONAL VERSION®. NIV®. Copyright © 1973, 1978, 1984 by International Bible Society. Used by permission of Zondervan Publishing House. All rights reserved.

Contents

Part 3
Historical Perspectives

11

Grace, Election, and Contingent Choice: Arminius's Gambit and the Reformed Response

RICHARD A. MULLER

The Arminian controversy of the first two decades of the seventeenth century marked a major turning point in the history of Protestant teaching.[1] The great Reformers of the sixteenth century, whether Luther, Bucer, Zwingli, Calvin, Bullinger, Vermigli, or their various contemporaries, had taught a doctrine of justification by grace alone through faith and had anchored faith itself in the grace of God. All held one or another of the views of predestination found in the Augustinian exegesis of Paul and elaborated in the Augus-

---

1. On Arminius and the Arminian controversy, see Carl Bangs, *Arminius: A Study in the Dutch Reformation* (Nashville: Abingdon, 1971); Gerald McCulloh, ed., *Man's Faith and Freedom: The Theological Influence of Jacobus Arminius* (Nashville: Abingdon, 1962); A. W. Harrison, *Arminianism* (London: Duckworth, 1937), 19–23, 29–30, 39–40; A. C. McGiffert, *Protestant Thought Before Kant* (London: Duckworth, 1911), 149–50; I. A. Dorner, *History of Protestant Theology*, trans. George Robson and Sophia Taylor, 2 vols. (Edinburgh, 1871), 1:417–19; Otto Ritschl, *Dogmengeschichte des Protestantismus*, 4 vols. (Leipzig: Hinrichs/Göttingen: Vandenhoeck und Ruprecht, 1908–1927), 3:314–39; Hans Emil Weber, *Reformation, Othodoxie und Rationalismus*, 2 vols. (Gütersloh: Gerd Mohn, 1937–1951), 2:98–100; and Richard A. Muller, *God, Creation, and Providence in the Thought of Jacob Arminius: Sources and Directions of Scholastic Protestantism in the Era of Early Orthodoxy* (Grand Rapids: Baker, 1991).

tinian tradition of the Middle Ages. In addition, none of the writers, certainly not Calvin, assumed that the doctrine of predestination was a form of fatalism or philosophical determinism that removed human responsibility.[2] Calvin explicitly states that the "universal operation" by which God "guides all creatures" in no way prevents a creature "from having and retaining its own quality and nature and from following its own inclination."[3] Nor, on the other side of the question, did Bullinger, who held a doctrine of single predestination and who emphasized the reciprocity of God and man in covenant, teach anything other than that grace alone was the ground of salvation, that human beings were incapable of inaugurating the work of salvation, and that faith itself is the result of God's gracious activity.[4]

There is, as indicated in the initial examples from Calvin and Bullinger, a spectrum of opinion in the Reformed theology of the sixteenth and the seventeenth centuries. It is not the case that there was a monolithic Reformed doctrine of predestination, and while it is certainly true that Calvin's doctrine represents one of the strictest formulations of the divine decree and perhaps the formulation that is least sensitive to traditional discussions of divine permission and secondary causality, it is also the case that his views were balanced out in the Reformed tradition by the milder formulations of Bullinger and by the more traditional and more technically adept formulations of Vermigli and Musculus. As for Calvin's successor, Theodore Beza, we must recognize (contrary to much received opinion) that Beza softened somewhat the impact of this doctrine of predestination by stressing, far more than Calvin, the concept of divine permission and the role of secondary causality.[5]

Related to the diversity of the Reformed tradition is another issue crucial to our understanding of the character of Arminius's protest: the development of Protestant scholasticism. Much of the discussion of this subject has linked scholasticism and predestinarianism, as if the rise of a scholastic form of Re-

2. Cf. John Calvin, *Institutes of the Christian Religion* (1559), ed. John T. McNeill, trans. Ford Lewis Battles, 2 vols. (Philadelphia: Westminster, 1960), 1.16.8; 3.23.6; with Paul Jacobs, *Prädestination und Verantwortlichkeit bei Calvin* (Neukirchen: Neukirchner Verlag, 1937); and note also the extensive rebuttal of these charges in the theology of Calvin's contemporary, Peter Martyr Vermigli, *Loci communes* (London, [2]1583), 3.1.5.

3. John Calvin, *Treatises Against the Anabaptists and Against the Libertines*, trans. and ed. Benjamin Wirt Farley (Grand Rapids: Baker, 1982), 242–43.

4. See Heinrich Bullinger, *Confessio et exposition simplex orthodoxae fidei* (Zürich, 1566), 10.1–2; 15.5; 16.1; text in Philip Schaff, *The Creeds of Christendom: with a History and Critical Notes*, 3 vols., 6th ed., rev. and enl. (New York: Harper and Row, 1931; reprint, Grand Rapids: Baker, 1983), 3:233–306; translation, 831–909.

5. Cf. Richard A. Muller, *Christ and the Decree: Christology and Predestination in Reformed Theology from Calvin to Perkins* (Durham, N.C.: Labyrinth, 1986; 2d printing, with corrections, Grand Rapids: Baker, 1988), 39–96; John S. Bray, *Theodore Beza's Doctrine of Predestination* (Nieuwkoop: DeGraaf, 1975), passim; and Tadataka Maruyama, *The Ecclesiology of Theodore Beza: The Reform of the True Church* (Geneva: Droz, 1978), 22, 138–48, 198–99.

formed theology is causally linked to the creation of a more rigid and increasingly supralapsarian doctrine of predestination. This view must be rejected categorically. In the Middle Ages, the strict Augustinian predestinarianism of Gregory of Rimini was no more scholastic in its exposition than was the refined semi-Pelagianism of Gabriel Biel. Among the Reformers, the scholastically trained Vermigli taught a more nuanced doctrine of predestination, with more attention to issues of freedom and contingency than did Calvin, who, as far as can be determined, was not trained in scholastic theology and who certainly never developed a great liking for its distinctions.[6] The development of a more scholastic theological method in followers and students of Calvin, among them Beza and Daneau, led to the introduction of qualifying concepts such as the divine permission. And it is easily shown that Arminius's theology not only reflects that of Biel at certain points, but that it is just as scholastic in its method as the theology of Reformed writers like Junius, Perkins, and Gomarus. Arminius did not reject the renewed scholasticism of the age nor did he simply react against the more strict voices in the Reformed tradition.[7]

As Arminius makes clear in his *Declaration of Sentiments*, he found repugnant not only the supralapsarian views of Perkins and Gomarus but also the infralapsarian views of Bullinger, the Belgic Confession, Ursinus, and Junius. He argued that the supralapsarian view stood in contradiction to the Reformed confessions but then rejected the infralapsarian view as well by defining his objections in terms of the mild Lutheran synergism of Melanchthon and Hemmingsen.[8] His own formulations dealing with the issues of election, grace, free will, and the related problem of the extent of divine concurrence in free or contingent events looked beyond the Lutheran synergists to the refined metaphysics of the Jesuit teachers, Francis Suárez and Luis de Molina.[9]

6. Cf. J. C. McClelland, "The Reformed Doctrine of Predestination according to Peter Martyr," *SJT* 8 (1955): 255–71; with John Patrick Donnelly, *Calvinism and Scholasticism in Vermigli's Doctrine of Man and Grace* (Leiden: Brill, 1975).

7. Cf. Richard A. Muller, "Arminius and the Scholastic Tradition," *CTJ* 24, 2 (November 1989): 263–77 with idem, *God, Creation and Providence*, 15–51.

8. Jacob Arminius, *Declaration of Sentiments*, in *The Works of James Arminius*, trans. James Nichols and William Nichols, 3 vols. (London, 1825, 1828, 1875; reprint with an intro. by Carl Bangs, Grand Rapids: Baker, 1986), 1:613–53. This "London" edition is preferable to the often reprinted American edition of Bagnall both because of the supplementary materials included by Nichols in volume 1 and because of the inclusion of the *Examination of the Theses of Dr. Francis Gomarus* in volume 3. I have compared and occasionally emended the Nichols translation on the basis of the Latin text of Arminius as found in Jacobus Arminius, *Opera theologica* (Leiden, 1629) and Jacobus Arminius, *Examen thesium D. Francisci Gomari de praedestinatione* (Amsterdam, 1645). The latter work does not appear in the Latin *Opera* of 1629, even though it had already been published in Leiden in 1613; it is, however, translated in *Works*, 3:521–658.

9. Cf. Muller, "Arminius and the Scholastic Tradition," 263–77 with idem, *God, Creation, and Providence*, 43–46, 155–64, 254–55.

Arminius's theology was not, therefore, a protest against philosophical determinism or even against a denial of human freedom and responsibility. Neither of these problems was resident in the Reformed theology of the six-teenth century, certainly not in the infralapsarian teachings of the Reformed confessions. Nor was Arminius's theology, considered as a whole, simply a protest against the Reformed doctrine of predestination. It was an attempt to produce a large-scale alternative to the entire Reformed theological system, indeed, to review and to revise the Protestant understanding of the relation-ship between God and world in terms not merely of the doctrines of grace and predestination but also in terms of the doctrines of God, creation, provi-dence, covenant, and the person and work of Christ.[10]

Arminius and the Doctrine of Predestination

Arminius's theological training in Leiden and Geneva was, of course, strongly Reformed; but it was not, as often stated, so rigidly supralapsarian as to produce a massive reaction against Reformed orthodoxy in the young Arminius.[11] In Leiden he sat under Guilhelmus Feuguereus and Lambert Da-neau. The former was a biblical scholar and the editor of Augustin Mar-lorat's *Scripture Thesaurus* (1574) and the latter, though a scholastic in method, was influenced deeply by his studies of the Fathers and was dis-tinctly infralapsarian in both his placement and his exposition of predestina-tion. Arminius's studies in Geneva (1582–1587) present a similar picture: de-spite the supralapsarian tendencies of Beza, the *Harmony of Reformed Confessions* produced in that era and the student theses in the Academy—we have a set in print from 1585—were infralapsarian in their teaching. Indeed, the *Harmony* chose as its central document Bullinger's Second Helvetic Con-fession. There is no evidence of a rigid "Bezan" predestinarianism in Geneva in the late sixteenth century. On the contrary, Arminius would have imbibed there, as in Leiden, a Reformed theology that respected Bullinger as well as Calvin, Ursinus and Zanchi as well as Beza.[12]

10. See Richard A. Muller, "The Federal Motif in Seventeenth Century Arminian Theolo-gy," *Nederlands Archief voor Kerkgeschiedenis* 62, 1 (1982): 102–22; "The Christological Problem in the Thought of Jacobus Arminius," *Nederlands Archief voor Kerkgeschiedenis* 68, 1 (1988): 145–63; and "God, Predestination, and the Integrity of the Created Order: A Note on Patterns in Arminius' Theology," in *Later Calvinism: International Perspectives*, ed. W. Fred Graham, Sixteenth Century Essays and Studies (Kirksville, Mo.: Sixteenth Century Journal Pub-lishers, 1993), 431–46.
11. Cf. the discussion in Muller, *God, Creation and Providence*, 3–30, with Carl Bangs, *Arminius: A Study in the Dutch Reformation* (Nashville: Abingdon, 1971), 68–69, 139–41.
12. Muller, *God, Creation, and Providence*, 19–22.

The last decade of the sixteenth century found Arminius again in Leiden and immersed in the study of Paul's Epistle to the Romans. He first directed his attention to the seventh chapter and the problem of the will. He then addressed the problem of predestination in the ninth chapter and engaged in a detailed and exceedingly cordial epistolary debate on that doctrine with Franciscus Junius. In the first of these enquiries, Arminius moved away from the traditional Augustinian pattern of the Reformers and argued that the inward struggle of Paul was a preconversion, not a postconversion, struggle. Here already are hints of a synergism in which the human will takes the first step toward grace.[13] In the second study, Arminius argued that Isaac and Ishmael, Jacob and Esau are not individuals but types and that the ninth chapter of Romans does not refer to individual predestination.[14] Similar arguments appear in the debate with Junius.[15] Arminius then encountered William Perkins's *De praedestinatione modo et ordine* (1598) and reacted strongly against its doctrine—not only against the supralapsarianism of Perkins, but against the general implications of the Reformed doctrine of predestination.[16] Since these documents were not immediately published, the Reformed community did not become aware in detail of the changes in his position, although his preaching "procured him . . . little favor with most of his ministerial brethren" and brought accusations of departure from the teaching of the confessions even during his first years of ministry.[17]

As Carl Bangs has shown, we can no longer look to the controversy over the theology of Dirk Coornhert for the wellsprings of Arminius's thought: there is no evidence that Arminius was ever called upon to engage in the debate.[18] Instead, we must hypothesize a fairly long development of Arminius's thought. Not only did Arminius intentionally work through a series of key biblical and theological loci related to the problems of grace, human will, and predestination, he also became acquainted with a series of Lutheran and Roman Catholic views in which alternative approaches to these problems were to be found. Thus, he later commented that "the Lutheran and Anabaptist churches, as well as that of Rome" view the Reformed doctrine of predestination as erroneous, and he noted in particular the teachings of

13. Jacob Arminius, *Dissertation on the True and Genuine Sense of the Seventh Chapter of the Epistle to the Romans*, in *Works*, 2:491–92, 497–98, 541–44.

14. Jacob Arminius, *A Brief Analysis of the Ninth Chapter of St. Paul's Epistle to the Romans*, in *Works*, 3:490–99.

15. Jacob Arminius, *Friendly Conference . . . with Francis Junius, about Predestination, carried on by Means of Letters*, in *Works*, 3:93.

16. Jacob Arminius, *Modest Examination of a Pamphlet, which that Learned Divine, Dr. William Perkins, published . . . On the Mode and Order of Predestination*, in *Works*, 3:276, 284–85, 294, 296–98.

17. Caspar Brandt, *The Life of James Arminius, D.D.*, trans. John Guthrie, with an intro. by T. O. Summers (Nashville: Stevenson and Owen, 1857), 67; cf. Bangs, *Arminius*, 140–41.

18. Bangs, *Arminius*, 138–41.

Melanchthon and of the Danish Lutheran theologian, Hemmingsen, as offering an alternative view. Even in the church of the Netherlands, he continued, strict Reformed predestinarianism was declared problematic by such ministers and theologians as Koolhaes, Herberts, Wiggertson, and Sybrants.[19]

In 1603, Arminius, still a virtually unknown quantity, succeeded Junius as professor of theology at Leiden.[20] The appointment process itself was marred by controversy, particularly by the opposition of Francis Gomarus, then professor of theology. Gomarus claimed to have known of Junius's opposition to Arminius and to have seen the unpublished correspondence, but he could produce no solid evidence of problems in Arminius's theology.[21] Shortly after his appointment, however, Arminius began to manifest more publicly the change of mind that had taken place in his theology over the past decade. His two sets of *Disputations*, public and private, indicate both the refinement of Arminius's thought during his years of teaching in the university and a certain reluctance, particularly in the *Public Disputations*, to argue his case against early Reformed orthodoxy. The first rumblings of dispute arose as rumor and accusation about his approach to theology in the classroom.[22] Eventually, Arminius's pronouncements on predestination, as expressed in a public disputation against a set of theses by his colleague, Gomarus, and his views on Christ's divinity, debated in a christological controversy with another colleague, Trelcatius, brought down on him the ire of the theological faculty.[23] These debates occupied the remainder of Arminius's life.

Arminius's most complete discussion of his doctrine of predestination is found in the *Declaratio sententiae* or *Declaration of Sentiments* he offered before the States of Holland at The Hague in 1608. In this work, he both analyzes various views of predestination found among the Reformed and presents his own mature teaching. As is true of other writings of Arminius, however, both the highly politicized context of the document and his training in Reformed theology led to elements of ambiguity in his thought and created the possibility that many of his statements could be read as quite in accord with the Reformed confessions and, on certain distinct issues, even in accord

---

19. Arminius, *Declaration of Sentiments*, in *Works*, 3:641–43; on Koolhaes, Herberts, Wiggerston, and Sybrants see Gerard Brandt, *The History of the Reformation and Other Ecclesiastical Transactions In and About the Low Countries, down to the Famous Synod of Dort*, 4 vols. (London, 1720–1723; reprint, New York: AMS, 1979), 1:367–69, 382, 388, 392, 404–6, 450–51; 2:33.

20. Bangs, *Arminius*, 231–39.

21. Ibid., 234.

22. Cf. Muller, *God, Creation, and Providence*, 24–28, 39–42, with Bangs, *Arminius*, 261–64.

23. See Arminius, *Examination of the Theses of Dr. Francis Gomarus*, in *Works*, 3:526–658; *Declaration of Sentiments*, in *Works*, 1:691–95; Arminius, *Letter to Hippolytus à Collibus*, in *Works*, 1:690–96; and cf. Bangs, *Arminius*, 263–64, 281–82, and Muller, "The Christological Problem in the Thought of Jacobus Arminius," 145–63.

with specific teachings of his most vociferous detractors, notably Gomarus. The problem of Arminian theology must be understood and examined, therefore, with close attention to the broader context of Arminius's teaching in his own theology and to the rather finely nuanced definitions and distinctions characteristic of the Protestant scholasticism of his day.

The *Declaration of Sentiments* does make immediately clear from its rejection of doctrines that Arminius denied both the supralapsarian and the infralapsarian perspectives of the Reformed. In addition, rather than follow the Reformed doctrine of a single eternal decree and its series of logically ordered objects he outlined four decrees resting on an order of priorities in the mind of God and on a distinction between the antecedent or absolute and the consequent or conditional and respective divine will. The identification of four distinct degrees was itself viewed as a suspect and excessively speculative development by Reformed theologians of the day.[24] Furthermore, only the first two of the four decrees are defined by Arminius as absolute; the third stands relative to the administration of temporal means, and the fourth is clearly consequent upon the divine foreknowledge of human choice. Indeed it was the language of Arminius's fourth decree that raised the most difficulties among the Reformed.

According to Arminius, the first decree is made without reference to individuals—it is a general decree expressive of the antecedent gracious will of God:

> The first absolute decree of God concerning the salvation of sinful man, is that by which he decreed to appoint his Son, Jesus Christ, for a Mediator, Redeemer, Savior, Priest, and King, who might destroy sin by his death, might by his obedience obtain the salvation which had been lost, and might impart it by his own efficacy *(virtute sua communicet).*[25]

Like the Reformed, Arminius views predestination as grounded in Christ, and like many of the infralapsarians, he understands a single decree of predestination to salvation. Unlike the Reformed view, however, this first decree embodies a general will of God to make salvation available, perhaps although not explicitly related to the universal call of the gospel, and not directed toward the salvation of particular individuals. Also, quite distinct from the Reformed, Arminius tends to subordinate the Son to the decree of the Father. In his Christology, in a parallel fashion, he emphasizes the subordination of the Son in the order of the Persons. The result is that the second person of the Trinity is, in the Arminian system, subordinate to the decree

---

24. Pierre DuMoulin, *The Anatome of Arminianisme: or, The opening of the Controversies lately handled in the Low-Countryes* (London, 1620), 5.
25. Arminius, *Declaration of Sentiments,* in *Works,* 1:653; cf. Arminius, *Certain Articles,* 15.1, in *Works,* 3:718–19.

and not, as the Reformed insist, at the same time electing God and elected or anointed Mediator.[26]

The relationship of the will of God to the effecting of salvation in individuals is the subject of Arminius's second decree, like the first, an antecedent will of God.

> The second precise and absolute decree of God is that in which he decreed to receive into his favor those who repent and believe, in Christ, for His sake and through Him, to effect the salvation of such penitents and believers as persevered to the end; but to leave in sin and under wrath all impenitent persons and unbelievers, and to damn them as aliens from Christ.[27]

This second decree presumes the first, so that salvation continues to be defined as occurring in Christ, but this decree also appears to rest salvation on foreknowledge of human repentance, belief, and perseverance. Indeed, it is hardly a decree at all; rather it is a decision to receive those who accept the general offer as determined by the first decree. In addition, this decree still relates to humanity in general, not to specific individuals: it is decreed apart from consideration of individual people. From a Reformed point of view, such teaching has a decidedly Pelagian tendency inasmuch as it raises in eternity the issue of the priority of human choice.

In the third decree Arminius still refers to an antecedent willing in God, without reference to specific human beings:

> The third divine decree is that by which God decreed to administer in a sufficient and efficacious manner the means which were necessary for repentance and faith; and to have such administration instituted (1) according to the Divine Wisdom, by which God knows what is proper and becoming both to his mercy and his severity, and (2) according to Divine Justice, by which He is prepared to adopt whatever his wisdom may prescribe and to put it in execution.[28]

By means, Arminius indicates preaching, sacraments, and the instrumental order of grace as a whole—it is a grace sufficient and efficacious, he notes, but the sufficiency and efficacy are always qualified by human choice. In addition, his argument is quite similar to, and probably based upon, Molina's hypothesis of a divine middle knowledge or *scientia media*:[29] here God provides the conditions for the future contingent acts of individual human beings.

26. Cf. Muller, "The Christological Problem," 150–52, with the discussion of the Reformed perspective in idem, *Christ and the Decree*, 154–71.

27. Arminius, *Declaration of Sentiments*, in *Works*, 1:653; cf. Arminius, *Certain Articles*, 15.2, in *Works*, 2:719.

28. Arminius, *Declaration of Sentiments*, in *Works*, 1:653; cf. Arminius, *Certain Articles*, 15.3, in *Works*, 2:719.

29. Cf. Muller, *God, Creation, and Providence*, 162–63, 250–51.

Finally, in a fourth decree, Arminius arrives at the actual effecting of salvation. The three previous decrees had defined no more than preparation of causes and conditions and the establishment of the divine will toward sinners antecedent to their decision to believe and, in quite a few of their phrases, could have been construed in a favorable relationship to the doctrine of the Reformed confessions. In the fourth decree, Arminius points more clearly toward his divergence from the Reformed:

> To these succeeds the fourth decree, by which God decreed to save and damn certain particular persons. This decree is grounded in the foreknowledge of God, by which he knew from eternity those individals who, according to the administration of those means which are suitable and proper for conversion and faith, through his prevenient grace, would believe, and through his subsequent grace would persevere; [and, by which foreknowledge,] he likewise knew those who would not believe and persevere.[30]

Salvation and damnation, then, according to Arminius, are eternally decreed on the basis of foreknown belief and unbelief. The antecedent will to save is juxtaposed with a consequent will to save particular human beings, and the effective will of God, therefore, rests on the foreknowledge of a future contingency. Although this point in itself ran counter to the tendency of Reformed theology, there is nonetheless a subtlety and a vagueness in Arminius's definition that might, even in this discussion of a consequent divine willing, yield a result not utterly out of conformity with the Reformed position: Arminius does insist that repentance, faith, and perseverance rest on a prevenient divine grace. The question that his discussion of the decrees leaves unanswered is whether the reception of grace itself rests on human choice. It is therefore to Arminius's teaching on grace that we now turn.

Grace, Free Choice, and Future Contingents in Arminius's Thought

Grace and the problems of the will and free choice also occupied Arminius's thought and became subjects of controversy as his theology developed, although not with the intensity or in the detail of the debate over predestination.[31] Here, too, granting the political context of some of the documents,

---

30. Arminius, *Declaration of Sentiments*, in *Works*, 1:653–54; cf. Arminius, *Certain Articles*, 15.4, in *Works*, 2:719.

31. The chief sources of Arminius's position are the *Letter to Hippolytus à Collibus*, in *Works*, 2:700–701; *Declaration of Sentiments*, in *Works*, 1:659–64; *Public Disputations*, 9–11; and *Private Disputations*, 42–43; and extended treatment of Arminius's doctrine is available in John Mark Hicks, "The Theology of Grace in the Thought of Jacobus Arminius and Philip van

Arminius's teaching is worded carefully and, at some points, vaguely. Thus, Arminius's *Letter to Hippolytus à Collibus* was an attempt to clear his name of charges of heterodoxy that had been spread as far as the Rhenish Palatinate: the addressee was the ambassador of the Palatinate to the United Provinces of the Netherlands. Although its order of topics is different, the *Letter* covers much the same ground as the *Declaration of Sentiments* and contains what may be Arminius's clearest summary statement on the topic of grace and its necessity in salvation. "Free choice," Arminius asserts, "is unable to begin or to perfect any true and spiritual good, without grace." It follows, therefore, that "grace . . . is simply and absolutely necessary for the illumination of the mind, the ordering of the affections, and the inclination of the will to that which is good" and that "this [grace] begins salvation, supports it, perfects and consummates it."[32] The *Letter*, however, neither fully defines grace nor indicates the precise relation of the will and its power of choice to the work of grace—and Arminius refers the ambassador to his public disputation on free choice.[33]

Grace receives clearer definition in the *Declaration of Sentiments*, where Arminius makes a series of three distinctions on grace relating to God, the human subject, and the work of the Spirit. In the first place, grace is "a freely given affection by which God is positively moved *[bene affectus est]* toward a miserable sinner." Second, it is "an infusion of all the gifts of the Holy Spirit that pertain to regeneration and renovation into the intellect and also into the will and affections of a human being." And third, grace is also the "ongoing assistance or continuing assistance of the Holy Spirit" that brings about good thoughts and desires, enabling the will to direct itself toward the good.[34] Arminius's language both here and in his letter to Hippolytus à Collibus is not overtly synergistic, although it is probably significant that he consistently places intellect prior to will and affections, rather than argue, as had Calvin, a distinct priority of the will in matters of sin and salvation.[35] In addition, while Arminius did insist on the necessity of grace in "the commence-

---

Limborch: A Study in the Development of Seventeenth-Century Dutch Arminianism" (Ph.D. dissertation, Westminister Theological Seminary, 1985).

32. Arminius, *Letter to Hippolytus à Collibus*, in *Works*, 2:700; cf. the Latin text in *Opera*, 944: the Nichols translation speaks of "grace and free will," but the Latin text speaks of "gratia et liberum arbitrium," that is, "grace and free choice."

33. *Public Disputations*, 11.7, 12, and cf. *Private Disputations*, 43.1–2.

34. Arminius, *Declaration of Sentiments*, in *Works*, 1:661–62.

35. Cf. Richard A. Muller, "Fides and Cognitio in Relation to the Problem of Intellect and Will in the Theology of John Calvin," *CTJ* 25, 2 (November 1990): 207–24, and idem, "The Priority of the Intellect in the Soteriology of Jacob Arminius," *WTJ* 55 (1993): 55–72, with Bangs, *Arminius*, 342–44, where Bangs argues Arminius's monergism on the ground of the necessity of grace for salvation in Arminius's thought. This teaching, however, is not the determiner of monergism unless the necessary grace is the sole "mover" or "worker" in the initiation of salvation. See the discussion in Hicks, "Theology of Grace," 64–69.

ment, the continuance, and the consummation" of salvation, he also insisted that "many persons resist the Holy Spirit and reject the grace offered."[36]

On this issue of prevenient grace and its character, Arminius does make a fairly clear declaration in his *Apology or Defense*. It was alleged against him that he claimed, in semi-Pelagian fashion, that a man might do good apart from grace and that he accepted a late medieval, semi-Pelagian maxim, "To those who do what is in them, God will not deny grace."[37] Arminius countered that no good could arise apart from grace and that even Adam needed the assistance of grace to do good. Furthermore, when he had used the late-medieval maxim, he meant that the person "who does what he can by the primary grace already conferred upon him" will receive from God further grace. Although this understanding does not deny the need of grace, it is distinctly semi-Pelagian, inasmuch as it is precisely the interpretation placed on the maxim by Gabriel Biel, the late-medieval semi-Pelagian whose theology Luther so vociferously rejected at the outset of the Reformation. In Arminius's theology, as in Biel's, the saying indicates that the prevenient grace of God is offered to all and is not irresistible.[38] The point represents a clear and fundamental departure from Reformed teaching, and in the eyes of Arminius's Reformed contemporaries was surely understood as a recrudescence of late medieval semi-Pelagianism. This resistibility of grace stands, moreover, in clear systematic relation with Arminius's understanding of the fourth and final decree of election as consequent upon human choice.

Furthermore, Arminius's discussion of calling, particularly when read in the context of his Reformed contemporaries' emphasis on effectual calling, carries an implicitly synergistic emphasis on the possibility of human rejection of the divine call. Calling, writes Arminius, is accepted by faith "by which a man believes that, if he complies with the demand, he will enjoy the promise; but that if he does not comply with it . . . the contrary evils will be inflicted upon him, according to the nature of the divine covenant."[39] As in his doctrine of election, so too in his concept of calling, Arminius places his emphasis on the rejectability of the call and on the choice of the individual. Nor does Arminius broach the distinction raised by the Reformed between effectual and ineffectual calling. The "efficacy" of calling, according to Arminius, results from the concurrence of the external calling of the preached Word with the internal calling of the Spirit, but this is an efficacy that may be rejected by the hearer of the Word who may resist the divine counsel and the work of the Spirit.[40]

---

36. Arminius, *Declaration of Sentiments*, 4:664.
37. Arminius, *Apology Against Thirty-one Theological Articles*, in *Works*, 2:19.
38. Cf. Arminius, *Apology Against Thirty-one Theological Articles*, in *Works*, 2:20, with Oberman, *The Harvest of Medieval Theology: Gabriel Biel and Late Medieval Nominalism*, rev. ed. (Grand Rapids: Eerdmans, 1967), 132–35.
39. Arminius, *Private Disputation*, 43.2.
40. Ibid., 42.10–12; cf. *Declaration of Sentiments*, in *Works*, 1:664.

Accordingly, Arminius's identification of faith as the "instrumental cause" of justification lacks the qualifications, found in many Reformed systems, that the subjective reception of justification by faith is passive and that faith and justification are in fact simultaneous.[41] Arminius insists, against Perkins, that the decree of predestination rests on divine foreknowledge of faith or belief. All who are predestined to salvation by God are first foreknown to be grafted into Christ by faith.[42] Indeed, faith must intervene between the universal love of God for the world and the application or effecting of the promise of salvation. All human beings are, therefore, genuinely offered the promise of salvation on the condition of repentance and faith—so that even those who do not ultimately believe "may be admonished of their duty, and may be invited and incited to faith and conversion."[43] Thus, God "does not lead" human beings "to life or to death, except after certain precedent actions of theirs."[44] In contrast to Arminius's view of calling, the Reformed hold that the external calling of the Word is extended to all, while the internal and graciously effective calling of the Spirit is extended to the elect alone.[45] The nonelect are called outwardly and are thrown back without excuse on their human inability, while the elect are saved in their inability by grace alone. This Reformed view Arminius rejects in his response to Perkins.[46]

From the Reformed perspective, as seen first in the response of Arminius's colleagues in the University of Leiden and subsequently in the response of the Synod of Dort to his followers, this understanding of predestination was a synergism inimical not only to the Reformed, Augustinian, and Pauline doctrine of predestination but also to the fundamental teaching of the Reformation that salvation is by grace alone. Indeed, the Arminian distinctions between antecedent and consequent divine wills and the Arminian assumption that prevenient grace is both universal and resistible led toward the development of a theory of grace and human choice quite opposed to the Reformed doctrines of salvation, grace, and calling, and toward their acceptance of a

---

41. Cf. Arminius, *Private Disputations*, 48.7, with the citations in Heinrich Heppe, *Reformed Dogmatics, Set Out and Illustrated from the Sources*, foreword by Karl Barth; rev. and ed. Ernst Bizer; trans. G. T. Thomson (1950; reprint, Grand Rapids: Baker, 1978), 555–58.
42. Arminius, *Examination of Perkins' Pamphlet*, 296–97.
43. Ibid., 310.
44. Arminius, *Examination of Gomarus*, in *Works*, 3:560.
45. Cf. William Perkins, *A Golden Chaine, or, The Description of Theologie*, in *The Workes of . . . Mr. William Perkins*, 3 vols. (Cambridge, 1612–1619), 1:78.1B; with idem, *Certaine Propositions Declaring How Farre a Man may Goe in the Profession of the Gospell, and yet be a Wicked Man and a Reprobate*, in *Workes*, 1:356.2B; idem, *A Treatise of the Manner and Order of Predestination*, in *Workes*, 2:719.2B, 725.1–2, and Heppe, *Reformed Dogmatics*, 515–18.
46. Arminius, *Examination of Perkins' Pamphlet*, 306–7, 310.

view of the divine foreknowledge of future contingents inimical to the Reformed doctrine of the sovereignty of God.[47]

God's eternal will to save certain individuals is consequent upon human choice, as allowed by the distinction between an antecedent and consequent or absolute and respective divine will (*voluntas Dei antecedens et consequens* and *voluntas Dei absolutiva et respectiva*) present in Arminius's doctrine of God.[48] In both of these forms, the distinction indicates a twofold character of the divine will: antecedently and absolutely considered, God's will is ultimate and utterly prior to the acts and choices of all finite agents, but consequently and respectively, God's will follows upon his knowledge of the acts and choices of finite agents. The consequent will of God is consequent to and consequent upon human choice.[49] Arminius does speak of prevenient and co-operating grace, but the former can be rejected and the latter serves only to reinforce and enable human choice. In his doctrine of predestination, the first three decrees indicate the antecedent and absolute will of God, while the fourth decree indicates a consequent and respective will: the divine decision to save some and not others is ultimately conditioned by human choice.

Granting his emphasis on human choice in the work of salvation and on an antecedent and consequent divine willing distinguished by the intervening choice to believe, what remained for Arminius was the definition or redefinition of divine knowing in such a way as to rest the consequent will of God on foreknown human action while at the same time relieving that action of dependence on the divine will. His resolution of this problem arose out of the context of early Protestant orthodoxy and of the revival and modification of Aristotelianism and scholasticism characteristic of the late sixteenth century—notably out of a broad and detailed acquaintance with the works of his teachers and predecessors in the young Protestant tradition, thinkers such as Ursinus, Zanchi, Beza, Danaeus, Junius, Chemnitz, and Hemmingsen, and with the ongoing Roman Catholic theological and philosophical tradition as represented by such writers as Driedo, Molina, Suárez, and Bellarmine.[50]

---

47. Cf. my comments on the limitation of divine dominion over against the world order in *God, Creation, and Providence*, 237–43, and in "God, Predestination, and the Integrity of the Created Order," 438–41, 446–47.

48. Cf. Arminius, *Private Disputations*, 19.6, with *Public Disputations*, 4.40–42, and with *Examination of Gomarus*, in *Works*, 3:555, 560, 567–68.

49. For further definition of these and related terms, see Richard A. Muller, *A Dictionary of Latin and Greek Theological Terms: Drawn Principally from Protestant Scholastic Theology* (Grand Rapids: Baker, 1985), s.v. *voluntas Dei*.

50. Discussion of the impact of the scholastic revival on Protestant thought is found in Hans Emil Weber, *Die philosophische Scholastik des deutschen Protestantismus in Zeitalter der Orthodoxie* (Leipzig: Quelle and Meyer, 1907); idem, *Der Einfluss der protestantischen Schulphilosophie auf die orthodox-lutherische Dogmatik* (Leipzig: Deichert, 1908); Ernst Lewalter, *Spanisch-jesuitisch und deutsch-lutherische Metaphysik des 17. Jahrhunderts* (Hamburg, 1935;

From the medieval and Reformed orthodox traditions Arminius inherited the standard distinction between two categories of divine knowing, the *scientia necessaria* or *scientia simplicis intelligentiae seu naturalis et indefinita* (necessary knowledge or knowledge of uncompounded intelligence or natural and indefinite knowledge) and the *scientia libera seu visionis et definita* or *scientia voluntaria* (free or visionary and definite knowledge or voluntary knowledge).[51] There is, on the one hand, a "necessary" knowledge that God has in the simplicity of the divine understanding that relates to all possibility: it is necessary inasmuch as God, who is omniscient, must have it. It is called "natural and indefinite" because it belongs naturally to God as a prior knowledge of possible existences that are not yet defined by God's will as existent or actual. From this knowledge of possibility God wills to bring into existence some things and not others. On the other hand, there is the voluntary or free knowledge that God has by "vision" or "sight" of all actual things: it is voluntary inasmuch as their existence depends on his will, free because his will is not constrained to actualize one particular set of possibilities rather than another. By this visionary or free knowledge, which is grounded in the eternal decree, God knows all things that he wills or permits and all that his creatures (as willed by him) will or permit.[52] It is, in short, God's knowledge of all actuality. Arminius points out that God's knowledge of things does not invariably impose necessity: God not only knows all things, he knows also the mode of a thing, whether necessary or contingent. What he knows as contingent is, therefore, established with certainty as contingent.[53] In none of these definitions did Arminius contradict the teaching of his Reformed contemporaries and colleagues. As Bangs indicates, Gomarus was present during Arminius's presentation of his thesis that the divine knowledge of contingents established them with certainty as contingent and did not object to the point.[54]

---

reprint, Darmstadt: Wissenschaftliche Buchgesellschaft, 1968); and Paul Dibon, *L'Enseignement philosophique dans les Universités neerlandaises à l'epoque précartesienne* (Amsterdam: Elsevir, 1954); on Arminius's relationship to these developments, see John Platt, *Reformed Thought and Scholasticism: The Arguments for the Existence of God in Dutch Theology, 1575–1650* (Leiden: Brill, 1982), 148–59; Muller, "Arminius and the Scholastic Tradition," 263–77; and idem, *God, Creation, and Providence*, 31–48.

51. Heppe, *Reformed Dogmatics*, 72–74.

52. *Synopsis purioris theologiae, disputationibus quinquaginta duabus comprehensa ac conscripta per Johannem Polyandrum, Andream Rivetum, Antonium Walaeum, Antonium Thysium* (1626), editio sexta, curavit et praefatus est Dr. H. Bavinck (Leiden: Donner, 1881), 6.32; Benedict Pictet, *Theologia christiana ex puris ss. literarum fontibus hausta* (Geneva, 1696), 2.5.16.

53. Arminius, *Public Disputations*, 4.38; cf. *Private Disputations*, 17.7.

54. Cf. Bangs, *Arminius*, 253; Bangs finds Gomarus's silence inexplicable, but see Franciscus Gomarus, *Disputationes theologiacae*, in *Opera theologica omnia* (Amsterdam, 1644); and Heppe, *Reformed Dogmatics*, 75–77, 144–45; note the typographical error on 75, where the quotation from Bucan should read, "This universal knowledge does not imply necessity of effects. Prescience itself is *not* the cause of things. . . ."

From Suàrez and Molina, Arminius learned the theory of another category of divine knowing, a category intervening between the other two, just as foreknown faith intervened between the antecedent will of God to save all people and the consequent will to save those who believe: middle knowledge or *scientia media*. Here Arminius moves beyond the bounds of Reformed doctrine. Middle knowledge intervenes between the divine knowledge of all possibility and the divine knowledge of those actualities directly willed by God as a knowledge of "things which depend on the liberty of created choice or pleasure."[55] Certain things exist by the direct act of God, others by God acting in and through the acts of creatures, and still others, Arminius argues, "by the intervention of creatures, either by themselves, or through them by God's . . . concurrence and permission."[56] These latter things or effects, which exist by the "acts" or "intervention of creatures . . . by themselves," and which seemingly occur outside of the general divine willing or will to actualize, are known by the *scientia media*. Indeed, Arminius can follow Molina to the point of holding that the divine concurrence or continuing ontological support flows not into the activity of the will, but into its effect, leaving the will entirely free while at the same time providentially supporting its result: here too, there are moments in the framework of volitional contingency that arise entirely from the creature and, inasmuch as they are known to God, belong to the *scientia media*.[57]

The Problem of Middle Knowledge from a Reformed Perspective

Recently, one scholar has proposed Molina's concept of a divine foreknowledge of future contingents lying outside of or prior to the divine will as a possible point for dialogue between Arminians and Calvinists—as if the concept had never before been proposed by Arminianism, and as if the concept actually offered a middle ground between the Arminian and Calvinist theologies.[58] For *scientia media* to become the basis for such rapprochement, however, the Reformed would need to concede virtually all of the issues in debate and adopt an Arminian perspective, because, in terms of the metaphysical foundations of the historical debate between Reformed and Arminian, the idea of a divine *scientia media* or middle knowledge is the heart and

55. Arminius, *Private Disputations*, 17.12.
56. Ibid., 4.34.
57. Ibid., 10.9; cf. Muller, *God, Creation, and Providence*, 253–55.
58. William Lane Craig, "Middle Knowledge: A Calvinist-Arminian Rapprochement?" in *The Grace of God, the Will of Man: A Case for Arminianism*, ed. Clark H. Pinnock (Grand Rapids: Zondervan, 1989), 141–64.

soul of the original Arminian position. Middle knowledge is not a middle ground. It was the Arminian, just as it was the Jesuit view, in the controversies over grace and predestination that took place in the late sixteenth and early seventeenth centuries.[59]

From the historical Reformed perspective, as from the Dominican, Thomist perspective, the notion of a divine foreknowledge of future contingents lying outside of the divine willing of actuality undermines the divine sovereignty, assaults the doctrine of salvation by grace, and in addition proposes an ontological absurdity. In the first place, if the salvation of human beings rests on divine foreknowledge, the human being is clearly regarded as the first and effective agent in salvation, and God is understood simply as the one who responds to an independent human action. In the second place, it must be asked whether future contingents lying outside of or prior to the general divine willing that actualizes all things are in fact possible. The Reformed orthodox enter the discussion with the assumption that God alone is original, self-existent, and necessary and that the entire contingent order depends on God for its existence. Or, to make the point in another way, prior to the act of creation, God alone exists as an actual or actualized being; the created order is simply a series of possibilities or potentialities in the mind of God. Out of all of the possibilities that God knows, God wills to create some. Once created, moreover, the things and actions of the finite order do not become self-existent, but continue to have their existence from God—or, to make the point in Thomistic language, all things have their existence by participation in the being of God.[60] The power of being, self-existence, and potential for the existence of others does not belong in any absolute sense to the created order.

Creation and providence, therefore, are two sides of the same issue. It is not as if God becomes a deistic *Deus otiosus,* an "idle God" or God on vacation, after the moment of creation. As Perkins comments, "if God should foresee things to come, and in no sort will or nill them, there should be an idle providence."[61] God actively maintains the created order in its being: all things not only exist, but continue to exist by the will of God. Granting that God alone is fully actualized being, without the divine will that things exist, the creation would not continue. Contingent things and events lying outside of this divine will cannot consistently be argued to exist, unless we overturn the whole doctrine of creation and argue that some things existed prior to

---

59. See Muller, *God, Creation, and Providence,* 151–66, 251–57, 272–74.
60. See Robert L. Patterson, *The Conception of God in the Philosophy of Aquinas* (London: Allen and Unwin, 1933), 259, 262.
61. William Perkins, *A Commentary on Galatians,* ed. Gerald T. Sheppard; introductory essays by Brevard S. Childs, Gerald T. Sheppard, and John H. Augustine, *Pilgrim Classic Commentaries,* vol. 2 (New York: Pilgrim, 1989), 157. (This volume contains a reprint of the Cambridge 1617 edition of Perkins's commentary.)

and apart from the creative work of God and continue to exist outside of God's providence. This problem appears in the Molinist and Arminian view of divine concurrence: Molina and Arminius after him argue that the divine action or concurrence that supports the existence of works or effects brought about by contingent agents enters the finite order of events in the effect, not in the secondary or finite cause. God thus supports the effect and gives it actuality while not strictly bringing it about or willing it. The finite agent acts independently in bringing about the action or effect.[62]

In response, the Reformed and the Thomists note that this theory may claim to account for the effect, but actually falls into ontological absurdity, because it does not account for the existence or action of the finite agent: it is impossible for any finite being to bring either itself or anything else from potency to actuality without the divine concurrence.[63] In other words, freedom and contingency not only are compatible with an eternal decree that ordains all things, but also depend upon it. Against the Roman Catholic theologian Albert Pighuis, whose views on foreknowledge and predestination adumbrated those of Arminius, Calvin argued,

> You ascribe a prescience to God after your own fashion, representing him as sitting in heaven as an idle, inactive, unconcerned spectator of all things in the life of men. Whereas, God himself, ever vindicating to himself the right and the act of holding the helm of all things which are done in the whole world, never permits a separation of his prescience from his power. Nor is this manner of reasoning mine only, but most certainly Augustine's also. "If (says that holy father) God foresaw that which he did not will to be done, God holds not the supreme rule over all things. God, therefore, ordained that which should come to pass, because nothing could have been done had he not willed it to be done."[64]

Calvin's point is not that all things occur by absolute necessity, but that the ability of creatures to have their own "quality and nature" and "follow [their] own inclination" depends on the divine ordination and conservation

---

62. Cf. Arminius, *Public Disputations*, 10.9, with Molina, *Concordia*, 2, q. 14, art. 13, disp. 26.5; and note Muller, *God, Creation, and Providence*, 254–55.

63. Cf. DuMoulin, *Anatome of Arminianisme*, 15–16; and see Reginald Garrigou-Lagrange, *God: His Existence and His Nature. A Thomistic Solution of Certain Agnostic Antinomies*, trans. Dom Bede Rose, 2 vols. (St. Louis: Herder, 1946), 470: "Molinism restricts God's universal causality and even the universality of the principle of causality. According to this view, the transition to act of the secondary cause does not come from God; and as potency cannot, of itself alone, pass into act, this transition is without cause"; and cf. idem, "Thomisme," in *Dictionnaire de théologie catholique*, vol. 15/1, col. 870. On the relationship between the Thomist-Molinist and the Reformed-Arminian debates, see Muller, *God, Creation, and Providence*, 155–66, 272–75.

64. John Calvin, *A Defense of the Secret Providence of God*, in *Calvin's Calvinism: Treatises on the Eternal Predestination of God and the Secret Providence of God*, trans. Henry Cole (London, 1856; reprint, Grand Rapids: Reformed Free Publishing Association, n.d.), 280–81.

of their existence.[65] In the more precise language of Turretin, "No effect can be understood as future, whether absolutely or hypothetically, without the divine decree, inasmuch as no creature can exist in the world apart from the divine causality; so also no future conditionals can be knowable prior to the divine decree."[66]

Thus, from the Reformed and the Thomistic perspective there can be no middle knowledge inasmuch as its proposed objects cannot exist. The two original categories of divine knowing—necessary and voluntary—are exhaustive: they refer to all possibility and all actuality. On the assumption of the divine creation of the world out of nothing, moreover, there can be no actuality that arises apart from the divine will.[67] As Voetius argued, since all actuality ultimately rests on God's willing, there is nothing outside of the divine willing: the object of middle knowledge, therefore, is nothing. Knowledge of nothing is no knowledge at all—and middle knowledge, so-called, cannot exist any more than can its purported objects. In order for future contingents to exist there must be an effective divine will that actualizes them as contingents, and the divine knowledge of future contingents must be an absolutely certain knowledge, eternally in God, of those possible contingents that God wills to actualize.[68] From the Reformed perspective, a middle knowledge is not necessary to account for future contingents or for the divine knowledge of future contingents. The free or voluntary knowledge of God is an eternal knowledge of all actual things, whether (from the perspective of the creature) past, present, or future, and whether necessary, contingent, or freely willed.

This is precisely the point made by the definitions of the immutable decree and its relation to the world order found in the Westminster Confession and many Reformed systems:

> God from all eternity did, by the most wise and holy counsel of his own will, freely and unchangeably ordain whatsoever comes to pass; yet so as thereby neither is God the author of sin, nor is violence offered to the will of creatures, nor is the liberty or contingency of second causes taken away, *but rather established.*[69]

65. Cf. Calvin, *Treatises Against the Anabaptists and Against the Libertines*, 242–43.

66. Franciscus Turretinus, *Institutio theologiae elencticae* (Geneva, 1677–1689; editio altera, Edinburgh: John Lowe, 1847), 3.13.10.

67. Heppe, *Reformed Dogmatics*, 75, 190–92.

68. Cf. Perkins, *A Commentary on Galatians*, 158, with the excerpt from Voetius in Heppe, *Reformed Dogmatics*, 79; note also Venema, *Institutes of Theology*, trans. Alexander Brown (Edinburgh: T. and T. Clark, 1850), 1:153–55, and Mastricht, *Theoretico-practica theol.* (Utrecht, 1724), 2.13.20–23.

69. Westminster Confession, 3.1, italics added; the text of the confession is found in Schaff, *Creeds of Christendom*, 3:600–73; cf. Pictet, *Theologia christiana* 3.1.13; and the discussion in Heppe, *Reformed Dogmatics*, 143–45.

The point is that the contingent order cannot exist and, therefore, free and contingent acts within that order cannot exist, unless God wills their actuality and wills it in such a way that they are established as free and contingent.[70] Or, again, in the discussion of providence,

> Although in relation to the foreknowledge and decree of God, the first cause, all things come to pass immutably and infallibly, yet by the same providence, he ordereth them to fall out, according to the nature of second causes, *either necessarily, freely, or contingently.*[71]

The Reformed orthodox theologians view this argument as far more sound and consistent—and certainly far more in accord both with Scripture and with the demands of soteriology—than the Arminian claim of a *scientia media,* inasmuch as middle knowledge, with its corresponding view of divine *concursus,* presupposes that some events belong to chains of cause and effect that lie outside of the divine willing. How, one wonders, if such events can actually occur, can they belong to or be drawn into God's plan of salvation? From the Reformed perspective, the Arminian God is an interventionist, not in control of his own world, and not particularly successful in effecting his will to save all human beings.[72]

Grace, Election, and Human Freedom in Reformed Theology

One of the historical errors typical of the many Arminian critiques of Calvinism is to assume that the older Reformed theology disavows human free will and undercuts human responsibility. Quite to the contrary, the theology of Calvin and of the Reformed orthodox assumes the freedom of the will from external constraint and assumes also human responsibility before God. What it denies is freedom of choice in matters of human sinfulness, grace, and salvation. It is not the case, as proponents of Arminianism allege, that the use of biblical examples by Calvin and other Reformed theologians to argue their case for predestination indicates "a divine determinism of all human actions."[73] The issue debated between the Arminians and the Reformed was not philosophical determinism but soteriology. The biblical ex-

---

70. Cf. the citations in Heppe, *Reformed Dogmatics,* 258–62, 267–70.

71. Westminster Confession, 5.2, italics added; cf. *Synopsis purioris theologiae,* 11.11 (virtually verbatim, the same point), and Pictet, *Theologia christiana,* 6.2.8; 4.9.

72. Leonhard Riissen, *Summa theologiae didactico-elencticae* (1695; Frankfurt and Leipzig, 1731), 3.31, controversia 3, argumentum.

73. Bruce R. Reichenbach, "Freedom, Justice, and Moral Responsibility," in *The Grace of God,* 291.

amples drawn by the Reformed typically point to the bondage of human beings in sin, to their inability to choose salvation, and, therefore, to the
necessity of grace in salvation—not to a determination of human actions in
general and, especially, not to a determination of human beings to commit
individual transgressions. It was never the Reformed view that the moral acts
of human beings are predetermined, any more than it was ever the Reformed
view that the fall of Adam was willed by God to the exclusion of Adam's free
choice of sin. The divine ordination of all things is not only consistent with
human freedom; it makes human freedom possible. As J. K. S. Reid has argued of Calvin's theology, the divine determination so belongs to the ultimate order of being that it cannot be understood as a philosophical determinism in and for the temporal order of being: human responsibility is assumed
and God is not the author of sin.[74] This overarching providential determination (which includes the divine ordination of and concurrence in freedom
and contingency) is, moreover, distinct from predestination: predestination
is the specific ordination of some to salvation, granting the inability of
human beings to save themselves. Again: this is not a matter of philosophical
determinism, but of soteriology.

Thus, Bullinger argued in the Second Helvetic Confession that human beings were created with the faculty of free will and continue to possess it in
their sinful condition. After the fall, Bullinger writes, human beings were deprived neither of understanding nor of will: the fallen will has become sinful,
infected, as it were, with an "infirmity," but it remains free. "As touching evil
or sin, man does evil, not compelled either by God or the devil, but of his own
accord; and in this respect has a most free will."[75] Even after grace, the will
remains weak and the flesh wars against the Spirit. The Reformed view presupposes free will while at the same time assuming the inability of human beings to save themselves:

> in outward things no man denies but that both the regenerate and the unregen-
> erate have their free will; for man has this constitution common with other
> creatures (to whom he is not inferior) to will some things and to nill other
> things. So he may speak or keep silence, go out of his house or abide within. . . .
> In this matter we condemn the Manicheans, who deny that the beginning of
> evil unto man, being good, came from his free will. We condemn, also, the Pe-
> lagians, who affirm that an evil man has free will sufficiently to perform a good
> precept. Both of these are confuted by the Scripture, which says to the former,
> "God made man upright" (Eccles. 7:29); and to the latter, "If the Son made you
> free, then you shall be free indeed" (John 8:36).[76]

74. See Reid's introduction to John Calvin, *Concerning the Eternal Predestination of God*
(London: James Clarke, 1961), 25–27.
75. Second Helvetic Confession, 9.2.
76. Ibid., 9.10–11.

Calvin held a similar assumption. "Three kinds of freedom are distinguished: first from necessity, second from sin, third from misery," he wrote, "the first of these so inheres in man by nature that it cannot possibly be taken away, but the other two have been lost through sin."[77] Similarly, the Westminster Confession declares that "God hath endued the will of man with that natural liberty, that is neither forced nor by any absolute necessity of nature determined to good or evil."[78] The issue is not that events are predetermined by God and freedom removed, but that "man, by his fall into a state of sin, hath wholly lost all ability to will any spiritual good accompanying salvation."[79] The confessional position of Reformed theology is hardly "a divine determinism of human actions." More precisely, the Reformed view is not a form of necessitarianism: when God ordains "whatsoever comes to pass" he does so in such a way as to establish and give certainty to "the liberty and contingency of second causes."[80] In fact, the underlying soteriological issue addressed by Reformed theology is that human beings have free will, have used it wrongly, and have thereby fallen into a condition of alienation from God that cannot be remedied by the liberty that remains to the will in its fallen condition.

All of the biblical examples cited by Calvin and the Reformed—the selection of Abraham, the choice of Isaac over Ishmael and of Jacob over Esau, the hardening and punishment of Pharaoh, and so forth—are examples of divine determination relative to the salvation of God's chosen people identified following the Pauline example of Romans 9. Reformed doctrine in no way denies that some events are genuinely contingent, having "a cause that could by its nature have acted differently," that others result from divine persuasion, and that still others are the result of human free agency or deliberation.[81] Reformed doctrine only insists that the beginning of the redeemed life is solely the work of God, and therefore distinguishes between the general decree of providence that establishes all things, whether as necessary, contingent, or free, and the special decree of predestination that establishes salvation by grace alone. Far from being a rigid metaphysical determinism of all human actions, a form of necessitarianism (which was never Reformed doctrine in any case), predestination applies only to the issue of salvation.[82] And the Reformed exegesis of biblical passages related to predestination, far from indicating a determinism of all human actions, indicates the ultimate determination of God in matters pertaining to salvation.

---

77. Calvin, *Institutes*, 2.2.5.
78. Westminster Confession, 9.1.
79. Ibid., 9.2.
80. Ibid., 3.1.
81. Heppe, *Reformed Dogmatics*, 266, 271–72.
82. Ibid., 145–46, 151–52.

The issue is complicated somewhat by the frequent translation of both Latin terms, *voluntas* and *arbitrium*, as "will." The former term, *voluntas*, indicates the faculty of the will that belongs to all human beings. The latter term, *arbitrium*, is better translated as "choice." Thus, in the chapters of Calvin's *Institutes* that address the problem of sin and human freedom, what is denied consistently is the ability of the free choice of sinless acts. Calvin assumes the freedom of the human will from compulsion and he consistently affirms both Adam's responsibility for the fall and subsequent human responsibility under God's law.[83] When Calvin speaks of the necessity of sinning and of the bondage of the will in sin, he denies not a general freedom to choose but only a freedom and an ability to cease being sinful or to abstain from acting sinfully. Calvin can, with consistency, enjoin obedience to the moral law and indicate the ability of human beings to refrain from overt transgressions of the law such as blasphemy, adultery, or murder at the same time that he can insist on the sinful character of the actions of all fallen human beings. Human obedience is invariably imperfect. Even so, Calvin's assumption of the necessity of grace and denial of synergism or cooperation with prevenient grace rests not on a metaphysical determinism but on a thoroughgoing doctrine of original sin and on the view that "the whole of Scripture proclaims that faith is a free gift of God."[84]

Arminian responses to this doctrine typically argue that it is inconsistent or that it portrays God as unjust: how can the gospel and the grace of salvation be genuinely offered to all people, when only a portion of the human race is elected to salvation? The Reformed assumption, however, is that all human beings have fallen short of the obedience and righteousness willed by God and that all are worthy of damnation. In willing to save some, God is manifest as merciful; in willing to damn others for their sins, God is manifest as just. The offer of the gospel to all leaves without excuse those who do not accept it—granting that their nonacceptance is entirely because of their own fallenness.[85] It is certainly true that, without the grace of God, human beings cannot come to faith and salvation, and true also that, in the Reformed view, those who receive their fully merited damnation are no more unworthy of salvation than the elect. It may also be the case that, from the perspective of the human wisdom of salvation through merit, this view of the divine work appears both unjust and foolish. It does, however, respect the mystery of salvation by grace alone, it clearly sets limits both to human merit and to human wisdom, and it does manifest the consistency of divine will with salvific re-

83. Calvin, *Institutes*, 2.2.7–12, 26–27 on will and choice; cf. ibid., 2.1.4–6.
84. Ibid., 2.3.5–8.
85. Cf. Heppe, *Reformed Dogmatics*, 180–81, citing *Synopsis purioris theologiae*, 24.46: "Election is the positive *principium* of salvation, but reprobation strictly speaking is not a principle but the removal of a principle. Nor can it be said strictly that men were ordained from eternity to damnation, unless with this addition: on account of sin."

sult: those intended by God for salvation are indeed saved. Nor does the Reformed view lapse into antinomianism, granting that it serves only to define salvation as entirely of grace and never to argue against the redeeming effects of God's free grace in the lives of the faithful.[86]

From the Reformed perspective, there is a far deeper problem in the Arminian contention that God wills the salvation of all people and that the salvation of some relates only to the acceptance or the rejection of God's grace. The Reformed of the seventeenth century noted this problem as the untenable hypothesis of contradictory wills in God: Arminian theology claimed that God antecedently wills the salvation of all people but consequently wills not the salvation of all, but only of some, on the grounds of certain conditions.[87] Reformed theologians certainly assumed distinctions in the divine will, such as the distinction between the ultimate divine good pleasure *(voluntas beneplaciti)* and the outwardly designated divine will *(voluntas signi)*, or the similar distinction between a hidden will *(voluntas arcanum)* and a revealed will *(voluntas revelatum)*. In neither case do the distinctions indicate contrary wills in God, but only the fact that the entirety of God's will is never revealed to finite creatures. They also argue, against the Arminians, the soteriological consistency of the original divine intention with the result of God's willing.[88] Similarly, when Reformed theologians approached the concept of an antecedent and a consequent divine will, they understood that the former referred to the absolute or decretive will and the latter to the preceptive will of God. Thus the former "was determined by God from eternity before any created things existed" while the latter rests on the eternal decree without contradicting it: the divine precepts fully concur with the righteousness of the eternal decree, are consequent upon it, and may be ignored or disobeyed by sinful human beings.

The "neo-Pelagian" Arminians, however, understand the antecedent will of God as prior to the acts of the creature; and the consequent will they rest not on this *voluntas antecedens,* but on the will of the creature that precedes it in time. God, thus, antecedently wills salvation of all people and consequently wills salvation only for those who have chosen to believe. God from eternity wills the salvation of Judas, while at the same time knowing that

---

86. Calvin, *Institutes,* 3.2.10–20; 14.4–6; 17.11; 22.10–11; cf. John Calvin, *Commentary on the Epistle of James,* in *Commentaries on the Catholic Epistles,* trans. John Owen (1855; reprint, Grand Rapids: Baker, 1979), James 2:20–23, in loc. (314–17).

87. Riissen, *Summa theologiae,* 3.31, controversia 1; cf. *Synopsis purioris theologiae,* 4.35; against the Arminian counter that it is the Reformed who hold contrary wills in God, see Heppe, *Reformed Dogmatics,* 86–88.

88. See Muller, *Christ and the Decree,* 171–73, 178–82; idem, *Post-Reformation Reformed Dogmatics* (Grand Rapids: Baker, 1987), 1:2.4; idem, "Perkins' A Golden Chaine: Predestinarian System or Schematized Ordo Salutis?" *The Sixteenth Century Journal* 9, 1 (April 1978): 69–81; and cf. Lynne Courter Boughton, "Supralapsarianism and the Role of Metaphysics in Sixteenth-Century Reformed Theology," *WTJ* 48 (1986): 63–96.

Judas will disbelieve, and on the basis of that knowledge, permits Judas to remain in its infidelity and perish. Who, questions Riissen, would be so foolish as to attribute such wills to God? According to this doctrine God genuinely wills that which he knows will never happen, indeed, what he wills not to bring about![89] In this view, the covenant of God with human beings depends entirely on the human will and, indeed, only those who have chosen God through faith and repentance will be chosen or elected by God.[90]

In the era of Reformed orthodoxy, the sacrifice of Isaac (Gen. 22:1–18) became a standard text in the debate over the distinctions in the will of God. It is a false objection, argued Riissen, to claim that, according to Scripture, God first willed the death of Isaac and then afterward willed his life: "God did not will or decree [Isaac's death], rather he commanded it."[91] The distinction between the ultimate will or decree of God and a divine command is significant, since the former refers to the ultimate good pleasure of God, the *voluntas beneplaciti,* while the latter refers to the revealed will of God, the *voluntas signi:* God does not, therefore, "will and not will in the same manner and relation." God thus wills the sacrifice of Isaac according to his revealed or preceptive will in order to test Abraham's obedience, but does not will the sacrifice according to his ultimate good pleasure. Riissen states categorically, *"Non datur contrarietas in voluntate Dei"*—"There are no contraries in the will of God."[92] Even so, Poole, following Calvin and the older tradition of interpretation of the text, commented on Genesis 22:12, "for now I know that thou fearest God," as the conclusion of Abraham's trial but not a discovery on God's part:

> God knew the sincerity and resolvedness of Abraham's faith and obedience before and without this evidence, and from eternity foresaw this fact with all its circumstances; and therefore you must not think that God had now made any new discovery: but this is spoken here, as in many other places, of God after the manner of men, who is then said to know a thing when it is notorious and evident to a man's self and others by some remarkable effect.[93]

Similar considerations obtain in the distinction of an absolute and conditional will in God. The rectitude of the distinction depends upon its defini-

89. Riissen, *Summa theologiae,* 3.31, controversia 1, argumentum 1; cf. DuMoulin, *The Anatome of Arminianisme,* 30–32.
90. Riissen, *Summa theologiae,* 3.31, controversia 1, argumentum 4; cf. the citations in Heppe, *Reformed Dogmatics,* 90–92.
91. Riissen, *Summa theologiae,* 3.31, controversia, obj. 2.
92. Ibid., margin at 3.24; similarly Johannes Braun, in Heppe, *Reformed Dogmatics,* 85–87.
93. Matthew Poole, *Annotations on the Holy Bible;* republished as *A Commentary on the Holy Bible,* 3 vols. (London: Banner of Truth, 1962), 1:52; and cf. John Calvin, *Commentaries on the First Book of Moses called Genesis,* trans. John King, 2 vols. (Calvin Translation Society, 1847–1850; reprint, Grand Rapids: Baker, 1979), 1:570–71.

tion: "it is possible to allow," writes Riissen, "a *voluntas conditionata*" or "conditioned will" in God "but not in an *à priori* and antecedent sense, as if dependent on a [prior] condition, rather in an *à posteriori* and consequent sense, given that some condition in the creature intervenes between the will and its execution"; and then "only to the extent that the condition does not belong to the internal divine act or volition, but to the external object or thing willed."[94] In other words, the conditional will remains an immutable will, willed eternally by God, but it is understood as being directed toward a contingent or conditional event: the condition, strictly understood, obtains not in the divine will but in the temporal event. What is to be rejected, Riissen adds, is a "neo-Pelagian" form of the distinction that distinguishes an absolute will, independent of all external conditions, from a conditional will, "dependent on a condition *extra Deum*"—"outside of God." Such a concept is repugnant to the independence, wisdom, and power of God inasmuch as it renders these attributes "doubtful and uncertain," dependent on the mutable will of human beings, and by extension "ineffective and capable of disappointment."[95] "An ineffective will cannot be attributed to God, since it would imply either a divine ignorance, which does not know events that are not going to follow, or an impotence, which is not able to effect what it intends."[96]

Applied to the order of salvation, this view of distinctions in the divine will reinforces the Reformed doctrine of salvation by grace alone. Perkins argued pointedly against the claim that "certaine circumstances of the creature" were prior to and somehow determined or limited the will of God in the work of salvation. The assumption that God willed "indefinitely and upon condition, that all and every man of all ages should be saved" is foreign to the teaching of Scripture and indicates "a finite power and insufficiencie in him that willeth," which is impossible in God.

> to beleeve and to persevere is a certaine kind of good action; and on the contrarie, not to beleeve, or not to persevere is an evill action. And every thing that is good is through the effectuall will of God; and so farre forth as there is, or existeth that which is good, so farre forth God willeth it, and maketh it to exist by willing it. And that evill which commeth to passe, commeth to passe God not hindring it. . . . Hereupon it is certaine, that God willeth that some should beleeve, & persevere unto the end, & that other some not so. . . .[97]

94. Riissen, *Summa theologiae*, 3.31, controversia 3.

95. Ibid., 3.31, controversia 3, argumentum; cf. the clear establishment of conditions *extra Deum* in Arminius, *Examination of Gomarus*, in *Works*, 555.

96. Riissen, *Summa theologiae*, 3.31, controversia 2, argumenta.

97. Perkins, *A Treatise of the Manner and Order of Predestination*, in *Workes*, 2:711.1B–C.

God foresees future events because he has willed them to be: such events cannot exist apart from his willing. He therefore foresees faith in some and not in others "because it is his will to give one man faith, and not another."[98] Nor does this teaching remove the freedom of the will. Perkins insists that fallen human beings retain "freedom from compulsion or constraint, but not from all necessitie."[99] Even so, the good angels, who are utterly unable to sin, are not for that reason deprived of free will; they freely will the good without compulsion or restraint. Since, moreover, sin is a privation and a form of bondage, beings who are capable of doing either good or evil are not as free as those who can do only the good.

In the case of human beings, "the libertie of will, since the fall of man, is joyned with a necessitie of sinning; because it stands in bondage under sinne"—but this sinfulness so belongs to human nature that it is not a matter of compulsion and does not, therefore, remove the freedom of choice.[100] The certainty of the divine decree, which establishes all things in their necessity, freedom, and contingency, does not impinge on or abolish this self-limited freedom of the human will, but establishes it and concurs in its actions. Thus, a broad freedom "to will or nill, or to suspend" remains in human beings after the fall as the basis of free acts in "naturall, humane, and ecclesiaticall" matters. Human beings move about with a natural freedom, can eat and drink; they can also exercise their humanity freely in the arts, trades, and other occupations; they can practice "civill vertue, justice, temperance, liberalitie, chastitie"; and they may freely exercise the ecclesiastical duties of outward worship.[101] The weakness or bondage of the will, however, is such that in its sinful condition it cannot will the good demanded by God as the ground of its own salvation—and it cannot will to have faith.[102]

Salvation, therefore, must begin with God. Nonetheless, this divine beginning in effectual calling and regeneration, Perkins argues, is not temporally prior to the human turning of the will toward God:

> everie cause is before his effect, if not in time, yet in prioritie of nature. The will converted, so soone as God hath begunne to renew it, wils to be renewed: and it could not will the conversion of it selfe, unlesse it had formerly tasted the goodnesse thereof. . . . Will in the act of working, effecting, producing of our conversion or regeneration, is no cause at all, but in it selfe considered, a meere patient or subject to receive the grace of conversion wrought and given by God.[103]

---

98. Ibid., 2:719.2B.

99. Perkins, *Treatise of Gods Free Grace and Mans Free Will*, in *Workes*, 1:703.2C; cf. DuMoulin, *Anatomy of Arminianisme*, 282–88.

100. Perkins, *Treatise of Gods Free Grace and Mans Free Will*, in *Workes*, 1:703.2D.

101. Ibid., 1:704.1A, 709.2C–710.1C.

102. Cf. DuMoulin, *Anatomy of Arminianisme*, 300–13.

103. Perkins, *Treatise of Gods Free Grace and Mans Free Will*, in *Workes*, 1:715.2D, 716.1B.

There is no metaphysical determinism of all human actions here: Perkins and the other Reformed theologians of his time assume genuine freedom and contingency as established by God's overarching willing of all things. Without this divine willing, moreover, nothing would exist, and outside of it nothing does exist. There is, of course, a certain determinism in the order of grace. Salvation is inaccessible to fallen humanity, outside of the range of human free willing, available by grace alone. As Perkins's comments indicate, however, grace does not wrench or force the will; it regenerates and reforms the will in order that it might freely choose to believe. The doctrine conforms to the requirements of the Reformed insistence on the freedom of the will, of the Reformed doctrine of the will's inability in matters of salvation, and of the Reformed conception of a divine concurrence that must be active for free willing to occur.

Concluding Remarks

The theology of Jacob Arminius has, over the centuries since the controversies of the early seventeenth century, become the basis of much Protestant soteriology. The irony of this development lies in the direct opposition of the Arminian system to the theology of the Reformation. Indeed, when the Arminian understanding of the relationship of grace and human choice has been spelled out—particularly in terms of Arminius's own interpretation of the medieval maxim, "to those who do what is in them God will not deny grace"—Arminianism, like the Molinist theology on which it drew, is little more than the recrudescence of the late medieval semi-Pelagianism against which the Reformers struggled. It tenets are inimical to the Pauline and Augustinian foundation of Reformed Protestantism.

In the Arminian system, the God who antecedently wills the salvation of all knowingly provides a pattern of salvation that is suitable only to the salvation of some. This doctrinal juxtaposition of an antecedent, and never effectuated, divine will to save all and a consequent, effectuated, divine will to save some on the foreknown condition of their acceptance of faith reflects the problem of the *scientia media*. The foreknowledge of God, in the Arminian view, consists in part in a knowledge of contingent events that lie outside of God's willing and, in the case of the divine foreknowledge of the rejection of grace by some, of contingent events that not only thwart the antecedent divine will to save all people, but also are capable of thwarting it because of the divinely foreknown resistibility of the gift of grace. In other words, the Arminian God is locked into the inconsistency of genuinely willing to save all people while at the same time binding himself to a plan of salvation that he foreknows with certainty cannot effectuate his will. This divine inability results, presumably, from the necessity of those events that lie within the divine foreknowledge but outside of the divine willing remaining outside of the effective will of God. Arminian theology posits the ultimate contradiction that God's antecedent will genuinely wills what he foreknows can never come to pass and that his consequent will effects something other than his ultimate intention. The Arminian God, in short, is either ineffectual or self-contradictory. Reformed doctrine, on the other hand, respects the ultimate mystery of the infinite will of God, affirms the sovereignty and efficacy of God, and teaches the soteriological consistency of the divine intention and will with its effects.

12

Augustine, Luther, Calvin, and Edwards on the Bondage of the Will

John H. Gerstner

Augustine on Grace and the Bondage of the Will

Will as will is called by Augustine *voluntas,* but willing well and freely is the work of the *liberum arbitrium.*[1] *Voluntas* is in itself a good gift of God but liable to abuse, as are, for example, eyes and feet. *Liberum arbitrium* is man's inclining to the good when God so inclines the *voluntas.* To will perfectly, according to Augustine, requires a perfect righteousness, which created man had but could and did lose. With his loss of perfect righteousness went his *liberum arbitrium.*

Evil will is not from God, though it is occasioned by him.[2] This is the sense in which God could be said to have two wills (deficient and efficient) with their differing effects on the will of man, an insight from the neo-Platonists that delivered Augustine from the Manichean grip. In both wills, God is absolutely sovereign and man is absolutely and voluntarily subordinate.

1. *Libero Arbitrium* 2.19, 51.
2. *Spirit and Letter* 31, 54. That is how Augustine explains Shimei's cursing though he was led by God into it (2 Sam. 16:5–6).

Once into original sin, man's will is inclined only to sin, although man still has natural power to will the good. He did not become a "puppet,"[3] though fallen men cannot will what is good in order to believe or to be regenerated. As Louis Berkhof has well stated: "Augustine's sinner is totally depraved but still possesses 'natural good' but cannot will that which is good in the sight of God. The will of man stands in need of renewal, and this is exclusively a work of God from start to finish: a work of divine grace."[4] Grace alone can deliver from the bondage of the fallen will.

The Augustinian system was condemned at the important Second Synod of Orange (529) in favor of a modified Augustinianism. The synod gave everything to Augustine except the irresistibility of grace; but, by that the church fell immediately into faith bringing regeneration rather than the reverse and then the deeper error of baptism bringing faith.[5] As historian Loofs once put it: Augustine has irresistible predestination and grace versus free will. Popular Catholicism could not become accustomed to this and finally declared itself Augustinian although it adopted semi-Pelagianism.

In the garden of Eden the free will, indwelt by God, chose good, but that same will separated from God chooses evil. So it is with respect to saving grace. This weight *(pondus)* toward evil from which the fallen person suffers is fatal. Only the elect in heaven does God never again leave so as to let them fall. (In heaven, God will by his eternal presence cause man to choose what he will have them choose: namely, good, never to forsake them.) So their still sinful nature, in itself, apart from God's presence, will never again express its *fall ability* because God will never cause or permit it to do so.

Augustinian ideas concerning grace and bondage are clearly defined, as the following list shows:

Cause: Whatever God produces in the creature by his presence or absence.

Conversion: When God takes imperfect and varying residence in a fallen creature.

Evil: Whatever God, by his absence, occasions the creature to cause.

Fallen creature: One in whom God never dwells to cause good but is always withdrawn to occasion evil.

---

3. This is the charge of J. M. Rist, "Augustine on Free Will and Predestination," in *Augustine. A Collection of Critical Essays,* ed. R. A. Markus (Garden City, N.Y.: Anchor Books, 1972), 235; against Etienne Gilson, whose "Augustine is a moral determinist: fallen men are puppets." Gilson escapes the compulsion of the Jansenists but not determinism. All that Rist proves is that he cannot conceive of a "determinism" (as Augustine and Gilson [and Luther, Calvin, and Edwards] could).

4. *The History of Christian Doctrines* (Grand Rapids: Eerdmans, 1953), 139. Roman Catholic writers fight this "Calvinistic" interpretation of Augustine to the bitter end of resistible grace (197, 198).

5. Cf. ibid., 142.

Free will: That by which man chooses whatever God causes him by God's presence or absence to choose.

Good: Whatever God produces in the creature by his presence within said creature.

Mercy: God's pardon, purchased by Christ, for the elect's benefit has come into expression.

Righteousness: Created man's condition before his deficient nature is allowed by God to express itself.

Saved sinful creature: One in whom God dwells in a varying but imperfect degree, thereby causing him to choose a mixture of good and evil. God may withdraw altogether and the person perishes in hell. God never withdraws altogether at the moment of the death of an elect person, who therefore goes, possibly via purgatory, to heaven.

Source of knowledge of good and evil: The Bible.

Let me comment concerning Augustine on Adam's free will and the fall. This is the theological area of the greatest difficulty for Reformed theology, Augustine's included. How man, created upright, would seek out his own devices defies explanation; indeed, explanation always hovers near the abyss of blasphemously charging God with authoring sin. I do not have the space to go into the detail necessary for elucidation, but Augustine in *The Enchiridion of Faith, Hope and Love* summarizes the matter classically for the whole tradition:

> Wherefore, God would have been willing to preserve even the first man in that state of salvation in which he was created, and after he had begotten sons to remove him at a fit time, without the intervention of death, to a better place, where he should have been not only free from sin, but free even from the desire of sinning, if He had foreseen that man would have the steadfast will to persist in the state of innocence in which he was created. But as He foresaw that man would make a bad use of his free-will, that is, would sin, God arranged His own designs rather with a view to do good to man even in his sinfulness, that thus the good will of the Omnipotent might not be made void by the evil will of man, but might be fulfilled in spite of it.[6]

Two items later, Augustine makes his profoundest statement on grace and the bondage of the will to be found anywhere in all his works; grace is necessary not only for the fallen will but also for the unfallen will:

> The former immortality man lost through the exercise of his free-will; the latter he shall obtain through grace, whereas, if he had not sinned, he should have

---

6. Edited and with an introduction by Henry Paolucci. Includes the historical analysis by Adolf von Harnack from *The History of Dogma* (Chicago: Regnery, 1961), 122.

obtained it by desert. Even in that case, however, there could have been no merit without grace; because, although the mere exercise of man's free-will would not have sufficed for his maintenance in righteousness, unless God had assisted it by imparting a portion of His unchangeable goodness. Just as it is in man's power to die whenever he will (for, not to speak of other means, any one can put an end to himself by simple abstinence from food), but the mere will cannot preserve life in the absence of food and the other means of life; so man in paradise was able of his mere will, simply by abandoning righteousness, to destroy himself; but to have maintained a life of righteousness would have been too much for his will, unless it had been sustained by the Creator's power. After the fall, however, a more abundant exercise of God's mercy was required, because the will itself had to be freed from the bondage in which it was held by sin and death. And the will owes its freedom in no degree to itself, but solely to the grace of God which comes by faith in Jesus Christ; so that the very will, through which we accept all the other gifts of God which lead us on to His eternal gift, is itself prepared of the Lord, as the Scripture says.[7]

If the Augustinians have a problem explaining how a good tree produced bad fruit, Arminians have a greater problem. How did a non-tree produce good or bad fruit? Their first man was no person at all but only a potential for becoming one, when he first made a choice for which, alas, he had no inclination whatever!

Martin Luther on Grace and the Bondage of Sin

For Luther, it is God's, not man's, will that determines all things. Man's will does not decide God but God's will determines man's will. The double predestination of the German Reformer puts human decision in the perspective of eternity. Luther was a theologian of Romans 9, of verse 18 especially: "God has mercy on whom he wants to have mercy, and he hardens whom he wants to harden." When God takes salvation out of our hand and puts it in his own, that does not destroy the human will but implies that if it works at all, it is in accord with the divine will, be it mercy or in hardening.[8]

The God Luther preaches was seeking in grace the salvation of sinners, but Luther's "hidden God" had another end in view. Luther does not shrink from the whole truth he believed: that God "does, however, will damnation" according to his inscrutable will.[9] This is hard doctrine but ultimately neither

7. Ibid., 124–25. Cf. also my "Augustine and Irresistible Grace," in *Life Religion: Essays in Honor of H. Evan Runner*, ed. Henry Vandergoot.
8. Luther's *Works*, vol. 33, *Career of the Reformer 3*, ed. Philip S. Watson, general ed. Helmut T. Lehman (Philadelphia: Fortress, 1972), 185.
9. Paul Althaus, *The Theology of Martin Luther*, trans. Robert C. Schultz (Philadelphia: Fortress, 1966), 274ff., has a fine, full discussion of this tension in Luther.

paradoxical nor unscriptural. Rather it is the prevailing view of our, and even Luther's, day that God wills only to save and men do the free willing that destroys them. But Luther sees no human will different from that of God. God changes one person's will and not another's. Luther, although he shudders, acknowledges and even acquiesces in both wills of God as well as both wills of man (the one that God turns toward him and the one that God allows to turn from him).

But how is man to will if he does not know God's will for him? Luther answers (as virtually all Reformed thinkers do): Obey the will you do know, not the one you do not know. God's revelation calls you to will faith whatever his hidden will may have decided. Decide with reference to the revealed God of profound mercy, not the hidden God of decreed wrath.[10]

Luther agreed with Calvin that hell was made for the overly curious. Yet neither of these theologians kept this dark secret from people but kept them from brooding about it. Luther knew that all God did was right. That was enough for Luther.

So, in God, there is nothing but "will, will, will." What does all this spell for the will of man? That is exactly what Europe was asking Luther when he failed to answer Erasmus's *Diatribe on the Free Will*. Seven Strassburg preachers (23 November 1524) wrote to the Reformer about Erasmus:

> What is he up to? Does he not everywhere brush aside the authority of scripture. . . .We therefore implore you for Christ's sake: Don't let yourself be appeased by flesh and blood! . . . Out with the trimmings of the Latin language: away with the awe of learning which dims the praise of Christ. His Word saves us; the words of others lead us to ruin. . . .[11]

This urgency provoked the classic response on *The Bondage of the Will* (1525), in which the Reformer proved to the foremost scholar of his day that man's will is not free but enslaved. Already in *The Heidelberg Theses of 1518* he had written that the will is free in name only. "When man does what is in him he commits mortal sin." The free will is not free to choose one thing or another but is an imprisoned slave though free from all compulsion (Zwang). He cites Pope Gregory in support, and Genesis 8:21 is quoted to show how enslaved man's will is.

In *The Bondage of the Will*, Luther calls it a *Keinwille* (no will),[12] for apart from election no fallen will would choose God. Yet God works through evil although God cannot do evil, being good himself. But he uses tools

---

10. *Weimar Ausgabe*, 18:685.
11. Heinrich Bornkamm, *Luther in Mid-Career 1521–1530*, trans. E. Theodore Bachmann (Philadelphia: Fortress, 1983), 417.
12. *Weimar Ausgabe*, 28:630–31.

(Werkzeuge) that cannot draw away from his use. This all belongs to the mystery of his majesty and incomprehensible judgment (Rom. 11:33). Luther is blunt with reference to Judas:

> . . . if God foreknew that Judas would be a traitor, Judas necessarily becomes a traitor, and it was not in the power of Judas or any creature to do differently or to change his will, *though he did what he did willingly* and not under compulsion, but that act was a work of God, which he set in motion by his omnipotence, like everything else. In it is an irrefutable and self-evident proposition that God does not lie and is not deceived. There are no obscure or ambiguous words here, even if all the most learned men of all the centuries are so blind as to think and speak otherwise.[13]

Maybe Luther was at his simplest in his *Smaller Catechism:* "92. By whom was sin brought into the world? Sin was brought into the world by the *devil,* who was once a holy angel but fell away from God, and by *man,* who of his own free will yielded to the temptation of the devil."
A modern Lutheran writer puts it this way:[14]

> In his famous treatise known as *The Bondage of the Will,* Luther presented fifty-seven arguments against the heresy [of free will]. Below are three of them:
> Argument 16: Universal unbelief proves "free-will" to be false.
> In John 16:8 Jesus says that the Holy Spirit will "convict the world of guilt in regard to sin." In verse 9 he explains that the sin is "men do not believe in me." Now this sin of unbelief is not in the skin or in the hair, but in the mind and the will. All men without exception are as ignorant of the fact of their guilty unbelief as they are ignorant of Christ himself. The guilt of unbelief has to be revealed to them by the Holy Spirit. So all that is in man, including "free-will," stands condemned by God and can only add to the guilt of which he is ignorant until God shows it to him. The whole of scripture proclaims Christ as the only way of salvation. Anyone who is outside Christ is under the power of Satan, sin, death and the wrath of God. Christ alone can rescue men from the kingdom of Satan. We are not delivered by any power within us but only by the grace of God.
> Argument 18: Knowing that salvation does not depend on "free-will" can be very comforting.
> I confess that I wouldn't want "free-will" even if it were given to me! If my salvation were left to me I would be no match for all the dangers, difficulties and devils that I have to fight. But even if there were no enemies to fight, I could never be certain of success. I would never be sure I had pleased God or whether there was something more I needed to do. I can prove this from my own painful experience over many years. But my salvation is in God's hands and not my

---

13. Luther's *Works*, vol. 33, *Career of the Reformer 3*, 185.
14. Sheridan B. Manasen, D.M.D., in *Christian News Encyclopedia* (Washington, Mo.: Missourian Publishing, 1992), 5:3752.

own. He will be faithful to his promise to save me, not on the basis of what I do but according to his great mercy. God does not lie and will not let my enemy the devil snatch me out of his hands. By "free-will," not one person can be saved. But by free grace, many will be saved. Not only so, but I am glad to know that as a Christian I please God, not because of what I do but because of his grace. If I work too little or too badly he graciously pardons me and makes me better. This is the glory of all Christians.

Argument 19: God's honour cannot be tarnished.

You may be worried that it is hard to defend the honour of God in all this. "After all," you might say, "he condemns those who cannot help being sinful who are forced to stay that way because God does not choose to save them." As Paul says: "Like the rest, we were by nature objects of wrath" (Ephesians 2:3). But you must look at it another way. God should be reverenced and respected as one who is merciful to all he justifies and saves, although they are completely unworthy. We know God is divine. He is also wise and just. His justice is not the same as human justice. It is beyond our human understanding to grasp fully, as Paul exclaims in Romans 11:33: "Oh the depth of the riches of the wisdom and knowledge of God! How unsearchable his judgments and his paths beyond tracing out!" If we agree that God's nature, strength, wisdom and knowledge are far above ours, we should also believe that his justice is greater and better than ours. He had promised us that when he reveals his glory to us, we will see clearly what we should believe now—that he is just, always was and always will be.

Here is another example. If you use human reason to consider the way God rules the affairs of the world, you are forced to say either that there is no God or that God is unjust. The wicked prosper and the good suffer (see Job 12:6 and Psalm 73:12) and that appears to be unjust. So, many men deny the existence of God and say that everything happens by chance. The answer to this problem is that there is life after this life and all that is not punished and repaid here will be punished and repaid there. This life is nothing more than a preparation for, or rather, a beginning of the life that is to come This problem has been debated in every age but is never solved, except by believing the gospel as found in the Bible. Three lights shine on the problem: the light of nature, the light of grace and the light of glory. By the light of nature, God seems to be unjust for the good suffer and the wicked prosper. The light of grace helps us further but it does not explain how God can condemn someone who, by his own strength, can do nothing but sin and be guilty. Only the light of glory will explain this on this coming day when God will reveal himself as a God who is entirely just, although his judgment is beyond the understanding of human beings. A godly man believes that God fore-knows and fore-ordains all things and that nothing happens except by his will. No man, or angel, or any other creature, therefore, has a "free-will." Satan is the prince of this world and holds all men captive unless they are released by the power of the Holy Spirit.

Among our four champions of an enslaved will that only grace can liberate, Luther is clearly the least lucid though perhaps the most fervent. While the others elucidate and answer problems raised against this central doctrine, Luther swallows them all, God having given him a strong stomach. Grace is necessary and grace is sovereign and that is that.

Calvin on Grace and the Bondage of the Will

For John Calvin, "the human soul consists of two faculties, understanding and will." He insists "that no power can be found in the soul that does not duly have reference to one or the other of these numbers. . . and in this way we include sense under understanding."[15] A diagram makes clear Calvin's view:

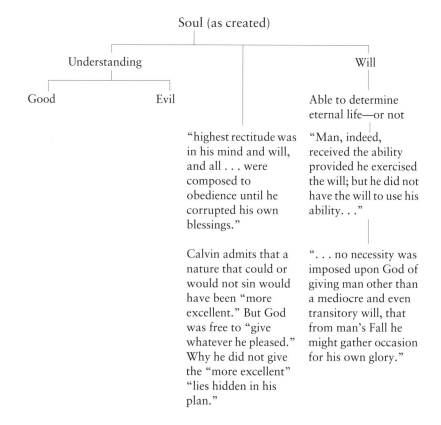

This deals with Calvin on the *original* free will of created man. He defends the man who had the will to choose eternal life if he would and refuse it if he

---

15. John Calvin, *Institutes of the Christian Religion,* The Library of Christian Classics, ed. John T. McNeill, vol. 20, trans. Ford Lewis Battles (Philadelphia: Westminster, 1960), 1.25.8.

would not. Calvin, the great opponent of free will, was the opponent of free will in *fallen* humanity. Chapter 5 of book 2 is given over to the "Refutation of the Objections Commonly Put Forward in Defense of Free Will." This is the Genevan's biblical defense of the "Grace of God and the Bondage of the Will" against the semi-Pelagians of the past and the Arminians of the present.

Opponents argue that if sin is necessary, it is not sin; if it is voluntary, it can be avoided. But, Calvin points out, sin is "not from creation but from corruption . . ."[16] in which "Adam willingly bound himself over to the devil's tyranny." And "all men are deservedly held guilty of this rebellion." Bernard is cited as teaching that "necessity is voluntary." The Calvinistic answer to the argument that choices being voluntary means sin can be avoided is a mere reminder: the *necessary* can be voluntary.

The answer to the second objection, that reward and punishment lose meaning if there is no free will, is the same. Man's punishment is because man is responsible for having lost his free will in the garden. As for reward, Calvin begins with Augustine's "God does not crown our merits but his own gifts." He ends with an observation of his own that these gifts of God are rewarded to us because "he makes them ours."[17] This idea is not developed here, but Calvin means that although the Christian's so-called good works are not good enough in themselves to deserve reward, the imputation of Christ's righteousness gives them merit fit to be rewarded. Edwards spells this out more specifically in his "Justification by Faith."

According to the critics, not only rewards and punishments would disappear if there were no free will in fallen man, but present good and evil would be meaningless also. God is the source of good, and if some fall away from it, well, God does not choose to give all the gift of perseverance, says Calvin (very uncalvinistically).[18]

All exhortations would be meaningless without free will, say the voluntarists. For Calvin it is not free will but God who gives the grace to respond to warnings, threatenings, promises as he sovereignly chooses. Apart from him Christians can do nothing. "When he [God] addresses the same Word to the reprobate, though not to correct them, he makes it serve another use: today to press them with the witness of conscience, and in the Day of Judgment to render them the more inexcusable."[19] "Paul points out that teaching is not useless among the reprobate, because it is to them 'a fragrance from death to death.'" A free will is necessary to respond properly to a divine exhortation. A bondaged free will is all that is necessary to respond culpably!

16. Sect. 1.
17. Sect. 2.
18. Sect. 3.
19. Sect. 5.

Why are there commands if there is no ability to respond? Full of Augustine here, Calvin even ends with the latter's immortal "Let God give what he commands and command what he wills."[20] The command can be fulfilled not by free will but by free grace.

Calvin notes three kinds of commands. First, God commands us to convert and to be converted because the command drives us not to free will but to God's grace, which alone can fulfill the command. Second, the commands to follow God's teaching are balanced by "countless passages that bear witness that whatever righteousness, holiness, piety, and purity we can have are gifts of God." Third, the exhortations to persevere are matched by being "strong in the Lord." Calvin addresses the difficult text, Jeremiah 31:32–33, which "cannot be refuted by any cavils: that the covenant of God made with the ancient people was invalid because it was only the letter; moreover, that it is not otherwise established than when the Spirit enters into it to dispose their hearts to obedience."[21] Central in Augustine's *Spirit and Letter,* the heart of Luther's *Bondage of the Will,* exegeted precisely in Edwards's *Notes on the Bible,* Calvin puts it in a nutshell here: Law is law and grace is grace.

The tenth section deals with the enemies' citation "of promises in which the Lord makes a covenant with our wills: 'Seek good and not evil, and you will live.'" It is interesting that Calvin cites objections earlier made against Luther. These promises, offered to believers and unbelievers, have significance for both. Using arguments already cited, Calvin concludes: "the Lord neither attributes to us the free capacity to will or to hearken, nor yet does he mock us for our impotence." Section 11 continues with the explanation of rebukes, and then Calvin concludes by dealing with special passages and incidents in Scripture.

On Deuteronomy 30:11, Calvin admits that the "you can do it" referring to God's commandments might be problematical, but Paul "our sure interpreter" shows that Moses was talking about the gospel. Moreover, if Moses meant that God's people could keep God's commandments he would be leading them "to dash into ruin." Paul conforms to this testimony: in the gospel, salvation is not offered under the hard, harsh, and impossible condition laid down for us by the law—that only those who have fulfilled all the commandments will finally attain it—but under an easy, ready, and openly accessible condition. Therefore, this Scripture (Rom. 10) has no value in establishing the freedom of the human will.[22] (The human will—as fallen, understood.)

Next it is pointed out, in favor of free will, that Hosea has God going to his place until his people seek his face (5:15). Here Calvin gives a *tu quoque*

20. Sect. 7.
21. Sect. 9.
22. Sect. 12.

argument: that even the free willers insist that some grace must be involved in God's people seeking him. Moreover, the Lord's withdrawing (by holding back his Word) is "for no other purpose than to compel us to recognize our own nothingness."[23]

Calvin next writes, on works being called "ours": "I will object in turn that the bread that we petition God to give us is also called 'ours.'"

To the further protest that Scripture affirms that we worship and serve God, he answers: "In who is such a fool as to assert that God moves man just as we throw a stone?"[24] But when God is working in converted persons, Calvin's answer is taken again from Augustine: "To will is of nature but to will aright is of grace."

The role of free will in regeneration is next addressed. Here Calvin seems to agree with Augustine but alters his view. For Augustine, "grace does not destroy the will but rather restores it," while Calvin sees God as considering "it necessary to put a new nature within."[25] The grand result: "we ourselves are fitly doing what God's Spirit is doing in us." Here Calvin solemnly warns the Arminians of the ages: "any mixture of the power of free will that men strive to mingle with God's grace is nothing but a corruption of grace. It is just as if one were to dilute wine with muddy, bitter water."

After a rather abstruse argument about Cain's ability to master his appetite,[26] one finds the surprising use of Romans 9:16 in favor of free will by those who interpret "so it is not upon him who wills or upon him who runs but upon God who shows mercy." In answer to those who infer that God's mercy makes up for the deficiency in man's willing and running, Calvin (after recovering from the shock of such an interpretation) says: "Paul's meaning is simpler: it is not the will; it is not the running that prepares the way to salvation for us. Only the mercy of God is here."[27]

We can now turn to Christ's words in Luke 10:30, where he tells of the traveler left "half-alive" by the thieves. Free willers make that mean that fallen man is not altogether dead but that something of his free will is left. Disgusted with this twisting of allegory, Calvin nevertheless asks, even if man had judgments of honesty and awareness of divinity, "what do these qualities amount to?" He ends his masterful discussion with this exclamation:

Therefore let us hold this as an undoubted truth which no siege engine can shake: the mind of men has been so completely estranged from God's righteousness that it conceives, desires, and undertakes only that which is impious, perverted, foul, impure, and infamous. The heart is so stupid in the poison of

23. Sect. 13.
24. Sect. 14.
25. Sect. 15.
26. Sect. 16.
27. Sect. 17.

sin, that it can breathe out nothing but a loathesome stench. But if some men occasionally made a show of good, their minds nevertheless ever remain enveloped in hypocrisy and deceitful craft and their hearts bound by inner perversity.[28]

Calvin is nothing if not clear about free will. Even in the garden, its freedom was to fall. However, Calvin, unlike Augustine, Luther, and Edwards, is not much troubled about how the created good tree (man) could bring forth bad fruit. Once we have a bad tree (sinful man), Calvin lets it fall on all free-willers and grind them to theological death. The fallen will of man freely chooses indeed—to remain fallen. Only when God by grace makes a good tree does it willingly will to produce good fruit. From the garden of Eden to the Vine of Christ the will is what God leaves it to be or makes it to be.

Jonathan Edwards on Grace and the Bondage of the Will

Surely Jonathan Edwards believed that man's chief end is to glorify God and to enjoy him forever. This is what makes man superior to animals. If, therefore, man's superior mentality is not used accordingly, it becomes a liability. "If men have no other end to seek but to gratify their senses, reason is nothing but an impediment."[29] The animals are better off. And if worship be the essential duty of man, his will is his most important feature.

"If men be very careful in temporal things to their families, or greatly promote the temporal interest of the neighborhood, or of the public; yet if no glory be brought to God by it they are altogether useless"—"unless in their destruction."

Before his fall, man's soul was pure and his reason ruled his will (for a while), in sharp contrast to what prevails after the fall. "At the very same time that wicked men are tempted to commit some sin, and their reason then tells them that it will expose them to the eternal wrath of God, and that it will therefore be a dreadful folly for them to do it, *yet they will do it.*"[30] Again, on their coming to Christ, "their will is in this also inconsistent with itself."[31]

---

28. Sect. 19.
29. Manuscript sermon on Ezekiel 15:2–4; *Works,* 2:125–29 (Hickman edition, currently published by the Banner of Truth, which I use throughout this piece unless otherwise indicated). This part of the essay is based largely on my *Rational Biblical Theology of Jonathan Edwards,* vol. 2 (Powhattan, Va.: Berea Publications; Orlando, Fla.: Ligonier Ministries, 1992), chap. 20, 237–84 and passim.
30. *Rational Biblical Theology of Jonathan Edwards,* 245 (italics added).
31. Ibid., 247.

Edwards understands the soul to have two parts: understanding and will. Not only is *Freedom of the Will* based on this dichotomy; that dichotomy underlies *Religious Affections* as well. Jeremiah Day,[32] Enoch Pond,[33] and others have criticized Edwards for ignoring "sensibility," which they thought was between understanding and will. However, Edwards did not ignore "sensibility" but saw it as belonging to the understanding.

Edwards agreed with the English Puritan, John Preston, that the mind came first and the heart or will second. "Such is the nature of man, that no object can come at the heart but through the door of the understanding. . . ."[34] In the garden, man *could have* rejected the temptation of the mind to move the will to disobey God. After the fall he could not, although Arminians and Pelagians thought otherwise. Their notion of the "freedom of the will" made it always possible for the will to reject what the mind presented. This perverted notion, Edwards said in *Original Sin,* "seems to be a grand favorite point with Pelagians and Arminians, and all divines of such characters, in their controversies with the orthodox."[35] For Edwards, acts of the will are not free in the sense of uncaused. "If will determines its own acts, that determination is an act of the will."[36] Conrad Cherry cites philosopher Murphy approvingly: for Edwards, acts of the will are effects that have causes.[37]

"When God first made man he had a principle of holiness." But now "man is born with no other principle but self-love to direct his powers."[38] In the application, Edwards says that Adam, too, had the self-love principle but it was subject to the love of God and, therefore, good.

Edwards's sermon on 1 John 4:12 tells us that holiness was a supernatural principle in Adam and did not properly belong to human nature.[39] Human nature as such exists apart from a principle of holiness. The unregenerate are true, although utterly evil, men.

The sermon "Jesus Christ the same yesterday, to-day, and for ever" leads to an oblique reference to the changeability of mere man and his will:

32. *An Examination of President Edwards's Inquiry on the Freedom of the Will* (New Haven, Conn.: Durrie and Peck, 1841), 14.

33. "Review of Edwards on the Will," *Literary and Theological Review* (1834).

34. Sermon on Hebrews 5:12, "Every Christian should make a business of endeavoring to grow in the knowledge of divinity," *Works 2,* 158. Cf. unpublished sermon on 2 Peter 1:19 (4), "When God first made man he had a principle of holiness in his heart," 1, to the Mohawks at the Treaty, 16 August 1751. The text for the sermon reads, "We have also a more pure word of prophecy."

35. *Works* (New Haven, Conn.: Yale University Press), 3:375.

36. Miscellany 1075 in Harvey Townsend, *Philosophy of Edwards,* 165.

37. *Theology of Jonathan Edwards,* 433.

38. Unpublished sermon on Matthew 10:17, "That the nature of man is so corrupted that he is become a very evil and hurtful creature," 3, two sermons, before 1733.

39. Unpublished ms. sermon on 1 John 4:12, "True grace in the hearts of the saints is something divine," 5 December 1738.

We learn from the truth taught in the text, how fit Christ was to be appointed as the surety of fallen man. Adam, the first surety of mankind, failed in his work, because he was a mere creature, and so a mutable being. Though he had so great a trust committed to him, as the care of the eternal welfare of all his posterity, yet, not being unchangeable, he failed, and transgressed God's holy covenant. He was led aside, and drawn away by the subtle temptation of the devil. He being a changeable being, his subtle adversary found means to turn him aside, and so he fell, and all his posterity fell with him. It appeared, therefore, that we stood in need of a surety that was unchangeable, and could not fail in his work. Christ, whom God appointed to this work, to be to us a second Adam, is such an one that is the same yesterday, to-day, and for ever, and therefore was not liable to fail in his undertaking. He was sufficient to be depended on as one that would certainly stand all trials, and go through all difficulties, until he had finished the work that he had undertaken, and actually wrought out eternal redemption for us.[40]

The Holy Spirit was originally with the originally righteous man. The medievalists had an originally nonrighteous man who would be pulled apart by the tension between body and soul were it not for the superadded gift *(donum superadditum)* to hold him in harmony. When man failed to control the tension by failing to use this special gift, he fell into sin. Why man as created did not use this gift was the scholastics' problem as it was Augustine's before them. He called it the *aidiutorium*.

Edwards's problem is far more difficult. His superadded gift was none other than the Spirit of God. The Holy Spirit could not fail to keep changeable man from freely changing from good to evil, and man could not overpower him if he were tempted to do so. If the Holy Spirit were resident in the first man, man would never have fallen (as will be the case later in heaven where, for that reason, he never can fall). If the Spirit were not resident, but merely offering to remain within man, it still remains difficult to understand why such a man would ever reject such a Gift.

Man was made with a holiness principle (the Holy Spirit) but this was not essential to human nature. It was lost by the fall without humanity ceasing to be. As a matter of fact, all the motivation that is necessary to human nature per se is self-interest, not God-interest. Yet man should know from his rational nature that it is to man's self-interest to be controlled by God-interest. He was at first aided toward this by the "supernatural principle of holiness" (the presence of the Holy Spirit himself) in Adam, but being deceived by the devil he let his self-interest overthrow his God-interest.

Edwards goes into a deep discussion of Adam's "free" first sin—probably deeper than Augustine, Luther, Calvin, or any other Reformed theologian. And Edwards wrote his greatest most profound work, *On the Freedom of the*

40. Ms. sermon on Hebrews 13:8, printed, *Works,* 2:949–54.

Will, as an evangelistic tract to refute the Arminian errors pertaining to the subject that in his mind was undermining the "doctrines of grace"—to wit, the gospel.

What Edwards detailed biblically, theologically, and philosophically in his great treatise, he preached constantly. "That wicked men are servants and slaves to sin" is the doctrine of Edwards's sermon on John 8:44.[41] The text clearly indicates that men are bondservants of sin though they deny that they feel any such servitude. Edwards's answer to that is "you can't see that you are under slavery now because of your blindness which is one effect of your servitude."[42] You will see it, he says, if you pay attention to this sermon. But in any case you will see it in the world to come when you are set free of the blindness. But men are under Satan's bondage and therefore they have no satisfaction even if they had the whole world. They are utterly devoted to the commission of sin even though their personal interests suffer by it. They are obedient to the point of jumping into the pit at Satan's command. The bondage of their wills appears most clearly in the fact that men receive no advantage from their servitude. There is no happiness for them. Even the earthly slave may have enough to keep alive, but sin utterly kills. Man's whole heart is given up to sin. Satan will not allow him to see one truth. He can open his eyes only when sin allows. His senses are also blindfolded. Sin makes him hate life itself (Prov. 21:4; Rom. 6:19). As an analogy Edwards refers to a practice in Guinea, of which he had heard, where victims were required to gather the fuel for their own burning.[43]

But withal this is a voluntary bondage. As Edwards says in another sermon, "we may learn the reason why natural men will not come to Christ: they *do* not come because they *will* not come."[44] Edwards says to the sinner who would use his sin as an excuse that "as long as you will not, it is no matter whether you have ability or no ability."[45] As long as a person is morally indisposed toward virtue it makes no difference, because moral inability is in and of itself reprehensible.

Natural inability of will does excuse, according to Edwards, while moral inability does not; but that refers only to an initial natural inability.[46] That is, if a person never had an ability to choose morally then he would not be morally blameworthy or praiseworthy. Naturally one asks at this point, "But, Mr. Edwards, suppose this person was created this way." Edwards, of course, does not believe he was created this way and he is not thinking of that possibility. He believes that God is a moral God who would never make a

---

41. Unpublished ms. sermon on John 8:44 (1).
42. Ibid.
43. Unpublished ms. sermon on Romans 2:5 (1).
44. Ms. sermon on Romans 5:10; printed, *Works*, 2:130–41. The quotation is on 138.
45. Ms. sermon on Romans 3:19; printed, *Works*, 1:668–79.
46. *Works* (Yale), 1:309–10.

person wicked and then blame him for being wicked. Nevertheless, he does not spell that out at this point and we have to assume that it is in his mind when he says that moral inability never excuses. Edwards is assuming that God would not create man morally unable. At least we assume he is assuming. (We remember the discussion on "The Entrance of Sin into the World.") He does have that awesome sentence in *Freedom of the Will* that seems to suggest that God might have created man with a disinclination to virtue. Edwards believed that moral inability was something that a person came by responsibly and was therefore a moral liability to him. In the sermon on Romans 11:10 he does say that this moral inability or bondage of will whereby we are bowed down to the earth and cannot stand erect, as was the case with Nebuchadnezzar and with the woman who was bowed down for eighteen years, came about by the first transgression of Adam, but men are given over when they reject the offer of mercy.[47] This is a rather surprising theme that Edwards apparently nowhere develops. His general teaching seems to be that fallen man is given over in infancy, at the moment of birth. He is born dead in trespasses and sins. Here Edwards seems to suggest that he is bowed down only after he willfully rejects mercy.

The utterly debilitating effect of sin in the life of the natural man is seen in the effect of the means of grace in his life or rather the noneffect of the means of grace in his life. The most earnest biblical preaching, the most fervent prayers, the most assiduous personal counseling and labor, every conceivable ordinance of God in the gospel and in providence is of no use to those who are in willful bondage to evil. It is an internal ailment that no amount of external medicine, including preaching, will ever heal.

The burden of the *Treatise on Grace* is to show that this moral inability is what makes supernatural grace absolutely necessary to the salvation of the human soul. We have no voluntary moral power "to make ourselves holy or work any holy inclination or affections or exert any one holy act any more than a dead body can raise itself to life."[48] Again elsewhere in this same sermon for a suicide he writes, "We are in ourselves utterly without any strength or power to help ourselves."

Though only God by supernatural grace can help a person in this state of voluntary moral inability, no one dare say that God is obligated to do so. Men have a habit of saying that because they cannot do something God must help them to do it. Any cogency in that kind of argument eludes Edwards. "Persons are not at all excused for any moral defect or corruption that is in them, that God doesn't help 'em to be otherwise."[49] The Bible says that every

---

47. Unpublished ms. sermon on Romans 11:10, "Some men are laid under such a curse that they are forever bowed down to the earth and never are able to lift up themselves," 5 June 1740.
48. Unpublished ms. sermon on Romans 5:6.
49. Unpublished ms. sermon on Deuteronomy 29:4.

voluntary act is a responsible one and a free one. Man will be accountable for his corruption even though God does not interfere.

With this doctrine of sin how does Edwards account for the apparent goodness of man? What is his explanation of what Augustine calls the "splendid vices of the heathen" and Martin Luther "civic righteousness"? When natural men do an act of justice it is not wrong as an act of justice, and when they do an act of liberality it is not wrong as an act of liberality. What is done is only a shadow without substance. There is the shell of the duty but the inside is hollow.[50] The natural man may have a shadow of morality but never the real thing. Edwards puts the same principle in somewhat more technical language:

> Thus when a natural man speaks the truth, when he is just in his dealings, when he gives to the poor, he does those things that are right as to the manner of them though altogether wrong as to the matter. As to what is visible in the action it is right. That which is as it were the body of the actions; but, if we look at the inward principle and aim which is, as it were, the soul of the act and is what God looks at and which the rule does chiefly regard it is altogether wrong.[51]

In a sermon that carries the title "Wicked men are the children of hell," Edwards does remark nevertheless that "there are many in a natural condition that are a very good sort of man are sober and moral in their behavior. . . ."[52] Of course he means moral in this outward sense of the word, because Edwards would never say that intentionally willing moral men are children of hell. Likewise, in a sermon entitled "The Gadarenes loved their swine better than Jesus Christ," Edwards remarks that if natural men ever part with anything it is not for Christ's sake but to avoid hell.[53] Thus even the morality of these swinish people is directed toward hell and not toward heaven.

50. Unpublished ms. sermon on Romans 3:11–12.
51. Ibid.
52. Unpublished ms. sermon on Matthew 23:15, "Wicked men are the children of hell," 5 January 1738/39.
53. Unpublished ms. sermon on Mark 5:16–17, "The Gadarenes loved their swine better than Jesus Christ," 6 April 1737.

13

John Wesley's Contention with Calvinism: Interactions Then and Now

Thomas J. Nettles

Spiritual Biography

John Wesley's life covers nearly the entire eighteenth century (1703–1791). He was one of nineteen children, nine of whom died as infants.[1] Although Wesley's great-grandfather and grandfather dissented from the Church of England and suffered for their convictions, Wesley's father, Samuel Wesley, left a dissenting college and a dissenting life, and subscribed to the Thirty-Nine Articles in order to enter Exeter College, Oxford. He obtained a curacy in London and married Susanna Annesley, the daughter of another well-known ejected clergyman. In 1696 he became rector of Epworth parish and remained there until his death in 1735.

John was elected to a fellowship at Oxford in 1726, was ordained priest in 1728, and reentered Oxford. He became a member and eventually leader of what some derisively called "the holy club," which met for prayer, discussion of the classics, study of the Greek New Testament, self-examination, and projects of charitable relief, including visiting prisoners and poor parish-

1. L. Tyerman, *The Life and Times of the Rev. John Wesley, M.A.*, 3 vols. (New York: Harper and Brothers, 1870), 1:15.

ioners. In pursuit of these projects they received the permission and the guidance of the bishop.[2]

In 1735, John and Charles Wesley accepted an invitation from the Society for the Propagation of the Gospel to go to Georgia on a mission to the Indians and the colonists. Though extremely disciplined on board ship and taking great pains to use every moment of time in godly conversation, instruction, learning, and devotion, John Wesley concluded because of fear at the roaring of the wind, "I was unfit, for I was unwilling to die."[3] Impressed with the courage and assurance of the Moravians on board, he became disturbed at his inability to answer confidently of a saving relationship with Christ. When questioned by Spangenberg, a pastor of the German pietists, Wesley judged his own answers to be "vain words."[4]

On the voyage back to England, begun 22 December 1737, Wesley gave free reign to his thoughts regarding his eternal state. He was convinced "of unbelief, having no such faith in Christ, as will prevent my heart from being troubled." He also lamented, "I went to America, to convert the Indians; but oh! who shall convert me! Who, what is he that will deliver me from this evil heart of unbelief." Strangely, however, in the same meditation he continued with some confidence, "I think verily, if the Gospel be true, I am safe."[5] Despondency about his spiritual state returned and he wrote, "I who went to America to convert others, was never myself converted to God." A later editorial footnote inserted at that point "I am not sure of this."[6]

Soon after landing in England, John met Peter Boehler, 7 February 1738, and had a number of interviews with him until Boehler left for Carolina on 4 May. Boehler taught that faith in Christ always produced "dominion over sin and constant peace from a sense of forgiveness." In addition he taught that "justification was instantaneous work."[7]

These conversations clearly convinced Wesley of his unbelief. On 24 May, a Wednesday, after arising early to read his New Testament and attending an afternoon service at St. Paul's, Wesley went to a society meeting in Aldersgate Street. There he heard Luther's preface to the Book of Romans read, and, according to his testimony, "I felt my heart strangely warmed. I felt I did trust

---

2. John Wesley, *The Journal of the Rev. John Wesley*, 4 vols. (London: J. Kershaw, 1827), 1:6, 7. Wesley and his friends took great pains to do all things in proper order, avoiding officiousness and always seeking the counsel of informed and wise people. Other names by which they "were sometimes dignified" were "the Godly Club," "Enthusiasts," and the "Reforming Club." Ibid., 10.

3. John Wesley, *Journal*, 1:17, 23 November 1735, and also 23 January 1736.

4. Ibid., 1:21, 7 February 1736.

5. Ibid., 1:67, 69; 8, 24 January 1738.

6. Ibid., 1:70, 29 January 1738.

7. Tyerman, *Life and Times*, 1:177, 399. Although he defended the Moravians from misrepresentations, Wesley's own investigations eventually led him to consider Moravian theology as antinomian.

in Christ, Christ alone, for salvation; and an assurance was given me, that He had taken away my sins."[8]

Even this experience gave way to further ambiguity of expression, possibly caused by his visit to Hernhutt. Wesley told his brother Samuel, "The seal of the Spirit, the love of God shed abroad in my heart, and producing joy in the Holy Ghost, . . . this witness of the Spirit I have not."[9] On 14 October, Wesley engaged in a series of meditations designed to conclude whether or not he was a new creature. On most counts he would conclude, "In this respect, I am a new creature." On some counts he felt "other desires often arise in my heart" and "I cannot find in myself the love of God or of Christ."[10] In December 1738 he concluded "there is in me still, the old heart of stone"; and, "there is in me still the carnal heart"; and "my desires, passions and inclinations in general are mixed; having something of Christ and something of earth." In January he wrote, "My friends affirm I am mad, because I said I was not a Christian a year ago. I affirm, I am not a Christian now. . . . That I am not a Christian at this day, I as assuredly know, as that Jesus is the Christ. . . . Though I have constantly used all the means of grace, for twenty years, I am not a Christian."[11]

These meditations revealed not only Wesley's dead earnestness about personal religion but also his penchant toward idiosyncratic definitions of words and reductionistic argumentation. His "friends," including his brother Samuel, were perplexed as to what he meant by "Christian" when he claimed not to be one. While they were thinking about justifying faith in Christ, Wesley insisted on using the word *Christian* for internal moral conformity to Christ. If his friends became confused, his eventual antagonists became incensed. Much of the frustration that crescendoed into rage when Calvinists took up a polemic against him can be traced to these tendencies. His opponents fumed over what they felt was simplistic reductionism and a squirminess and privatization of definitions.

These meditations also reveal a resistance to any system that seems to set forth ends without proper attention to means. He insisted that one could lay no claim to benefits from the objective work of Christ without corresponding evidences of the subjective. Thus he indulged such a great antipathy toward

---

8. Wesley, *Journal,* 1:97, 98, 24 May 1738.

9. Tyerman, *Life and Times,* 1:190.

10. Wesley, *Journal,* 1:155, 156, 14 October 1738.

11. Ibid., 164, 165, 14 January 1739. Wesley introduces the meditation, "One who had had the form of godliness many years, wrote the following reflections." His conclusion that he was not a Christian came from his identification of Christianity with full sanctification. He looked for a full display of the "fruits of the Spirit of Christ," an undiminished love for God in preference to anything in the world ["I have been, yea, and still am, hankering after a happiness, in loving, and being loved by one or another"], a joy in the Holy Ghost that was unspeakable and full of glory, and a peace that passes understanding, one which cannot be explained in terms of "health, strength, friends, a competent fortune, and a composed, cheerful temper."

antinomianism that it became just as dominant a theological principle from the negative standpoint as holiness was from the positive standpoint.

These contemplations came subsequent to a visit to Germany begun in June 1738 to experience the Christianity of the Moravian communities. There Wesley found "living proofs of the power of faith: persons saved from inward as well as outward sin . . . and from all doubt and fear"; he found that whereas Boehler made justification and assurance of it inseparable, Zinzendorf taught that one "may not know he is justified till long after"; and he heard Christian David preach four memorable messages concerning justification, peace with God, and the ground of faith. David taught that a sinner must not rely on his sense of contrition as a foundation for justification. If relied on, it would only hinder one's justification. Remission of sins is not a result of this "either in whole or in part." Instead he affirmed that the ground of justifying faith is "nothing wrought in you by the Holy Ghost; but it is something without you, viz. The righteousness and the blood of Christ."[12] Further discussions with Zinzendorf confirmed his view of the urgency of holiness he earlier had imbibed from William Law, Thomas a'Kempis, and Jeremy Taylor and settled a conviction in his mind that he had a call to "spread scriptural holiness over the land."

These contacts stirred Wesley to further thinking about justification and sanctification. He solicited the testimony of the experience of grace of friends and examined his own experience. This led him not only to the tumultuous struggle in his own soul but also to a critical appraisal of the Moravian treatment of justifying faith. He eventually concluded that the Moravians collapsed justification and sanctification and had no room for faith that "works by love" or for distinctive progressive holiness in the believer. Their discussions he described as "a heap of palpable self-contradiction" and "senseless jargon." He described his friends the Moravians as "the most plausible, and therefore the most dangerous of all the Antinomians now in England."[13]

Although he had preached in the open air in 1735, before George Whitefield was ordained,[14] Wesley pursued this practice more consistently beginning in 1739 with the encouragement of Whitefield. In the course of the next forty-two years he traveled some eight thousand miles a year and preached about one thousand sermons a year. He went to the remotest places of England and preached to the rudest, most ignorant, most brutal, and resistant. He knew England better than any living person and his journals serve well in social history as well as religious history. Had he kept his turnpike tolls and

---

12. Ibid., 1:101–12.

13. John Wesley, "A Short Review of the Difference between the Moravian Brethren (so called) and the Rev. Mr. John and Charles Wesley," in *The Works of the Reverend John Wesley, A.M.,* 7 vols. (New York: J. Emory and B. Waugh, 1831), 6:22–24.

14. Wesley, *Works,* 6:194.

inn tabs they would make an interesting history of prices in later eighteenth-century England.

Entries from 1790 will give a flavor of how an eighty-seven-year-old man fared. On Tuesday 5 October he wrote, "I went on to Rye. Though the warning was short, the congregation was exceeding large, and behaved with remarkable seriousness. While our people mixed with the Calvinists here, we were always perplexed, and gained no ground; but since they kept to themselves, they have continually increased, in grace as well as in number"; and on Wednesday the thirteenth: "In the evening I preached at Norwich; but the house would in no wise contain the congregation. How wonderfully is the tide turned! I am become an honourable man at Norwich. God has at length made our enemies to be at peace with us, and scarce any but Antinomians open their mouth against us."[15]

Controversy with Calvinists

Both notations show two of the enduring characteristics of Wesley, zeal for preaching and conflict with Calvinists. Though he desired his only enemies to be unbelief and the devil himself, and in spite of his 1865 opinion that a belief in predestination was "compatible with true Christianity," he came to consider Calvinism and the doctrine of unconditional election, if not equally intransigent, at least a close second. His correspondence often demonstrates this. He wrote to Lady Maxwell in September 1788: "You believe the doctrine of Absolute Predestination is false." If so, how could one give any foothold to it, seeing it is not only false but a "very dangerous doctrine," which hinders the work of God in the soul, feeds all evil and weakens good tempers, and turns "many out of the way of life" and drives them "back to perdition." Acknowledging these things, one should conclude that Calvinism is "the very antidote of Methodism, the most deadly and successful enemy which it ever had." To his preachers he wrote, "Nothing can more effectually stop the work of God than the breaking in of Calvinism upon you" and he urged earnestly that they would "calmly and diligently oppose it."[16]

Wesley's resistance to Calvinism was born initially of theological conviction; along the way several conflicts strengthened his stance against it both theoretically and practically. His unpleasant interaction with Augustus Toplady in 1770 brought the retort, "Arminians have as much right to be angry at Calvinists, as Calvinists have to be angry at Arminians."[17] He felt himself,

15. Wesley, *Journal*, 4:483, 485.
16. *The Letters of the Rev. John Wesley, A.M.*, 8 vols. (London: Epworth, 1931), 3:211–13; 8:95; 7:136.
17. Wesley, "What Is an Arminian," in *Works*, 6:134.

and many times rightly so, abused severely by Calvinist polemic. Polemical situations sometimes destroy even the most nobly irenic intentions. While Wesley aggressively asserted Arminian distinctives and engaged specific charges against himself whenever necessary, his love of Christian peace led him to seek to avoid personal confrontation, personal invective, bitterness, and rancor whenever possible. Each of his antagonists ostensibly sought the same. Wesley and his opponents, however, each equally felt the other in notable violation of the ideal.

George Whitefield

In 1740, Wesley preached a sermon based on Romans 8:32 entitled "Free Grace." He was prompted to this when controversy arose within his societies over the freedom given Calvinistic exhorters. The exhorters were dismissed. Whitefield heard of this and earnestly urged Wesley not to oppose the doctrines of grace. "I dread coming to England," Whitefield wrote Wesley from America, "unless you are resolved to oppose these truths with less warmth than when I was there last." One month later, in June 1740, he wrote, "For Christ's sake, if possible, never speak against election in your sermons." Again he implored Wesley, "Give me leave to exhort you not to be strenuous in opposing the doctrines of election and final perseverance." And after the sermon was in public Whitefield lamented, "If you think so meanly of Bunyan and the puritan writers, I do not wonder that you think me wrong."[18] Wesley's biographer, L. Tyerman, speaks paternalistically of Whitefield in this match with Wesley. While Wesley had "thoroughly sifted the subject for himself," Whitefield was "no theologian. His heart was one of the largest that ever throbbed in human bosom; but his logical faculties were small."[19] It is possible that Tyerman received his cue from Wesley in this; Wesley wrote Whitefield that it would be easy to "hit many other palpable blots, in what you call an answer to my sermon! And how, above measure, contemptible would you then appear to all impartial men, either of sense or learning."[20]

In the sermon itself, as he was wont to do, Wesley moved quickly from his definitions of unconditional election directly into reprobation. "God's decree concerning the election of grace . . . amounts to neither more nor less than what others call, 'God's decree of reprobation.'" After leveling eight objections to such a doctrine, including "it renders all preaching vain," it makes "the Christian revelation contradict itself," and "it is full of blasphemy," he concluded:

18. Tyerman, *Life and Times,* 1:314–17.
19. Ibid., 1:312.
20. Ibid., 1:325.

This is the blasphemy clearly contained in the *horrible decree* of predestination. And here I fix my foot. On this I join issue with every asserter of it. You represent God as worse than the devil. . . . Whatever that scripture proves, it never can prove this; whatever its true meaning be, this cannot be its true meaning. . . . But this I know, better it were to say it had no sense at all, than to say it had such a sense as this.[21]

In Whitefield's epistolary response to Wesley in December 1740 he remarked on Wesley's "equivocal definition of the word *Grace*, and your false definition of the word *Free*."[22] He also recognized that Wesley shifted the ground of argument from election to reprobation. "You knew people . . . were generally prejudiced against the doctrine of reprobation; and therefore thought, if you kept up their dislike of that, you could overthrow the doctrine of election entirely. For without doubt, the doctrine of election and reprobation must stand or fall together."[23] He had already in September remarked about Wesley's manner of thinking: "And you will not own *election*, because you cannot own it without believing the doctrine of *reprobation*. What then is there in *reprobation* so horrid? I see no blasphemy in holding that doctrine, if rightly explained. If God might have passed by all, He may pass by some."[24]

Whitefield expanded on this point in the open letter to Wesley. Surely, he believed, Wesley saw no injustice in the imputation of Adam's sin to his posterity. How then does the doctrine of reprobation assume that men are doomed "without any preceding offense or fault," as Wesley had said? If Adam's posterity fell in him, "God might justly have passed them **ALL** by, without sending his own Son to be our Savior for **ANY ONE**." Disagreement with this point would set Wesley opposed to the doctrine of original sin. But believing the doctrine of original sin, he must "acknowledge the doctrine of election and reprobation to be highly just and reasonable." If Adam's sin is imputed justly, and God might justly pass by all, then assuredly he might pass by some with no injustice. Election then becomes "amiable" instead of horrid.[25]

Wesley and Whitefield were reconciled through the mediation of Howell Harris. Annoyances continued, however, and, in 1751, Wesley published "Serious Thoughts upon the Perseverance of the Saints." He contended throughout that true believers may "so fall from God as to perish everlast-

---

21. Ibid., 1:320.
22. George Whitefield, *Life and Sermons* (New Haven, 1834), 631. The title page is missing from the volume to which I have access.
23. Ibid., 631.
24. Tyerman, *Life and Times*, 1:317.
25. Whitefield, *Life and Sermons*, 639, 640.

ingly."[26] Whitefield replied, "Strong assertions will not go for proofs with those who are sealed by the Holy Spirit even unto the day of redemption."[27]

John Gill

John Gill of the Particular Baptists said more. He responded with "The Doctrine of the Saints Final Perseverance Asserted and Vindicated."[28] Wesley's piece had asserted eight propositions, each concluding believers "may yet so fall as to perish everlastingly." Gill responded point by point to each assertion and each Scripture passage. He sought both to show the fallacy of Wesley's assertions and interpretations and to give a pure exposition of each passage in question. Wesley responded with his "Predestination Calmly Considered." It met the twofold purpose of correcting a tendency toward election in some of the Methodist Societies and of engaging Gill's pamphlet. When Gill read it he published again and asserted that Wesley had not attempted to answer "one argument advanced by me in vindication of" perseverance.[29] But beyond that, Wesley "was pleased to shift the controversy from perseverance to Predestination."[30] While Wesley's title promised a discussion of predestination, according to Gill, it delivered only a "harangue" against reprobation, "which he thought would best serve his purpose."[31]

Wesley believed that the sole support for Gill's exegesis was unconditional election. Destroy that and Gill's system falls. Tie unconditional election to reprobation and it is destroyed. Wesley only acted consistently with his past

26. Wesley, *Works*, 6:90.
27. Tyerman, *Life and Times*, 2:137.
28. John Gill, *Sermons and Tracts of John Gill*, new ed., 3 vols. (London: W. Hardcastle, 1815), 3:63–100.
29. An example of one of their literary exchanges comes from Hebrews 10:38. Wesley translated it, "If the just man that lives by faith draws back, my soul shall have no pleasure in him." Gill contended the translation was wrong and sought to demonstrate it both grammatically and from its origin in Habakkuk 2:4. Wesley asked that Gill please "show me wherein" the translation is wrong and sought to demonstrate that the writer of Hebrews had used the quote from Habakkuk in a way distinctly different from its original use. Gill responded, "I will tell him." "Ean, *if*, is by force removed from its proper place, even from one sentence back to another; inserting the word *that* before *live* is doing violence to the text; rendering *zesetai, that lives*, as if it was of the present tense, when it is future, and should be *shall live*. Leaving out *kai, and* or *but*, which distinguishes two propositions; so confounding them and making them one. . . . it is a clear case, that the just man in the text, and he that draws back, are two sorts of persons; it is most manifest, and beyond all contradiction, that in the original text in Hab. ii.4. the man whose *soul is lifted up* with pride and conceit of himself, *and is not upright in him,* has not the truth of grace in him, is the person who both according to the Apostle and the *Seventy* is supposed to draw back; from whom *the just* man *that lives by faith* is distinguished, and to whom he is opposed: and by the Apostle two sorts of persons are all along spoken of in the context, both before and after." Gill, "The Doctrine of Predestination," 3:130.
30. Ibid., 3:100.
31. Ibid., 3:101.

performances against any element of the doctrines of grace. He consistently argued that one could not consider "the doctrine of irresistible grace by itself, any more than that of unconditional election or final perseverance." It can never escape its connection "with unconditional reprobation, that millstone which hangs about the neck of your whole hypothesis."[32]

Gill's response made a positive case for predestination. A seven-point defense of election filled with short but pertinent Scripture exegesis preceded a discussion of reprobation as a second branch of predestination. Wesley said he would believe an election that did not imply reprobation; but "what election that can be," Gill responded, "the wit of man cannot devise."[33] Not even Wesley's notion of election can escape it, according to Gill.[34]

Although the doctrine of reprobation is not contrary to the nature and perfections of God, but is equally defensible with the doctrine of election, the Scriptures are "more sparing of the one than of the other, and have left us to conclude the one from the other," but not without clear and full evidence. Because of this, it seems "most proper and prudent, not so much to insist on this subject in our discourses and writing." This policy does not come from any weakness in the evidence but from the awfulness of the subject.

> This our opponents are aware of; and therefore press us upon this head, in order to bring the doctrine of election into contempt with weak or carnal men; and make their first attacks upon this branch of predestination, which is beginning wrong; since reprobation is not other than non-election, or what is opposed to election; let the doctrine of election be demolished, and the other will fall of course; but that will cost too much pains; and they find a better account with weak minds in taking the other method.[35]

Gill also challenged Wesley's caricature of the doctrine of perseverance. Wesley said it has a "natural, genuine tendency . . . either to prevent or obstruct holiness."[36] Wesley also stated it this way: "The doctrine of predestination naturally leads to the chambers of death." The entire Calvinistic sys-

---

32. Wesley, *Works,* 6:60.
33. Gill, "Doctrine of Predestination," 110.
34. This is a forceful and well-taken point to be treated later. It concerns Wesley's commitment to absolute foreknowledge of all events before creation and involves God as responsible for all events that occur just as much as if he had decreed them. In a later controversy with Augustus Toplady, Toplady makes the same point. "It is a position which follows even from the foreknowledge of God, putting all decrees quite out of the question. Only allow that some sinners actually will be condemned in the last day; and that God always knew and knows at this moment who those persons will be; and (not Mr. Wesley's, but) my consequence stands unshaken, that the condemnation of the reprobate is necessary and inevitable." *The Complete Works of Augustus Toplady,* a reprint of the 1894 one-volume edition (Harrisonburg, Va.: Sprinkle Publications, 1987), 746.
35. Gill, "Doctrine of Predestination," 112, 113.
36. Wesley, *Works,* 6:62.

tem, culminating in the doctrine of perseverance, gives careless sinners a carnal security, according to Wesley, which makes them conclude, "If I am elect, I may safely sin a little longer; for my salvation cannot fail." Gill was incredulous that Wesley could give such a caricature of the doctrine of perseverance and remonstrated, "Strange! that the doctrine of perseverance in grace and holiness, for no other perseverance do we plead for, should be so pleasing and agreeable to corrupt nature; that it obstructs holiness." How could Wesley not see that he was fulminating against a teaching that did not exist? The doctrine of perseverance, according to Gill, gives no encouragement to "professors to indulge their corruptions," but only intends to "promote holiness of heart and life."[37] Perseverance promotes no security for those satisfied with carnality but is a source of assurance only to those who love and seek to evaluate the purity of Christ and his commandments.

Gill concluded his remonstrance with an exposition of eight passages of Scripture that, according to Wesley, overthrow perseverance.[38] Wesley followed with his final response to Gill, a twelve-page pamphlet consisting entirely of hymns from "God's Everlasting Love."

James Hervey

The controversy over the meaning of imputed righteousness with James Hervey, the pupil and friend of Wesley, showed Wesley's growing discomfort with the tendency of Calvinism to invade the entire fabric of Christian theology. Hervey had written a theological dialogue entitled *Theron and Aspasio*. The discussion argued clearly that justification consisted not of forgiveness only but of the imputation of the perfect and complete righteousness of Christ. His obedience to God's law accomplished the righteousness that is credited to the sinner in his union with Christ. Wesley wrote Hervey about his discomfort with this language and received no response from him. Soon, Wesley wrote "A Preservative Against Unsettled Notions in Religion" to protect his people from the views of the imputation of the righteousness of Christ espoused in Hervey's work. Hervey considered this publication a violation of the rules of gentlemanly private correspondence and began to write a series of letters in answer to Wesley's reservations concerning imputation. Hervey did not publish the material in his lifetime (he was dying even as he began crafting his response) but the material was taken by others and quickly and inaccurately published. Eventually Hervey's brother published an edition of the letters in order to make the production more reputable editorially

---

37. Gill, "Doctrine of Predestination," 121, 122.

38. The eight passages are Ezekiel 18:24, 1 Timothy 1:19, Romans 11:17–24, John 15:1–5, 2 Peter 2:20, 21, Hebrews 6:4–6, Hebrews 10:38, Hebrews 10:29. An example of the exchange of Wesley and Gill has already been given.

and more accurate in content. In a private letter, October 1758, before he began his work Hervey indicated that Wesley was "so unfair in his quotations, and so magisterial in his Manner, that I find it no small Difficulty, to preserve the Decency of the Gentleman, and the Meekness of the Christian." He prayed that he might be aided to maintain both or else that God "not suffer me to write at all."[39]

Wesley heard that Hervey was working on this project and urged him to stop. Surely William Cudworth was the instigator. Wesley said, "Give no countenance to that insolent, scurrilous, virulent libel, which bears the name of William Cudworth."[40] Wesley had had a bitter exchange with Cudworth in 1745. He viewed Cudworth as a dangerous antinomian. Hervey was his dupe. Wesley feared that Hervey's insistence on the imputation of the active obedience of Christ as righteousness for the sinner would encourage antinomianism. "I have abundant proof, that the frequent use of this unnecessary phrase," Wesley wrote, "instead of furthering men's progress in vital holiness, has made them satisfied without any holiness at all."[41] Some that he knew interpreted imputed righteousness as a final and settled sanctification as well as justification. Personal progress in holiness was for them, therefore, as useless as it was impossible.[42]

Although at first blush this appears to be a controversy without Calvinist/Arminian overtones, the foundation of Wesley's resistance to imputed righteousness was its susceptibility to unilateral application and its apparent dependence on the covenantal obedience of Christ "for all his people." He smelled a Calvinist rat in this doctrine. In his response to Hervey's exposition of imputed covenantal righteousness Wesley said, "I could sooner be a Turk, a Deist, yea, an Atheist, than I could believe this."[43] In fact, when Hervey argued that God established a new covenant and Christ was charged with completing its conditions, Wesley challenged, "I deny both these assertions, which are the central point wherein Calvinism and Antinomianism meet."[44]

Wesley's denial forced a reworking of justification and made him maintain a doctrine that, according to Hervey, resembled that taught in the Council of Trent. In one letter to Hervey Wesley included a number of laconic remarks that were open to such conclusions: "The 'gift of righteousness' . . . signifies the righteousness or holiness which God gives to, and works in,

---

39. James Hervey, *Eleven Letters from the Late Rev. James Hervey, to the Rev. John Wesley containing an Answer to that Gentleman's Remarks on Theron and Aspasio* (London: J. F. and C. Rivington, 1790), v.

40. Wesley, *Works*, 6:685.

41. Wesley, "Preface to a Treatise on Justification," in *Works*, 6:120.

42. See "Dialogue between an Antinomian and his Friend" and "Second Dialogue between an Antinomian and his Friend," in *Works*, 6:68–81.

43. Wesley, *Works*, 6:116.

44. Ibid.

them; . . . [righteousness] was implanted as well as imputed; . . . Both the one [imputatively] and the other [intrinsically]. God, through him, first accounts and then makes us righteous."[45] Justification depends not only on the work of Christ for us externally, but also his work internally by which the believer perseveres in holiness and increases in purity of love for God.

Too close to popery for Hervey's comfort, this was. "This notion may pass current at Rome, not among the *Protestant* churches," said Hervey.[46] "Nobody can acquit your Principles, from halting between Protestantism and Popery. . . . You have unhappily adopted some specious Papistical Tenets."[47] Although Hervey had given a clear statement concerning the particular areas in which he feared Wesley's tendency toward Rome, Wesley said, "I know not which and should be glad any one would inform me."[48] Wesley only remarked that holding universal redemption did not prove the charge; but that was not the issue at stake. Imputed and infused righteousness were. Wesley's concerns were summed up in his 1762 "Thoughts on the Imputed Righteousness of Christ."

> And doth not this way of speaking naturally tend to make Christ the minister of sin? For if the very personal obedience of Christ (as those expressions directly lead me to think) be mine the moment I believe, can any thing be added thereto? Does my obeying God add any value to the perfect obedience of Christ? On this scheme, then are not the holy and unholy on the very same footing?[49]

The important issue for Wesley clearly seems to be couched in that phrase *this way of speaking*. In this tract, having denied that the term *righteousness of Christ* ever appears in Scripture[50] he did admit that the meaning of Romans 5 clearly insinuated the concept. To that he replied, "But this is not the question. We are not inquiring what he means, but what he says."[51] Although different persons may agree as to meaning they should not confine orthodoxy to the use of a manner of expression. "Therefore, though I believe he hath lived and died for me, yet I would speak very tenderly and sparingly of the former . . . for fear of this dreadful consequence." Wesley feared that emphasis on imputation of righteousness threatened to undo the potential

45. Ibid., 6:113, 114.
46. Hervey, *Eleven Letters*, 105.
47. Ibid., 123.
48. Wesley, *Works*, 6:122.
49. Ibid., 6:102.
50. Wesley wrongly had argued "'The righteousness of Christ' is an expression which I do not find in the Bible" and quoted 2 Peter 1:1 as mentioning only the "righteousness of God," seemingly unaware that the whole phrase should be translated "the righteousness of our God and Savior Jesus Christ."
51. Wesley, *Works*, 6:102.

universal benefits of the atonement. "Why do so many men love to speak of his righteousness rather than his atonement?"[52] Wesley thought he knew the answer: "It affords a fairer excuse for their own unrighteousness." Hervey, by his language, seemed intent on taking pains to increase the "swarm [of] antinomians on every side."[53]

The controversy with Hervey nevertheless pushed Wesley to preach the sermon "The Lord Our Righteousness." He gave a clear statement affirming that Christ's "whole and complete" human obedience is imputed to sinners at the moment of their belief. He still issued the warning, however, that use of that language was easily transformed into a cloak for unholiness.

With all his misgivings about the inferential language and the dangerous susceptibility to misunderstanding, Wesley did not reject the doctrine of imputed righteousness but, for a season, sought to maintain a semblance of evangelical unity on this matter. In a letter written in 1765 Wesley affirmed, "I think on justification, just as I have done any time these seven-and-twenty years; and just as Mr. Calvin does. In this respect, I do not differ from him an hair's breadth."[54] Even in the midst of the Minutes Controversy and the criticism of his funeral sermon for Whitefield, Wesley wrote, "In this respect there is not a hair's breadth difference between Mr. Wesley and Mr. Whitefield."[55]

The Minutes Controversy and Augustus Toplady

Wesley eventually found the "hair's breadth" to be too little distance between himself and the Calvinists, or at least his understanding of the tendency of Calvinist doctrine, and issued a short statement at the 1770 Methodist Conference that prompted immediate and intense controversy. If he was seeking to stir up attention to this issue, he succeeded.

David Lowes Watson indicates that the controversial elements of the Minutes might have been more calculated than careless.[56] Perhaps, Wesley wanted to provoke a reaction that would establish the difference between the

---

52. Wesley, "Preface to a Treatise on Justification," in *Works*, 6:115.
53. Wesley, *Works*, 6:113, 114.
54. Tyerman, *Life and Times*, 2:537.
55. Wesley, *Works*, 6:133.
56. David Lowes Watson sees the issue in Wesley's mind as reduced to an evangelistic concern. Evangelistically, Calvinism, according to Watson, relegated works to "secondary importance by grounding justification in an imputed status." Wesley, however, by "restricting the doctrine of justification to pardon, and consigning the fulfillment of the law to . . . sanctification gave faith and works equal importance—something which the Calvinist position failed to do." Wesley incorporated "good works into the gospel message no less than forgiveness" and affirmed that "good works were necessary, not only to proceed to sanctification, but even to retain the grace of justification." ("Christ Our Righteousness: The Center of Wesley's Evangelistic Message," *Perkins J* 37 [spring 1984]: 34–47, pp. 44, 45.)

spirits of Wesleyanism and Calvinism. The beginning of the document strongly suggests this in saying, "We have leaned too much toward Calvinism." One area of leaning was in regard to working for life. "Every believer," it is said, "till he comes to glory, works for as well as *from* life." The pyrotechnic part said:

> Review the whole affair: 1. Who of us is *now* accepted of God? He that now believes in Christ with a loving and obedient heart.
> 2. But who among those that never heard of Christ? He that feareth God and worketh righteousness, according to the light he has.
> 3. Is this the same with "he that is sincere"? Nearly if not quite.
> 4. Is not this "salvation by works"? Not by the *merit* of work, but by works as a *condition.*
> 5. What have we been disputing about for these thirty years? I am afraid, *about words.*
> 6. As to *merit* itself, of which we have been so dreadfully afraid; we are rewarded "according to our works," yea, "because of our works." How does this differ from, "For the sake of our works?" And how differs this from *secundum merita operum?* as our works *deserve?* Can you split this hair? I doubt I cannot. . . .
> 8. Does not talking of a justified or sanctified *state* tend to mislead men? almost naturally leading them to trust in what was done in one moment? Whereas we are every hour and every moment pleasing or displeasing to God, "according to our works";—according to the whole of our inward tempers, and our outward behaviour.[57]

This broadside gained for Wesley the support of Joseph Benson, a member of the faculty of Trevecca College, and John William de la Flechere [Fletcher], the president of Trevecca. This college was sponsored by Lady Huntingdon, a Calvinistic Methodist. Lady Huntingdon had set her influence against the doctrine of the Minutes and insisted that "whoever did not fully disavow them must quit the college."[58] Fletcher gladly pledged his loyalty to Wesley and his "doctrine to the last" with the hope that he would "gladly remove stumbling blocks out of the way of the weak" by altering "such expressions as may create prejudice in the hearts of those who are inclined to admit it."[59] Fletcher resigned his position at Trevecca. Wesley conceded to issue a careful clarification to Lady Huntingdon's group while receiving tacit apologies for overly zealous reaction from its leaders. Wesley also gained a new set of adversaries in Augustus Toplady and Richard and Rowland Hill.

57. Tyerman, *Life and Times,* 3:73.
58. Ibid., 3:89.
59. Ibid., 3:96.

The exchanges with Toplady produced some of the most remarkable outrage in the history of controversial literature. Tyerman concludes concerning Toplady, "The most charitable excuse for this angry writer is, that he had, in a paroxysm of mortified vanity, lost his balance, and was now *non compos mentis.*"[60] Tyerman's judgment, however, that the outburst was caused by an "honest abridgement" is not quite on target. Wesley had published an abridgment of Toplady's translation of *Absolute Predestination* by Jerome Zanchius. Toplady certainly became overly angry, but he felt terribly betrayed by Wesley's manner of abridgment in which Wesley's comments were often inserted as if they were part of Zanchius's original text. Toplady challenged Wesley to take Zanchius's "arguments in their regular connection and dependency on each other . . . in a manner worthy of a scholar and a divine," and that he should avoid relying on "mangled, castrated citations from Zanchius."[61] In addition, Wesley's piece, according to Toplady, amounted to subtle assertions without argument and gross reductions like "some clumsy bungling anatomist who in the dissection of an animal dwells much on the larger and more obvious particulars, but quite omits the nerves, the lymphatics, the muscles, and the most interesting parts of the complicate machine."[62]

Toplady admitted in the preface to his letter: "If, by anger, the ingenious animadverters mean a just and becoming disapprobation of Mr. Wesley's lying abridgment, and of the surreptitious manner in which he smuggled it into the world, I acknowledge myself, in this respect, angry."[63] Toplady characterized Wesley as a "red-hot Arminian" who had decided his theology by the casting of lots.[64] In a subsequent exchange with Wesley, Toplady wrote, "Much as I disapprove Mr. Wesley's distinguishing principles, and the low cunning with which he circulates them, I still bear not the least ill-will to his person. As an individual, I wish him well, both here and ever." He believed, however, that Wesley had an "exceeding strait gate to pass through before he gets to heaven."[65]

In this second exchange, "More Work for Mr. Wesley," Toplady spends much less time in fuming sarcasm and much more developing substantive ar-

60. Ibid., 3:82.
61. Augustus Toplady, "Letter to Rev. Mr. Wesley, relative to his abridgment of Zanchius on predestination," in *Works,* 722, 723.
62. Toplady, *Works,* 723.
63. Ibid., 720.
64. Ibid., 720, 721. Toplady misrepresents the lot-casting event. It is told with greater accuracy in Whitefield's letter to Wesley.
65. Toplady, "More Work for Mr. Wesley; or a Vindication of the Decrees and Providence of God," in *Works,* 730, 732. This Toplady production was in answer to Wesley's short tract entitled "The Consequence Proved." In that work Wesley sought to defend the logic of his summary of Toplady's earlier work with Zanchius: "The sum of all is this: One in twenty, suppose of mankind are elected; nineteen in twenty are reprobated. The elect shall be saved, do what they will: The reprobate shall be damned, do what they can." Wesley, *Works,* 6:141, 142.

guments. It is regrettable that much sniping persists, for that atmosphere hinders many from enjoying what is, in fact, a remarkable piece of polemical divinity. Serious interaction with Scripture and close reasoning on logical points permeate the work. Toplady dissects Wesley's major premises and the five "Consequences" of predestination and finds them "utterly void of judgment, strength, and truth."[66] Wesley's estimation, "one in twenty, suppose, of mankind is elected," Toplady called "palpably absurd." It formed no part of a legitimate argument to charge an opponent with "peremptory consequences, affirmed to be drawn from absolute premises" when in fact the consequence is hypothetical and founded on a "mere vague supposition." The second consequence, "The elect will be saved, do what they will," implies that "personal sanctification and practical obedience are unnecessary to salvation." Toplady answered by clearly affirming that the elect "cannot be saved without sanctification and obedience." Their salvation, however, is not precarious, for the "same gratuitous predestination which ordained the existence of the elect as men ordained their purification as saints." Ephesians 1 casts holiness as the necessary purposive result of election, as does Titus 2:14, and as Titus 1:16 certainly implies. Toplady argued his case for several long columns and concluded the discussion of this consequence with a flourish on Romans 8:31–35:

> Now if it be the Father's will that Christ should lose none of his elect; if Christ himself, in consequence of their covenant-donation to him, does actually give them eternal life, and solemnly avers that they shall never perish; if God be so for them that none can hinder their salvation; if nothing can be laid to their charge; if they cannot be condemned and nought shall separate them from the love of Christ; it clearly and inevitably follows that none of the elect can perish, but they must all necessarily be saved. Which salvation consists as much in the recovery of moral rectitude below, as in the enjoyment of eternal blessedness above.[67]

To the third consequence, "The reprobate shall be damned, do what they can," Toplady responded with shocked horror and theological power. In wording such an assertion few men ever "sunk deeper into the despicable, launched wider into the horrid, or went farther in the profane."[68] Toplady then gave an exposition and a defense both of God's justice in the condemnation of any and, should he so choose, every, sinner and his mercy in saving or forbearing to save any he pleases. God's mercy does not cease to be infinite because it is extended to a limited number any more than he ceases to be omnipotent because he has created a limited number of worlds. Toplady then

---

66. Toplady, "Vindication," in *Works,* 740.
67. Ibid., 740.
68. Ibid.

deploys an impressive arsenal of Scripture texts accompanied by expositions to defend the doctrine of reprobation.[69] The last two consequences concern the relationship of election and reprobation to the reality of moral responsibility and the possibility of future judgment. Toplady is quite sure, and writes lucidly if at times with acerbity, that no contradiction exists in maintaining all of these. Toplady seeks to show the noncontradictory relationship by amassing into a coherent argument a formidable wall of biblical texts and events. Important among these is the coexistence of the decretal certainty of Christ's death and the undeniable culpability of his murderers. In conclusion he wrote:

> I infer that God's decrees, and the necessity of event flowing thence, neither destroy the true free-agency of men, nor render the commission of sin a jot less heinous. They neither force the human will, nor extenuate the evil of human actions. Predestination, foreknowledge, and providence, only secure the event, and render it certainly future, in a way and manner (incomprehensibly indeed by us; but) perfectly consistent with the nature of second causes.[70]

Wesley's Personal and Theological Grounds for Rejecting Calvinism

Wesley's struggle with the doctrine of election emerges clearly in a letter to his mother written 29 July 1725. He had read Bishop Jeremy Taylor's *Rules and Exercises of Holy Living and Dying*, made some observations concerning that, and then posed the perplexities of predestination. "What shall I say of predestination?" he asks. An everlasting purpose of God to deliver some from damnation certainly means others are not chosen. And if none besides those so decreed may be saved, "a vast majority of the world were only born to eternal death, without so much as a possibility of avoiding it. How is this consistent with either the divine justice or mercy?"[71]

His mother soon gave her answer. She firmly believed that "God from eternity hath decreed some to everlasting life." This decree of election, however, "is founded on his foreknowledge," according to Romans 8. After quoting a large part of the critical passage she offered her explanation. In his eternal prescience, God saw who would make a "right use of their powers, and accept of offered mercy." These he did predestinate, and work in them all those things by which they would be conformed to the image of his Son. He "called them to himself, by his external Word, the preaching of the gos-

69. Ibid., 744–47.
70. Ibid., 750.
71. John Wesley, *Works,* ed. Frank Baker (Oxford: Clarendon, 1980), 25:174, 175.

pel, and internally by his Holy Spirit." They obey this call by faith and repentance, are thus justified, and because of the "merits and mediation of Jesus Christ" are finally received to glory. This view of predestination she considered "agreeable to the analogy of faith, since it never derogates from God's free grace, nor impairs the liberty of man." Also, the mere prescience of God can never be considered "the cause that so many finally perish, than that our knowing the sun will rise tomorrow is the cause of its rise." She also gave advice, which he followed always, that "the doctrine of predestination, as maintained by the rigid Calvinists is very shocking, and ought utterly to be abhorred."[72]

Two issues drive this correspondence and similarly drove Wesley in his lifelong resistance to Calvinism: one, the implication of reprobation lurked within every aspect of Calvinism; two, prescience, not decree, characterizes God's knowledge of the world and his purposes of grace.

The debate with Gill had brought out clearly Wesley's first objection in its most reduced state. Wesley moved to reprobation whenever any agitant stirred the cauldron of unconditional election. "Unconditional election I cannot believe . . . (to waive all other considerations) because it necessarily implies reprobation." If there were an election that did not imply reprobation, Wesley would "gladly agree to it."[73] When Rowland Hill in his controversy with Wesley spoke of "election doubters" Wesley responded by vowing that he would "chase the fiend, reprobation, to his own hell and every doctrine connected with it." He issued a call to arms to his Arminian friends, in light of Hill's bitter attack, exhorting them, "Let none pity or spare one limb of either speculative or practical antinomianism, or of any doctrine that naturally tends thereto."[74]

Wesley considered reprobation as destructive of his entire concept of God and man. If reprobation is true there can be no such thing as moral responsibility. Man "would not be capable of virtue or vice, of being either morally good or bad. . . . Yea, and it would be as absurd to ascribe either virtue or vice to him, as to ascribe it to the stock of a tree."[75]

Because reprobation, like all aspects of Calvinist soteriology according to Wesley, eradicates moral responsibility, it renders speaking of God's justice in condemnation an impossibility. Wesley, therefore, found nothing compelling about the Calvinist argument, mentioned by Whitefield in a letter, that if God might justly have passed by ("speak out," retorts Wesley, "'If God might justly have reprobated all men,'—for it comes to the same

72. Ibid., 178, 179.
73. Wesley, "Predestination Calmly Considered," in *Works,* 6:28, 29.
74. Tyerman, *Life and Times,* 3:144.
75. John Wesley, "On Predestination," in *Sermons On Several Occasions,* 2 vols. (New York: J. Emory and B. Waugh, 1829), 2:39.

point,") then he might justly pass by some. Wesley responded, "Are you sure he might? Where is it written? I cannot find it in the word of God. Therefore I reject it as a bold, precarious assertion, utterly unsupported by Holy Scripture." Wesley refused to apply such a case even to his own condition. "If you say, 'But you know in your own conscience, God might justly have passed by you:' I deny it. That God might justly, for my unfaithfulness to his grace, have given me up long ago, I grant: but this concession supposes me to have had that grace which you say a reprobate never had."[76]

In addition to its necessary implication of an amoral humanity, reprobation completely distorts the attributes of God. Every aspect of the doctrines of grace eventually collapsed into reprobation in Wesley's understanding; and reprobation, in his opinion, was self-evidently false by the absurdity it created of God's character. To postulate that God would be just in condemning the nonelect would assume that "his justice might have been separate from his other attributes, from his mercy in particular." Such a division is impossible. All of God's attributes "are inseparably joined: they cannot be divided, no not for a moment." God's sovereignty may never supersede his justice. Such is the "present objection against unconditional reprobation; (the plain consequence of unconditional election;) it flatly contradicts, indeed utterly overthrows, the Scripture account of the justice of God."[77]

The doctrine of predestination Wesley identified with the Muslim doctrine of a deceitful Allah and the government of fate and felt that every Christian should abominate the doctrine and take a vow against it in the way required of Muslim converts: "I do anathematize the blasphemy of Mohammed, which saith that God deceiveth whom he will, and whom he will he leadeth to that which is good. Himself doeth what he willeth and is himself the cause of all good and all evil. Fate and destiny govern all things."[78]

His resistance to it Wesley expressed in hymns also. In "Hymns of Universal Redemption" he prayed that those who believed in unconditional election might be taught better by God.

> Lord, if indeed, without a bound,
> Infinite Love Thou art,
> The HORRIBLE DECREE confound,
> Enlarge Thy people's heart!

He not only asked God to dislodge this teaching from the hearts of people but also pledged his own soul in opposition to it. Were such a thing true, Wesley felt that he could not enjoy the salvation of such a cruelly arbitrary

76. Wesley, "Predestination Calmly Considered," in *Works*, 6:32, 33.
77. Ibid., 33, 35.
78. Wesley, "A Predestinarian and His Friend," in *Works*, 6:67.

315

deity. "Cut off, exclude me from thy grace," he sang, "Unless for *all* the Saviour bled." He rather would find his identity with the damned than with the redeemed if the decree of salvation involved particularity on the part of God.

Verses like this prompted Whitefield's remark, "For Christ's sake be not rash! . . . Study the covenant of grace. . . . And then, instead of pawning your salvation, as you have done in a late hymn book, if the doctrine of universal redemption be not true, . . . you will compose a hymn in praise of sovereign, distinguishing love."[79] But Wesley insisted.

> If *all may* not Thy mercy claim,
> On *me* the vengeful bolt let fall;
> Take back *my* interest in the Lamb,
> Unless the Victim died for all.

The aspersions cast on the character of God by the contemplation of such a discriminatory decree filled his hymns with astonishment. This God was "a torturing God, . . . a fiend, a Molock gorged with blood!"

> Horror to think that God is hate!
> Fury in God can dwell!
> God could an helpless world create,
> To thrust them into hell!
> Doom them an endless death to die,
> From which they could not flee:—
> No, Lord Thine inmost bowels cry
> Against the dire decree![80]

No unconditional aspects of grace could coexist, in Wesley's opinion, with the goodness of God. God decreed from the beginning to save all who believe and to reprobate all who persist "obstinately and finally . . . in unbelief."[81] But prevenient grace gave all the same opportunity, while in his omniscient foreknowledge God saw who would believe and, thus, who would become elect. Wesley was not content with emotional repudiation of the Calvinist view as he perceived it; he wanted to establish a rhetoric that affirmed his views of foreknowledge and universal prevenient grace. God calls "as many souls as breathe, and all *may* hear the call." God's grace restores "a power to choose, a will to obey" so that all may find the savior.

79. Whitefield, *Life and Sermons*, 644.

80. Hymn samples taken from the *Poetical Works of John and Charles Wesley*, 13 vols., collected and arranged by G. Osborn, D.D. (London: Wesleyan Methodist Conference, 1868–1872), 1:311, 312.

81. Wesley, "A Predestinarian and His Friend," in *Works*, 6:67.

Those, however, that God foreknew would "not his grace refuse" were decreed, "Ordain'd in Jesu's steps to tread." These are the elect, the "consenting few, Who yield to proffer'd love."[82]

It seems strange that, given the ferocity of Wesley's objection to the supposed smallness of the number of the elect, he would call the elect the "consenting few." God knew beforehand, however, that even with his equitable method of prevenient grace, the number would be relatively small.

In all his years of controversy, Wesley argued from the explanation given by his mother in 1725. In Wesley's understanding of the order of salvation, God's timelessness is the foundation of everything. In his exposition of Romans 8, Wesley teaches that Paul has given us the order in which the "several branches of salvation constantly follow each other" in our experience. All of the elements of salvation occur then infallibly in the particular individuals that God has foreknown. His decree of election is based on his foreknowledge, not on a premundane decision to redeem one particular individual as opposed to another. All time, "or rather all eternity," is present to God at once and he sees all things, not in sequential order, but simultaneously from everlasting to everlasting. In this way, God sees "whatever was, is, or will be, to the end of time." God dwells in "one eternal now." But we must not make the mistake of thinking these things are because God knows them; rather, "he knows them because they are." This is illustrated by referring to his mother's analogy concerning the sun: "Just as I . . . now know the sun shines: yet the sun does not shine because I know it; but I know it because he shines."[83]

In "Predestination Calmly Considered" Wesley expands his exposition of election built on the foreknowledge of God. God, to whom all things are present at once, who sees all eternity at one view, "calleth the things that are not as though they were"; the things that are not yet as though they were now subsisting. For this reason he can call Abraham the "father of many nations" before Isaac was born and Christ "the lamb slain from the foundation of the world," though not slain, in fact, until generations after. In the same way, God calls true believers "elect from the foundation of the world," although they were not actually elect, or believers, until much later, in their own times. Only then were they actually elected, when they were made the "sons of God by faith." Then were they, in fact, "chosen and taken out of the world"; as Paul says "elect through belief of the truth"; or as Saint Peter expresses it, "elect according to the foreknowledge of God, through sanctification of the Spirit."[84]

---

82. *Poetical Works*, 1:311, 312.
83. Wesley, *Sermons*, 2:39, 40.
84. Wesley, *Works*, 6:28.

Summary

Two factors govern Wesley's exposition and polemics concerning Calvinism. One is reprobation. The doctrines of grace cannot be true, because they imply reprobation. Reprobation cannot be true, because it makes God unjust. It makes God unjust because it infallibly implies that he punishes people for the commission of sins that must have been caused by his decree. The second is foreknowledge. Foreknowledge equals absolute and pervasive cognition of all things simultaneously. God's election arises from this and is therefore not causative of the human experience of salvation, but reflective of his eternal awareness that these experiences will happen in time. My concluding section will offer several reasons to suggest that these objections do not show unconditional election and its attendant doctrines to be "utterly irreconcilable to the whole scope and tenor of the Old and New Testament."[85]

Foreknowledge

Wesley's discussions of foreknowledge never indicated that a serious word study of the New Testament term had been undertaken. He takes it for granted that "foreknowledge" is a simple synonym for prescience. God knows all the thoughts and actions of rational beings and all the events of history as a present reality in his mind though they have not yet come to pass in history. He has not decreed that they happen, except in isolated special cases, and he does not control their happening; he simply knows them as facts in the same way that we may know facts, and, because of past experience, even we "know" the future in some ways (such as the sun will rise tomorrow). Bengel, an older contemporary of Wesley's and a non-Calvinistic pietist, makes very few comments about the import of "foreknow." In fact, his comments on Romans 8:29–30 are less predestinarian even than Wesley's. For Bengel, Paul does not "make the number of those, who are called, justified, glorified, to be absolutely equal." He, in fact, believes (in consonance with Wesley) that "the believer may fail between the special call, and the glorification." "There are perhaps persons called, who may not be justified." When he does bring himself to remark on foreknowledge one can detect, even if only slightly, the power of the word when applied to God's type of knowledge when it relates to his work of redemption. In Acts 2:23 he identifies foreknowledge with "providence." He also treats the word as being defined by "determinate," as it indeed is. In 1 Peter 1:20 he translates it as "foreordained" when related to Christ. In Romans 8 he appears to share Wesley's view when he says "predestination accompanies foreknowledge,

---

85. Wesley, "Predestination Calmly Considered," in *Works*, 6:29.

for foreknowledge takes away reprobation." But in 1 Peter 1:1 he acknowledges that foreknowledge includes more than cognizance when he says, "It includes also good-will and love."[86]

Gill, a contemporary and sometime antagonist of Wesley, highlights especially this idea of goodwill and love in his definition of foreknowledge. It is not God's "eternal, universal, and infallible knowledge," and even less it is to be construed as "a bare prescience of men, and choice of them, upon a foresight of faith, holiness, good works, and perseverance therein." It is instead the "sovereign grace, good will, and pleasure of God, or the everlasting love of God the father . . . joined with affection, delight, and approbation; knowledge, and foreknowledge, as ascribed to the divine Being, do signify such things; see Psal. i.6. 2 Tim. ii.19. Rom viii. 29, 30." It is in effect "his pure love, and sovereign good will and pleasure." Again, in Romans 8, after eliminating several options (including Wesley's concept of prescience) Gill concludes, "This regards the everlasting love of God to his own people, his delight in them, and approbation of them; in this sense he knew them, he foreknew them from everlasting, affectionately loved them, and took infinite delight and pleasure in them."[87]

A contemporary New Testament scholar who defends this view of foreknowledge is Douglas J. Moo. After a careful and chaste discussion of its etymology and possible meanings he concludes that the use of the word in Romans 8:29 does not mean "know before" in the sense of "intellectual knowledge, or cognition" but to "enter into relationship with before" or "choose, or determine, before." So it is in Romans 11:2, 1 Peter 1:20, Acts 2:23, and 1 Peter 1:2. He also points out that the usage flows naturally from the Septuagintal translation of the Hebrew word for "know" when it "denotes intimate relationship."[88]

Wesley's view of foreknowledge also implies a tacit dualism in which the history of the created order has an independent existence apart from the wise providence of God.

Beyond that, this solution hardly escapes the problem Wesley sought so determinedly to avoid. This fact has been seen candidly and discussed from a variety of theological standpoints. Jonathan Edwards explores it fully in his work on the *Freedom of the Will*. Edwards claimed that "the absolute decrees of God are no more inconsistent with human liberty, on account of any Necessity of the event, which follows from such decrees, than the absolute

---

86. J. A. Bengel, *Gnomon Novi Testamenti,* published as *Bengel's New Testament Commentary* (Grand Rapids: Kregel, 1981); see his comments on the verses cited.

87. John Gill, *Exposition of the New Testaments,* 3 vols. (London: Mathews and Leigh, 1809; reprint, Paris, Ark.: Baptist Standard Bearer, 1989); see comments on 1 Peter 1:1 and Romans 8:29.

88. Douglas J. Moo, *The Wycliffe Exegetical Commentary: Romans 1–8* (Chicago: Moody, 1991); see comments on Romans 8:29.

Foreknowledge of God. Because the connexion between the event and certain Foreknowledge, is as infallible and indissoluble, as between the event and an absolute decree."[89]

Clark H. Pinnock, whose pilgrimage has taken him from the Augustinian model beyond Arminianism into a quasi-process view of history, began this pilgrimage when he found himself no longer able to define freedom in the context of causality. He began to doubt the existence of "an all determining fatalistic blueprint for history" and thought instead in terms of "significantly free creatures able to accept or reject his purposes for us." Pinnock also examined honestly the Calvinist argument that foreknowledge as *absolute* prescience has the same ultimate effect as absolute predestination; this kind of Arminianism left no more room for freedom than did Calvinism. He therefore rejected the Arminian concept of foreknowledge in acknowledging the force of the Calvinist argument that "exhaustive knowledge is tantamount to predestination."[90] Wesley would be greatly chagrined to see his friends forsaking a major component of his construction of biblical theology.

One of the strongest contemporary defenders of limited foreknowledge, Richard Rice, admits the same thing. "Traditional Calvinists," he says, "have a strong case when they argue that absolute foreknowledge excludes the freedom to do anything other than what God knows will occur."[91] This leads to what Rice calls a "severe tension within traditional Arminianism."[92]

It also leads to the view, shared by Pinnock, that God's omniscience does not include the future because the future is unknowable. This view has its own tensions, however, as well as incongruities as it seeks to make sense of biblical prophecy. The following remarkable paragraph is brim full of the latent inconsistencies of this position as it seeks to explain some "rather precise [biblical] descriptions [i.e., predictions] of what human beings will do."

> Since God knows the present exhaustively, he also knows everything that will happen as the inevitable consequence of past and present factors. This would be particularly applicable where the predicted event lay in the relatively near future. This might explain the accurate accounts of Pharaoh's actions, along with those of Judas' and Peter's behavior. Knowing their characters as intimately as God knows, one could accurately predict what they would do in certain situations. Genuine freedom excludes the concept that all human actions are predictable in this way, but it allows that some of them may be.[93]

89. Jonathan Edwards, *Freedom of the Will*, sect. 12.3. corol. 1.
90. Clark H. Pinnock, ed., *The Grace of God, the Will of Man: A Case for Arminianism* (Grand Rapids: Zondervan, 1989), 18, 25.
91. Richard Rice, "Divine Foreknowledge and Free-will Theism," in *The Grace of God, the Will of Man*, 128. Rice concedes Edwards's point on this in *God's Foreknowledge and Man's Free Will* (Minneapolis: Bethany House, 1985), 18.
92. Rice, "Divine Foreknowledge," 133.
93. Ibid., 135.

What should one make of this? If factors have "inevitable consequences" and God knows all the factors exhaustively, then he knows every succeeding moment exhaustively ad infinitum. If "characters" give rise to actions, why is it necessary that "genuine freedom" excludes the predictability of all human actions but allows it for some? Are those actions that are predictable because arising so certainly out of one's character then not considered "free"? If so, then "character" and "freedom" must be seen as mutually exclusive, and it is impossible, therefore, to judge any action that arises from one's character, certainly an unbiblical notion. But if character and freedom are not mutually exclusive, then causation cannot be detrimental to freedom as we experience it in this world. This leads naturally to a discussion of reprobation.

Reprobation

I speak of reprobation at this point only because Wesley raised it to such a high level of visibility. All that one need understand to set aside the ignominious reputation of the doctrine of reprobation is this: the freedom of moral actions and resultant responsibility for them are not eliminated by their natural and necessary connection with an intricate and complex series of causes and motivations.

Whatever the intricacies of the discussion raging around compatibilism and incompatibilism, it surely must seem acceptable to anyone that all actions occur in accordance with the strongest motivation at the time of the action. Whether pleasure, sacrifice, good judgment, fear, or the quickness of visceral reaction give rise to actions and no matter how complex the interaction of factors that precede and give rise to an action, no one could argue that an action is unfree because it is motivated. What could be the possible use of arguing that an action is free only if there is no reason for it? That would be saying that any time one has a reason for what he does, he would by definition be unfree. What a chaotic situation would exist and how useless all reasoning and argument would be if freedom could be maintained only in the absence of motivation, only when one acts without a reason.

Even a Wesleyan Christian who believes in prevenient grace but not effectual calling, who believes in the convicting work of the Spirit but not in the priority of regeneration to repentance and faith, must conclude that any action done under such conviction would not be a free act because it was done in accordance with persuasive motivation. Even the preacher must find it futile, and perhaps even wrong to seek to persuade, because actions are not done in accordance with motivation and if they are done so they are not free acts.

The chain of events that brings about the salvation of the elect and the damnation of the reprobate was established in eternity past in the wisdom of

God who works "all things according to the counsel of his own will." It is not fatalistic, because it is the wise design of an infinitely perfect personal God whose own glory is the most personal and just end of all things. It seems to me that there need be no hard-and-fast line drawn between the eternal determined purpose of God and the significant freedom of men. To divide them would be, on the microcosmic level, like dividing between human decision and the reasons for those decisions. God's wise well-considered decree serves as the foundation by which everything in reality occurs, gives all events in the world a personal and rational character, and serves as the initiatory energy by which we ourselves operate on the basis of planning, consideration, and motivation. God's freedom of action is not hindered in the least by the determining nature of his immutable moral character and his infinite wisdom; nor is the freedom of all his creatures hindered whether operating by reason or instinct (or both). In fact freedom is established by the reality that all of our actions are done as a part of a complex convergence of factors that we find persuasive in an unbroken continuum of thinking and doing. We continually do both and we always act freely and responsibly because our activity, mental, emotional, and physical, is in harmony with contextual preference.

By contextual preference, I mean that our choices are always in light of our context. Right now it is a beautiful September morning in northern Illinois, and instead of sitting in my study in my basement at my computer, I would prefer to be outside pitching with my baseball-playing son (and while I'm preferring, I would make the time about three and one-half years ago before he hurt his arm). But it is not three and one-half years ago, and he is away at college now, and I have an obligation as well as a sense of calling to finish this chapter. I choose freely, therefore, to keep writing because the reasons to do so are contextually more compelling than reasons not to do so. I am convinced that this is a perfectly free choice done in accordance with the "purpose of him who works all things after the counsel of his own will." And his will in this instance is now complete.

14

William Carey:
The Modern Missions Movement
and the Sovereignty of God

WILLIAM TRAVIS

An assertion made about Calvinism is that its belief in predestination and the doctrines of grace cuts the vitality from missionary endeavor. In a recent work, John Sanders refers to "those in the Reformed tradition, who have traditionally not evidenced much interest in missions despite their belief that the unevangelized are damned to hell."[1] One of the famous statements used to support this contention is one presumably made to William Carey (1761–1834) when, at a Baptist ministers' meeting in Northampton, England, in the late 1780s, he proposed discussion about sending missionaries to heathen nations: "Sit down, young man. When God pleases to convert the heathen, He will do it without your aid or mine." The irony of the situation is that William Carey was himself a Calvinist, one who saw no conflict between his Reformed theology and his desire to become a missionary; in fact, "[i]t was not in spite of, but rather because of his belief in the greatness of God and His divine purpose in election that Carey was willing 'to venture all' to proclaim the gospel in the far corners of the world."[2] The comment made to Carey that day represents a mi-

1. John Sanders, *No Other Name: An Investigation into the Destiny of the Unevangelized* (Grand Rapids: Eerdmans, 1992), 48 n. 24.
2. Timothy George, *Faithful Witness: The Life and Mission of William Carey* (Birmingham, Ala.: New Hope, 1991), 53. The story is repeated in several Carey biographies, but is also the subject of dispute: see George, *Carey*, 183 n. 14. Iain Murray (*The Puritan Hope* [London: Banner of Truth Trust, 1971]) says (139), "it is very doubtful if the story is true."

nority opinion in Reformed belief: while a few in the Calvinist tradition have been opposed to missions, the great majority have been strong advocates of missionary endeavor. This chapter points up a part of that history.

Within a few years after being told to sit down, Carey issued a call for missionary activity that since his time has been seen as the first major plea in modern Protestant missions. His *Enquiry into the Obligations of Christians, to Use Means for the Conversion of Heathens* (1792) was a call for missionary endeavor.[3] In the three center sections of the essay Carey gives a review of the history of missions, an account of the state of the world in his time with its millions of unreached people, and the practicality of doing missionary work in his era. Framing these center sections are two important contentions: the Great Commission given to the disciples in Matthew 28 is still binding on the church, and it is the duty of Christians to find the means to promote the work of carrying out the commission. This carrying out should first be done by prayer, and here Carey reminds his readers of the monthly concerts of prayer that had begun in the Great Awakening of the 1740s and were still continuing, and secondly by forming societies for the specific purpose of sending missionaries, including a society among his own Particular (i.e., Calvinistic) Baptists. The simple logic of carrying out his plan meant that the following year Carey sailed for India. And there he labored for the next forty years.

Before Carey

William Carey is often referred to as the father of modern missions, largely because the 1790s and the following decades mark an enormous increase in Protestant missionary work, and because his careful work laid out good principles of organizing the sending societies and the field work of missionaries. Yet his *Enquiry* correctly pointed out that other missionary work preceded his, and a good deal of the prior work by Protestants was done under Calvinist auspices.

The Reformers of the sixteenth century are often noted as having little interest in missionary work. Several lists of reasons for this have been drawn up, none of them totally satisfactory as explanations for the lack of missionary commitment.[4] Among the reasons cited for the failure to see missions as

---

3. The *Enquiry* is printed in several accessible places: as an appendix to the George biography, E1–E57, and an abridged version in Ralph D. Winter and Steven C. Hawthorne, eds., *Perspectives on the World Christian Movement: A Reader* (Pasadena: William Carey Library, 1981), 227–37. In October 1792 the organizing meeting was held, and the name chosen was "Particular Baptist Society for Propagating the Gospel amongst the Heathen," later simply called the Baptist Missionary Society. Leon McBeth, "The Legacy of the Baptist Missionary Society," *Baptist History and Heritage* 27 (July 1992): 7.

4. A summary of the reasons is conveniently listed in John H. Yoder, "Reformation and Missions: A Literature Survey," in *Anabaptism and Mission,* ed. Wilbert R. Shenk (Scottdale, Penn.: Herald, 1984), 40–50.

an obligation on the Reformers was the belief that the Great Commission was valid only for the apostolic age. Also, some felt that the gospel had already been sent to the whole world and therefore no further sending was needed. But there are indications that John Calvin, although not a missions advocate as some of his followers were to become, did have what can be called a missionary interest. The interest derived from his theology:

> Calvin's theology supports Christian missions. No theologian placed greater emphasis on the working out of the divine purposes in human history. Furthermore, Calvin explicitly believed that these purposes included the proclamation of the Gospel. "There is no people," Calvin wrote, "and no rank in the world that is excluded from salvation; because God wishes that the gospel should be proclaimed to all without exception. Now the preaching of the gospel gives life; and hence . . . God invites all equally to partake of salvation."[5]

The interest was shown in three regards: the training and support of pastors for Reformed churches in France; the use of Geneva as a center where exiles and others were trained and then went back to their home countries, ranging from Scotland to Hungary; and specific involvement in an ill-fated Huguenot mission to the Brazilian coast. Calvin wanted the gospel spread because "the knowledge of God must shine generally throughout the world and everyone must be partaker in it."

Among Dutch Calvinists of the seventeenth century a missiology was developed, one result of which was missionary activity connected with the Dutch East India Company. Hadrianus Savaria (1531–1613) argued for an episcopal system much like that in England, and stated that since bishops stood in the line of apostolic succession they were given authority to send out missionaries. Justus Heurnius (1587–1651) wrote in 1618 that an evangelical mission in India was warranted, and he stressed Bible translation and biblical preaching as the means for carrying out the mission. In personal response he served in India for fourteen years. Gijsbertus Voetius (1589–

---

5. John H. Leith, *Introduction to the Reformed Tradition: A Way of Being the Christian Community*, rev. ed. (Atlanta: John Knox, 1981), 51; Leith is quoting Calvin on 1 Timothy 2:4, *Commentaries on the Epistles to Timothy, Titus, and Philemon* (Grand Rapids: Eerdmans, 1948), 54–55. The second quotation in the paragraph is from Gordon D. Laman, "The Origin of Protestant Missions," *Ref R* 43 (autumn 1989): 58. Several scholars have argued for a mission-mindedness in Calvin's Geneva. Samuel Zwemer ("Calvinism and the Missionary Enterprise," *TToday* 7 [July 1950]: 206–16), himself in missions for more than fifty years, contends for such a mission-mindedness, and points out (215) that the first Protestant missionary to the Turks in the sixteenth century, Vaclav Budovec, was a Calvinist. Philip Edgcumbe Hughes ("John Calvin: Director of Missions," in *The Heritage of John Calvin*, ed. John Bratt [Grand Rapids: Eerdmans, 1973], 40–54), and W. Stanford Reid ("Calvin's Geneva: A Missionary Centre," *Ref Th R* 42 [September-December 1983]: 65–73) survey the Genevan situation. The Brazil expedition is detailed in R. Pearce Beaver, "The Genevan Mission to Brazil," *Ref J* 17 (July-August 1967): 14–20.

1676), professor at Utrecht, suggested in his *Politica Ecclesiastica* guidelines for a missions theology, including the conversion of pagans and the planting of the church. Johannes Hornbeeck (1617–1666) proposed an ambitious plan of a worldwide network of missionaries engaged in mutual support, and argued that universities ought to train missionaries, that governments should provide financial support to missionaries, and that the Protestant churches should surpass Roman Catholics in missionary enthusiasm.[6]

Dutch missionaries served in the seventeenth century in Ceylon, Java, the Moluccas, and Formosa. The work in Formosa provides an interesting case of how reaching the native Formosans (although not the immigrant Chinese) was a spinoff from school teaching and chaplaincy work connected with the trading company. Missionary activity in the Indies followed a similar pattern.[7]

For the English-speaking world one can trace the creation of a missions theology from the seventeenth-century Puritans through eighteenth-century Calvinist thinkers and on to later generations. Sidney Rooy's study of five Puritans—Richard Sibbes, Richard Baxter, John Eliot, Cotton Mather, Jonathan Edwards—leads him to conclude:

> The attitude of the Puritans toward missions was a positive one. We have seen how Sibbes' theological position stressed the need for conversion and for spreading the gospel. The implications were drawn out by Baxter, especially for the evangelization of heathen lands. Eliot's commitment to Reformed theology and lifetime dedication to the Indians united to form a powerful incentive to Protestant missions. The practical Mather and the theologically minded Edwards combined the chief Calvinistic doctrines, as understood by Sibbes, with active participation in New England mission and Indian unbelief.[8]

Jonathan Edwards (1703–1758) had an influence on missions in two regards. One was the influence exercised through Edwards's publication of *The Life of Brainerd*. The young David Brainerd (1718–1747) became ill in 1747, forcing him to leave his mission work among Indians in New Jersey, and he stayed in the Edwards home during the last months of his life, willing

6. Laman, "Origin," outlines the ideas of the four cited in the paragraph. Further details on Savaria are found in James Tanis, "Reformed Pietism and Protestant Missions," *HTR* 67 (1974): 65–73. Extensive analysis of Voetius is done by Jan Jongeneel, "The Missiology of Gisbertus Voetius: The First Comprehensive Protestant Theology of Missions," *CTJ* 26 (April 1991): 47–79.

7. The Formosan mission is recounted in Peter Herz, "A Century before Carey: The Dutch in Aboriginal Formosa (1627–1662)," *Presbyterion* 12 (spring 1986): 17–32. Brief surveys of early Dutch missions are in Rita Smith Kipp, *The Early Years of a Dutch Colonial Mission: The Karo Field* (Ann Arbor: University of Michigan Press, 1990), 24–26, and in Tanis, "Reformed Pietism."

8. Sidney H. Rooy, *The Theology of Missions in the Puritan Tradition* (Grand Rapids: Eerdmans, 1965), 310.

to Edwards his diary, from which Edwards compiled a biography. Through the middle of the nineteenth century the *Life of Brainerd* in its several editions had an unusual effect on the lives of those who went into missions, from William Carey to Henry Martyn to Adoniram Judson.[9]

On the theoretical side, Edwards laid down several principles as the basis for missions activity. Preaching was a core belief, Edwards seeing it as a major instrument of divine grace, both as the means by which the elect are brought to salvation and as a requirement for those who have faith—preaching is one of their good works. Edwards also had a postmillennial vision of the future, part of which included the end of heathenism, when "many shall go forth and carry the gospel unto them . . . and they shall be brought out of darkness into marvellous light."[10] Mankind's unity in sin is another basis for foreign missions; redemption is necessary in all parts of the world. Finally, there are the scriptural commands to take the gospel to all; when missionaries were sent from Stockbridge to the Iroquois in May 1753 Edwards preached on Acts 14:26–27, contending "Tis a special and glorious work of God to open the way for the propagation of the gospel among the Heathen."

Edwards's follower Samuel Hopkins (1721–1803) was noted for his concept of disinterested benevolence, a concept that had enormous influence in the United States on the matter of social reform (Hopkins was a strong abolitionist) and was also a factor in missionary motivation. It was Edwards in *The Nature of True Virtue* who introduced the concept of virtue as "benevolence to Being in general," and Hopkins fleshed out the idea to mean that a believer most reflected God's love when the believer acted benevolently. Benevolent action provided a spur not only for social reform, but for missionary activity as well, for the chief act of God's benevolence in his love for the world was the redemptive work of Christ, and it is our duty to see that "this

9. The influence of the Brainerd biography is charted by Joseph Conforti in "Jonathan Edwards's Most Popular Work: 'The life of David Brainerd' and Nineteenth-Century Evangelical Culture," *CH* 54 (June 1985): 188–201; Conforti says (196), "The *Life* had its greatest impact on American missionaries."

10. Earl R. MacCormac, "Jonathan Edwards and Missions," *Journal of the Presbyterian Historical Society* 39 (December 1961): 221 (from Edwards's *A History of Redemption*), 222 (from a sermon on Acts 14:26, 27). What has usually been seen as Edwards's optimism about America as a redeemer nation has recently been challenged by Gerald R. McDermott, "Jonathan Edwards, the City on a Hill, and the Redeemer Nation: A Reappraisal," *Am Pres* 69 (spring 1991): 33–47. For example (38), in 1743 Edwards excoriated New England's exploitation of Native Americans. Others who point to the influence of Edwards on missions include Rooy, *Theology of Missions*, 285–309; Charles L. Chaney, *The Birth of Missions in America* (South Pasadena: William Carey Library, 1976), 57–74; and William R. Hutchison, *Errand to the World: American Protestant Thought and Foreign Missions* (Chicago: University of Chicago Press, 1987), 40–41. Hutchison says (40) "it was Edwards's ideas about world evangelization that (along with those emanating from British and German evangelical sources) would have the most powerful and palpable influence in the century following."

good news should be published through the whole world, and the offer of this salvation be made to all mankind."[11]

The Scottish kirk was instrumental in a brief missions endeavor at the end of the seventeenth century. In 1698 the first of two expeditions went to Darien (the name given to Panama). The two ordained ministers who accompanied the trip died, one en route, the other a few weeks after arrival at Darien. The following year a second group of ships was sent, this time with four ministers aboard, one of whom died at sea. The other three took seriously their instructions to begin missionary work among the natives, attempting to learn the local dialect and making an exploratory trip to the nearby villages. The whole enterprise was brought to an end when a Spanish force overwhelmed the Scots early in 1700, and all had to flee.[12]

The Scottish church was a factor in eighteenth-century missionary work among the Indian population in North America. The Society in Scotland for Propagating Christian Knowledge (SSPCK; there was also a Society for Propagating Christian Knowledge [SPCK], founded in England in 1698) confined its work to the remote regions of Scotland from its founding in 1709 until 1730. In the latter year a board was established in Boston to work among Native Americans, but it ceased functioning in 1737, then was reconstituted in 1741 in New York. Among those it supported were Azariah Horton on Long Island and David Brainerd in Pennsylvania and New Jersey. In 1769 the Scottish society transferred its operations to a group of trustees connected with the College of New Jersey (Princeton), a Presbyterian school.[13]

Mention of work among Indian peoples in North America leads to what is a large topic, for several attempts were made at missionary work among the eastern tribes in America under Calvinist auspices other than through the SSPCK. The most noteworthy in the seventeenth century were those undertaken by John Eliot at Roxbury, near Boston, and by the Mayhew family on Martha's Vineyard off Cape Cod. The Mayhews began their ministry in 1642 when Thomas Mayhew (c. 1620–1657), son of the original patentee, was ordained pastor of the small English congregation, and who within two years after that began his evangelizing of the Indians. Regular preaching and a school followed within ten

11. Quoted in Chaney, *The Birth of Missions,* 79. Interestingly (Chaney, 77–80), Hopkins's words are from a sermon he preached in 1793 before the Providence [Rhode Island] Society for Abolishing the Slave Trade; he advocated both the end to the slave trade and missionary work in Africa. Chaney feels (74) that Edwards is more influential on the missionary movement than Hopkins; but see also Hutchison, *Errand to the World,* 50–51, and Oliver Wendell Elsbree, *The Rise of the Missionary Spirit in America 1790–1815* (reprint, Philadelphia: Porcupine Press, 1980), 146–52.

12. Two articles by Jack Ramsay recount the Darien colony: "Scottish Presbyterian Foreign Missions—A Century before Carey," *Journal of the Presbyterian Historical Society* 39 (December 1961): 201–18; "Francis Borland: Presbyterian Missioner to the Americas," *J Pres H* 62 (spring 1984): 1–17.

13. Elsbree, *Rise of the Missionary Spirit in America,* 16–17.

years. After Thomas's death in 1657, his father continued the work and a Congregational church was formed in 1670. Like other work among the New England Indians, King Philip's War in 1675–1676 had a deleterious effect on missions, and even though the Mayhew work continued for several more generations it was not as successful as before. John Eliot (1604–1690) was teacher at the Roxbury congregation from 1632 until his death and engaged in Indian evangelism from the 1640s on. In 1649 the Society for the Propagation of the Gospel in New England was formed to support Eliot and other workers among Native Americans, and several "praying towns" of Indian converts were founded under Eliot's auspices. After King Philip's War the work declined, although it continued into the eighteenth century.[14]

The eighteenth century saw a continuation of missions to Indians, inspired in part by the Calvinist Cotton Mather (1663–1728). Appointed a commissioner of Indian affairs for the New England Company in 1689, his attitude toward the Indians, which had been quite harsh up to that time, seemed to mellow thereafter, and he showed vigorous interest in Indian evangelization. Among his products from this interest were reports on progress of work among the Indians, helps for those who engaged in Indian evangelization, and agitation for continued Indian work.[15]

Other Indian missions were inspired and engaged in by Calvinists. Eleazar Wheelock (1711–1779) is noteworthy, for during the Great Awakening he began tutoring a Mohegan named Samson Occam, and from this he developed an interest in reaching other Native Americans. This led in 1754 to the opening of Moor's Charity School (the forerunner to Dartmouth College) as a training place for both white and Native American missionaries. Wheelock experienced only limited success in training Native Americans, but his life shows his great interest in reaching that population group.

Jonathan Edwards, noted for his role in the Great Awakening and for his acute theological thinking, was also for a time a missionary to the Indians. After the rupture with his church in Northampton led to Edwards's being released from the congregation, he moved to Stockbridge in western Massachusetts to serve a church with both white and Indian members.[16] Started in 1735, the mission at Stockbridge had not been very successful, and Edwards was there only briefly, because in 1755 he was called to the presidency of

14. The Mayhews and Eliot have been treated many times, but see in particular Lloyd C. M. Hare, *Thomas Mayhew: Patriarch to the Indians, 1593–1682* (New York: D. Appleton, 1932), and the section on Eliot (171–232) in *Five Missionary Pioneers* (Edinburgh: Banner of Truth Trust, 1965).

15. Chaney, *Birth of Missions*, 52–53. Solomon Stoddard, a contemporary of Cotton Mather and grandfather of Jonathan Edwards, can be mentioned here as having an interest in evangelizing Indians, particularly shown in his *Question Whether God is not Angry with the Country for Doing So Little Towards the Conversion of the Indians* (1723).

16. Edwards's years in Stockbridge are recounted in MacCormac, "Jonathan Edwards and Missions," 219–29.

Princeton. But he engaged in administration of Indian missions there, led in trying to persuade the learning of the English language, and even tried to mount a campaign of missions among the Iroquois.

While the ministry among Indians in North America had only limited success, it had far-reaching influence in the course of missionary history, for it served as a transition to the modern era of Protestant missions:

> The Indian missions of the seventeenth and eighteenth century, especially those undertaken and supported by Calvinists, provided great inspiration to those who played the most important role in the rise of the great Protestant missionary movement to the heathen at the end of the eighteenth and beginning of the nineteenth centuries.[17]

Carey and After

Historians have suggested a variety of reasons for the rise of modern Protestant missions, including the expansion of Europe, the rise of capitalism, the rise of an optimistic spirit about the future, and the postmillennial view that prior to Christ's second coming an era of great expansion of the gospel would occur. While not denying any of these as at least playing some role, and while recognizing that theologies other than Calvinism played some part in the rise of missions (among Moravians, for example, a theology Lutheran in background propelled that group into missionary activity beginning in the eighteenth century), the Calvinist missiology and work we have described played a major role in the missionary expansion that began with William Carey.

Although Carey was aware that he had been preceded by a host of others (as he noted in his *Enquiry*), yet there was a quickening of missionary interest in the decades following the 1790s that warrants our seeing the era from Carey on as a new epoch in the history of missions. The founding of many missionary societies, the rapid increase in numbers of missionaries, and the move toward a global missionary enterprise came within half a century of Carey's going to India. And here too, as before Carey's time, much of the sponsorship and personnel of missionary activity was in the hands of those in the Calvinist tradition. We cannot possibly cover every endeavor in a single chapter, but we will highlight the societies and major persons in the early nineteenth century that constitute the Calvinist missions activities. Our concentration is on the United States, with some passing references to Great Britain.

17. R. Pearce Beaver, "Methods in American Missions to the Indians in the Seventeenth and Eighteenth Centuries: Calvinist Models for Protestant Foreign Missions," *J Pres H* 47 (June 1969): 148.

The Baptist Missionary Society that delegated Carey to India was one among a number of organizations that spearheaded the nineteenth-century move into missionary activity.[18] In 1787 the Society for Propagating the Gospel among the Indians and Others in North America was established by Boston Congregationalists. Founded as a kind of extension of the SSPCK, it was as much interested in white frontier settlements as it was in Native Americans, although it sent individuals to both groups. But this was in keeping with the missionary enterprise in the decades after the American Revolution, for the western settlements were seen as equally "wilderness," whether the heathen there were white or red. For example, the New York Missionary Society was formed in 1796 by Presbyterian, Baptist, and Dutch Reformed clergy, and for more than twenty years the Society worked with Native Americans. In 1822 it united with several other home missionary societies in New York to form the United Domestic Missionary Society, which organization concentrated its work among white immigrant groups in New York State. When the Missionary Society of Connecticut formed in 1798, followed the next year by the Massachusetts Missionary Society (both founded by Congregationalists), the emphasis was on the white settlements being newly established in frontier areas. The term *missionary* applied equally to home and foreign missions and to the heathen in North America and Europe as well as those on the other continents until well into the nineteenth century.

The first and for half a century the largest missionary society in the U.S. was the American Board of Commissioners for Foreign Missions (ABCFM or American Board), a Congregational sending agency founded in 1810. Students from Williams College who attended the newly formed Andover Seminary petitioned the Congregationalists of Massachusetts in 1810 to organize the ABCFM. The first five missionaries sailed for India in 1812,

---

18. The birth of the SPGIONA is briefly told in Chaney, *Birth of Missions,* 138–40. That its sponsorship was Calvinistic is shown in that Jedediah Morse became mission secretary in 1802. Morse was an orthodox Calvinist much opposed to the growing Unitarianism in New England. When Harvard appointed a man of Unitarian sympathies to the Hollis Chair of Divinity in 1805, Morse founded a magazine, *Panoplist,* whose pages he used to attack the Unitarians. Along with Leonard Woods, Morse was instrumental in the founding of Andover Seminary (1808), an institution with a strong missions influence. The American Home Missionary Society, founded in 1826, is an example of the use of the term *missionary* to apply almost entirely to work done in white frontier settlements. Founded at a meeting supported by Congregationalists, Presbyterians, Dutch Reformed, and Associate Reformed, the society sent hundreds of missionaries to new settlements. For a full account of this and other home missions in the middle of the nineteenth century, see Victor B. Howard, *Conscience and Slavery: The Evangelistic Calvinist Domestic Missions, 1837–1861* (Kent, Ohio: Kent State University Press, 1990). Interest in missions to Native Americans did not wane as the century progressed, and here too, with the exception of the Methodists, there were many Reformed theology missionaries; note, for example, the references to Calvinism in William McLoughlin, *Cherokees and Missionaries, 1789–1839* (New Haven, Conn.: Yale University Press, 1984), 103, 132–33, 138–39, 151, 209, 238, 266, 329–30.

but only three of them remained with the American Board. Two of the five changed their position on baptism during the voyage—famed Baptists Adoniram Judson and Luther Rice—and later helped to found a Baptist missionary society. The first group went to India, but the most successful mission endeavor by the American Board was in Hawaii, where missionaries first landed in 1820. By 1877 the ABCFM was supporting 375 missionaries in a number of fields. And while it is true that American Congregationalism gradually moved in a more liberal direction after mid-century, from the beginning the missionaries, and the board, were in the Calvinist tradition.[19]

Included in their number was a significant contingent of Presbyterians, the Presbyterians not officially having a national mission board until 1837. In 1801 the Plan of Union was effected between the Congregationalists and the Presbyterians, the two agreeing to evangelize the frontier together, rather than engage in unnecessary overlap. Dominated by Calvinist thinking, the two groups worked together until the 1837 General Assembly revoked the union. Until that time, Presbyterians engaged in both home and foreign missions under terms of the union, so a number of missionaries who went out under the American Board did so with Presbyterian ordination.[20]

19. Even as late as 1865 the National Council "declared in substance its adherence 'to those ancient symbols [Westminster Confession and Savoy Declaration] as being' well and fully grounded upon the Holy Scriptures, 'the only sufficient and invariable rule of religion.' The whole action of the New England theology was within the frame of historic Calvinism." Gaius Glenn Atkins and Frederick L. Fagley, *History of American Congregationalism* (Boston: Pilgrim, 1942), 168. The same observation is made in a recent work, J. William T. Youngs, *The Congregationalists* (New York: Greenwood, 1990), 52, 140–48. The "Haystack Group" and its influence on the ABCFM is an oft-told story; a brief version is found in ibid., 129–31. The group who went to the Sandwich (Hawaiian) Islands went under the Westminster and Savoy standards of course; their theological commitment is fully explored in Sandra Wagner-Wright, *The Structure of the Missionary Call to the Sandwich Islands 1790–1830: Sojourners among Strangers* (San Francisco: Mellen Research University Press, 1990). Wagner-Wright says (10), "The foundation of the New England missionary enterprise rests upon the Calvinist theology of the Reformed tradition." This includes the wives among the several contingents of missionaries to Hawaii, as some recent historians acknowledge: Patricia Grimshaw, *Paths of Duty: American Missionary Wives in Nineteenth-Century Hawaii* (Honolulu: University of Hawaii Press, 1989), 75; Mary Zwiep, *Pilgrim Path: The First Company of Women Missionaries to Hawaii* (Madison: University of Wisconsin Press, 1991). Zwiep notes (11), "In the early 1800s, the young women and men applying for missionary work were united, not divided, by religion."

20. This joint operation (and some Dutch Reformed were also included), and the joint efforts noted in home missions activity, is part of the "society" (cross-denominational) approach to both social reform and missions in antebellum America, so we have both denominational and multidenominational missionary organizations, producing at times a confusing mix of agencies. By the 1830s the denominational mission boards begin to prevail as the norm for missionary activity (which norm in turn went back to a mix later in the nineteenth century, when faith missions were founded) as described in Fred J. Hood, *Reformed America: The Middle and Southern States, 1783–1837* (Huntsville: University of Alabama Press, 1980), 190–97.

The story of Presbyterian missionary organization is one with a Calvinistic basis, of course. Presbyterians sent a number of missionaries out under the American Board after its founding in 1810, but there were in place several missions organizations under Presbyterian auspices. From 1802 to 1828 there existed as an arm of the Synod of Pittsburgh the Western Missionary Society, which sent missionaries to settlers and Indians in Virginia, Ohio, and Pennsylvania. The General Assembly created a Standing Committee on Missions in 1802 and sent its first missionary out the following year. In 1816 the Standing Committee became the Board of Missions, and by this time was concentrating on supporting pastors in small congregations. In 1831 the Synod of Pittsburgh, under the prodding of the Reverend Elisha Swift of Second Presbyterian, Pittsburgh, formed the Western Foreign Missionary Society (WFMS).[21] The first missionary sent, to West Africa in 1833, was Princeton Seminary graduate John Pinney. Over the next few years, several more missionaries went out to Africa, India, and the American West. In 1837, when the Presbyterians split into Old School and New School factions (the two were reunited in 1869), the WFMS became the Old School's Presbyterian Board of Foreign Missions, the Board of Missions became the Board of Domestic Missions, and the New School continued to work through the ABCFM. The Southern Presbyterian denomination, not formed officially until after the American Civil War, marked its entrance into missionary activity with early efforts in China and the Congo. Through all this and the subsequent years, the Westminster Confession of Faith remained the standard for the various Presbyterian bodies.

The first national organization of Baptists took place in Philadelphia in 1814 with the formation of the Triennial Convention, whose specific aim was to engage in foreign missions, more specifically to support Adoniram and Ann Judson in Burma. It broadened to include home missions two years later, then began to reemphasize foreign missions in the

21. The story of the WFMS is told in Marjorie Barnhart, "From Elisha Swift to Walter Lowrie: The Background of the Presbyterian Board of Foreign Missions," *Am Pres* 65 (summer 1987): 85–96. Archibald Alexander (Barnhart, 87), one of the founders (and first professor) of Princeton Seminary, the quintessential Calvinist seminary in the nineteenth century, approved of the formation of the WFMS and made the contact on behalf of Pinney. David B. Calhoun ("Of Ships and Books: The Travel Journals of the Early Princeton Seminary Foreign Missionaries," *Presbyterion* 12 [spring 1986]) notes (37): "By 1862, the fiftieth anniversary of Princeton Seminary, 117 students had served on foreign mission fields." For a fuller account of Princeton Seminary and missions see Calhoun's "The Last Command: Princeton Theological Seminary and Missions (1812–1862)" (Unpublished dissertation, Princeton Theological Seminary, 1983). The Westminster Standards, together with the Nicene and Apostolic creeds, formed the basis for the uniting in 1890 of seven Presbyterian bodies working in China, including the Southern Presbyterians. "The Conference of Missionaries to China," *Presbyterian and Reformed Review* 1 (October 1890): 653–54.

mid-1820s; a separate American Baptist Home Mission Society was formed in 1832.[22] Baptists in America, while divided between general (Arminian) and regular or particular (Calvinistic), were probably most influenced by the Calvinistic view, and that largely through two confessions of faith. The first Baptist association of churches in America was formed in 1707 in Philadelphia; in 1742 the association adopted its Confession of Faith, to a large extent based on a Calvinistic confession drawn up in England in 1689. Both the Philadelphia association and its confession had a large influence on Baptists well into the national period of American history. In 1833, the New Hampshire Confession of Faith was drawn up to counter the Arminian teaching that had surfaced in New England. Originally adopted only by the Baptists in the state of New Hampshire, the confession and its moderate Calvinism became extensively influential among many Baptists in the U.S. In 1845, because of the split over slavery and the formation of the Southern Baptist Convention, the latter denomination formed its own missionary organization, the Foreign Mission Board. Although the SBC did not officially adopt a confession until 1925, that document was based on the New Hampshire Confession.

Probably the most famous Baptist in the nineteenth century was Charles Spurgeon (1834–1892), pastor of the Metropolitan Tabernacle in London, considered at the time to be the largest Baptist congregation in the world. That Spurgeon was a Calvinist is undoubted, influenced as he was by the Puritans, whom he quoted often, and seen in his combat in the "downgrade" controversy among English Baptists in the 1880s. His view of missions is captured well in these words:

> The greatest missionaries that have ever lived have believed in God's choice of them; and instead of this doctrine [of electing grace] leading to inaction, it has ever been an irresistible motive power, and it will be so again . . . How can men

22. Carey was among the first to advise American Baptists to form a missionary organization. The Judsons and Luther Rice, after their change to the Baptist point of view, first considered joining Carey's mission, but he thought it best for the Baptists in the U.S. to found their own society; McBeth, "Legacy of Baptist Missionary Society," 12. The full name of the 1815 society was The General Missionary Convention of the Baptist Denomination in the United States for Foreign Missions. The Philadelphia and New Hampshire confessions are printed in William Lumpkin, *Baptist Confessions of Faith*, rev. ed. (Valley Forge, Penn.: Judson, 1969). The first president of the Triennial Convention was a Calvinist Baptist pastor from South Carolina, Richard Furman (reelected to the post in 1817); see Thomas J. Nettles, "Richard Furman," in *Baptist Theologians*, ed. Timothy George and David S. Dockery (Nashville: Broadman, 1990), 140–64. Indications of the Calvinistic beginnings of both the SBC and its first seminary, The Southern Baptist Theological Seminary, are in Nettles, *By His Grace and for His Glory: A Historical, Theological, and Practical Study of the Doctrines of Grace in Baptist Life* (Grand Rapids: Baker, 1986), 161, 187.

say that the doctrine of distinguishing grace makes men careless about their souls?[23]

Spurgeon was an avid believer in missionary activity, both on the home front where the Tabernacle sponsored a whole series of enterprises, especially among the poor, and on the foreign front, about which he made many comments.

A brief mention of several smaller Reformed denominations will round out the survey in this chapter and will show that Calvinism and missionary activity continues into the late twentieth century. As already noted the Dutch Reformed at times engaged in missions activity in connection with Congregationalists and Presbyterians. The Dutch church in America was until after the American Revolution under the aegis of the Amsterdam classis (which classis was among the most missionary-minded in The Netherlands) and used the ABCFM and the American Home Missionary Society for its missions outreach. But in 1806 a standing committee on missions was formed by the General Synod, the national governing body. Its activity was quite limited, the Dutch Reformed (after 1867 called the Reformed Church in America) for some time willing to unite with Presbyterians and Congregationalists for missionary efforts. But in 1822 an independent missionary society came into being, and after the General Synod organized its own board of missions in 1831, the independent society became auxiliary to the synod board.[24]

The Christian Reformed Church was created in the U.S. in 1857 by a small group of seceders from the Dutch Reformed Church.[25] Although it was not a strong missionary denomination before World War I, this was due to factors other than theology, its strong Calvinism not at all opposed to missionary endeavor. The Orthodox Presbyterian Church was formed in 1936 when it left the parent body, the Northern Presbyterians, the break coming over the reorganization of Princeton Seminary that began in 1929, and over the rise

23. Cited in Iain Murray, *The Forgotten Spurgeon* (London: Banner of Truth Trust, 1966), 119. Spurgeon's theology is laid out by Lewis Drummond, "Charles Haddon Spurgeon," in *Baptist Theologians*, 267–88. Just months before his death Spurgeon with several other Baptist ministers issued a manifesto stating that "We hold and maintain the truths generally known as 'the doctrines of grace,'" the first of which was "The Electing Love of God the Father," *The Sword and the Trowel* 27 (August 1891): 446. *The Sword and the Trowel*, a monthly begun by Spurgeon in 1865 and edited by him until 1891, contains numerous reports about missionary activity on a variety of foreign fields and also Spurgeon's clear espousal of missionary activity.

24. The doctrinal standards for the Dutch Reformed Church/Reformed Church in America include three Calvinist creeds: the Belgic Confession, the Canons of Dort, and the Heidelberg Catechism.

25. Doctrinal standards of the Christian Reformed Church are the same as for the Reformed Church in America. Early CRC missions activity is described by Harvey A. Smit, "Mission Zeal in the Christian Reformed Church, 1857–1917," in *Perspectives on the Christian Reformed Church: Studies in Its History, Theology, and Ecumenicity*, ed. Peter De Klerk and Richard R. De Ridder (Grand Rapids: Baker, 1983), 225–40.

of liberalism in the larger denomination, including liberalism in missions policy. From the beginning, the OPC has had a strong missions emphasis.[26] The Presbyterian Church in America was formed in 1973 when a number of Southern Presbyterians refused to enter the merger that year with the national Presbyterian body. It too has engaged in strong missionary activity.[27]

Calvinism was a major factor in the limited Protestant missionary activity prior to William Carey and in the burst of missions that occurred during and after Carey's time. It is certainly noteworthy that the first three foreign missions boards founded were done so by groups adhering to the principles of Reformed theology. The American Board in 1810, founded by Congregationalists, and supported in part by Presbyterians and Dutch Reformed; the Triennial Convention of the Baptists founded in 1814; and the United Foreign Missionary Society, a smaller organization created in New York in 1817, supported by Presbyterian, Dutch Reformed, and Associated Reformed congregations—all had Calvinist associations. Charles Chaney contends that "[t]he early exponents of the missionary movement held consistently to the sovereign election of God in salvation. Among these men was an occasional advocate of a general atonement, but most insisted that the purpose of God in redemption had not been left to the caprice of sinful man but determined by the unmerited choice of God."[28] This may be too strong as a general description of the missionary movement in the U.S. down to the 1820s, but it makes abundantly clear that the notion that Calvinism and missions do not go together is a false notion.

Has missionary work been done only by those who emphasized the sovereignty of God? Of course not. But we have shown that Calvinism's emphasis on the doctrines of grace, rather than mitigating against missions, has been a catalyst for engaging in missions. Mission boards and individuals agreed with Calvin that God had ordained both the gospel of salvation to persons and the means for reaching those persons. The Calvinists believed that missions was God's choice because God's interest in salvation was global, that the Great Commission was still the mandate for believers, that God appointed means as well as ends, and that missions was done for the glory of God. William Carey could not "sit down"; expecting great things from God and attempting great things for God compelled him to stand and go.

26. The Orthodox Presbyterian Church uses the Westminster Confession of Faith as its doctrinal basis; a brief look at OPC missions is Victor B. Atallah, "Where Are We Going in Missions?" in *Pressing Toward the Mark: Essays Commemorating Fifty Years of the Orthodox Presbyterian Church*, ed. Charles G. Dennison and Richard C. Gamble (Philadelphia: Orthodox Presbyterian Church, 1986), 405–9.

27. The doctrinal basis for the Presbyterian Church in America is the Westminster Confession of Faith.

28. Chaney, *Birth of Missions*, 218–19.

Part 4
Theological/Philosophical Issues

15

The Place of Effectual Calling and Grace in a Calvinist Soteriology

BRUCE A. WARE

All those whom God hath predestinated unto life, and those only, he is pleased, in his appointed and accepted time, effectually to call, by his Word and Spirit, out of that state of sin and death, in which they are by nature, to grace and salvation, by Jesus Christ; enlightening their minds spiritually and savingly to understand the things of God, taking away their heart of stone, and giving unto them a heart of flesh; renewing their wills, and, by his almighty power, determining them to that which is good, and effectually drawing them to Jesus Christ: yet so, as they come most freely, being made willing by his grace.[1]

The purpose of this chapter is to explain the contribution made to Calvinism by the doctrine of God's effectual calling of sinners to saving faith through the provision of irresistible grace (indicated hereafter as the ECG doctrine, the doctrine of effectual calling and grace), and to defend the ECG doctrine as expressive of clear biblical teaching. As such, this doctrine provides strong evidence against an Arminian, and in favor of a Calvinist, soteriology. Furthermore, the strength of the ECG doctrine is greater for Calvinism than might be thought at first. Since the ECG doctrine both entails the Calvinist doctrine of unconditional election and precludes the Arminian doctrine of prevenient grace, establishing the ECG doctrine adds strength to the broader structure of a Calvinist soteriology.

---

1. The Westminster Confession of Faith, "Of Effectual Calling," 10.1.

It should be mentioned that I am holding together in a unity (i.e., the ECG doctrine) what is commonly expressed under two doctrinal headings. The twin Calvinist doctrines of God's *effectual call* to saving faith extended to the elect (as distinct from the general gospel call extended to all), and of the provision of *irresistible grace,* leading necessarily to the saving-faith response of the elect, are two aspects of one reality. Both doctrines may rightly be used to speak of the work of God's Spirit, through the word of the gospel, by which he opens the blind eyes and enlivens the hardened hearts of those dead in sin. For the first time, they then understand and embrace the gospel for what it is, namely, good news of God's salvation through faith in Christ. This saving work may be described variously as the Spirit's call to sinners to hear and to believe the gospel, rendered effectual by his supernatural enlivening work, or as the Spirit's provision of grace resulting in saving faith, rendered irresistible against all blindness, hardness, and unbelief. The Spirit supernaturally liberates the human heart from sin's clutches to turn from sin and joyfully accept God's gracious provision of salvation in Christ. For our purposes, then, these twin doctrines will be treated as a unity (i.e., the ECG doctrine) and understood as the doctrine of God's effectual calling of sinners to saving faith, by the word of the gospel and through the provision of irresistible grace.[2]

One other introductory comment is in order. I wish to affirm that my goal in this defense is primarily to contribute to the formulation a biblically responsible soteriology; only secondarily do I hope to support Calvinism, and this insofar as a proper biblical and theological understanding requires it. Calvinists and Arminians share, in principle, the same mindset: that theological systems must not be permitted to rule over the best and most responsible biblical understandings and theological formulations. But the theological system that grows out of and makes the best sense of those most compelling and responsible biblical understandings ought, then, to be upheld and commended. Calvinism ought to be defended not because of its inherent logic, symmetry, or comprehensive structure per se, but because the substance of its biblical understanding is more compelling than that of its rivals.

Arminian and Calvinist Structures of Soteriology

Calvinists and Arminians have more points of agreement than disagreement in their respective soteriologies. They agree on the doctrines of salva-

---

2. See also John Murray, *Redemption—Accomplished and Applied* (Grand Rapids: Eerdmans, 1955), 96: "God's call, since it is effectual, carries with it the operative grace whereby the person called is enabled to answer the call and to embrace Jesus Christ as he is freely offered in the gospel."

tion by grace through faith, justification by faith, adoption, union with Christ, sanctification as the outworking of one's justification and union with Christ, and the full and final salvation—glorification—of all who truly believe. In these shared convictions, we are evangelical allies.

In other areas significant disagreement arises. The two most critical differences between Arminian and Calvinist soteriologies concern the doctrines of divine election and of God's calling of sinners to saving faith through grace. That is, both on the question of how, in eternity past, the composition of the elect occurs, and of how, in the time-space medium of human history, sinners come to express saving faith in Christ, there is fundamental disagreement.

Arminian Soteriological Structure

Arminians hold the view that God's election of sinners to salvation is really his election of Christ to be Savior, so that all who place their faith in Christ thereby constitute the elect insofar as they are placed in Christ, God's elect One.[3] How, then, can God be said to elect certain *people* in Christ before the foundation of the world (Eph. 1:4)? According to classic Arminianism, God has exhaustive knowledge of all things, including exhaustive knowledge of the future. He knows from eternity past those who will in fact freely come. On the basis of this advance knowledge, God is said to "elect" in Christ those whom he knows will believe in Christ.[4] For the Arminian, election is primarily God's election of Christ, such that all who believe in Christ—whom God knows from

3. Arminius states: "The first precise and absolute decree of God for effecting the salvation of sinful man is that he has determined to appoint his Son, Jesus Christ, as a Mediator, Redeemer, Savior, Priest, and King, to nullify sin by his death, to obtain the lost salvation through his obedience, and to communicate it by his power. . . . The second precise and absolute decree of God is that he has determined graciously to receive in favor those who repent and believe, and, the same persevering, to effect their salvation in Christ, for Christ's sake, and through Christ, and to leave the unrepentant and unbelieving in sin and under wrath, and to damn them as strangers to Christ" (quoted in Carl Bangs, *Arminius: A Study in the Dutch Reformation* [Grand Rapids: Zondervan, [2]1985], 350–51). See also, for example, Robert Shank, *Elect in the Son* (Springfield, Mo.: Westcott, 1970); William W. Klein, *The New Chosen People: A Corporate View of Election* (Grand Rapids: Zondervan, 1990); and William G. MacDonald, "The Biblical Doctrine of Election," in *The Grace of God, the Will of Man: A Case for Arminianism*, ed. Clark H. Pinnock (Grand Rapids: Zondervan, 1989), 207–29.

4. Arminius states: "From this follows the fourth decree to save certain particular persons and to damn others, which decree rests upon the foreknowledge of God, by which he has known from eternity which persons should believe according to such an administration of the means serving to repentance and faith through his preceding grace and which should persevere through subsequent grace, and also who should not believe and persevere" (quoted in Bangs, *Arminius,* 352). Some contemporary Arminians are departing from this classic doctrine of God's exhaustive knowledge of the future. See, for example, Clark H. Pinnock, "From Augustine to Arminius: A Pilgrimage in Theology," in *The Grace of God, the Will of Man,* 25–27; and Richard

eternity past as part of his exhaustive knowledge of the future (in the classic Arminian view)—constitute those elect in Christ.[5]

Since God's election is of Christ primarily, and all who freely believe in Christ are thereby constituted the elect, it follows that all people must be able to accept or to reject Christ. That is, the moral responsibility and volitional freedom necessary to believe freely in Christ and so to be placed in Christ as the elect must be present with all humans, some of whom believe and thereby become part of the elect in Christ, and some of whom reject God's offer of salvation in Christ. But the point is, in whatever response, whether belief or rejection, each person must be able to act freely, apart from any causal determination that necessitated one response or the other. What enables this free human response?

If this doctrine of corporate election is accepted, one of three possible positions is required regarding the question of how, in the time-space medium of human history, sinners come to express saving faith in Christ. First, one may be morally and volitionally free in the Pelagian sense of being unaffected by Adam's sin and so able by nature to perform moral actions in one way or another, as one chooses. Second, one may retain, as the semi-Pelagian argued, the vestiges of a weakened, although still vital, moral will enabling one to choose for either good or evil, assisted only by the presence of divine grace. Arminius and those in the classic Arminian tradition have rejected both of these theological options. Sin has caused a "bondage of the will" (to use Luther's phrase and concept, which Arminius affirmed) such that, apart from grace, human nature cannot choose to act in ways that please God or honor the gospel of Christ.[6] So third, in Arminius's understanding, God provides commonly to all people his prevenient grace, a grace sufficient to overcome

---

Rice, "Divine Foreknowledge and Free-Will Theism," in ibid., 121–39. But for a staunch Arminian defense of God's exhaustive knowledge of the future, see William Lane Craig, *The Only Wise God* (Grand Rapids: Baker, 1987); and "Middle Knowledge, A Calvinist-Arminian Rapprochement?" in *The Grace of God, the Will of Man*, 141–64.

5. In the argument I develop, I purposely focus attention on the classic Arminian view, which holds to God's exhaustive knowledge of the future. I do so because this is a stronger Arminian view than the more recent and distressing neo-Arminian view advocated by Pinnock, Rice, and others, in which God knows all things past and present, but nothing (i.e., no real knowledge) of the future. This view is weaker than the classic Arminian view because it has no satisfactory answer to the question of how people could be spoken of as God's eternally elect ones. In the neo-Arminian view, surely God can have elected Christ in eternity past, but it is inconceivable how he would elect us in Christ before the foundation of the world (Eph. 1:4), since he had no way of knowing whether any people would in fact come to Christ, much less who those people would be who constitute the "elect" of eternity past.

6. Arminius states: "In this [sinful] state, the free will of man towards the true good is not only wounded, maimed, infirm, bent, and weakened; but it is also imprisoned, destroyed, and lost. And its powers are not only debilitated and useless unless they be assisted by grace, but it has no powers whatsoever except such as are excited by divine grace. For Christ has said, 'Without me ye can do nothing'" (quoted in Bangs, *Arminius*, 341). Regarding Arminius's position on the effects of sin on the human will, Bangs comments: "There is nothing here of grace as an *assistance* given to a man who is only weakened by sin" (ibid., 341).

the effects of sin, such that every person is made able either to accept in saving faith or to reject in disbelief the gospel of Christ.[7]

These temporal poles form the structure of an Arminian soteriology. In eternity past, God first elects Christ, and secondarily he elects in Christ the corporate body of those whom he knows (i.e., foresees) will freely respond in saving faith to the gospel. Then, in human history, he provides prevenient grace, commonly distributed to all, enabling all to believe while actually effecting the salvation only of those whom he previously knew would freely come.

Given this understanding, it should be clear how the doctrine of corporate election in the one elect Man, Christ, depends for its credibility on the corresponding doctrine of prevenient grace.[8] If God's election is of certain people to be saved (albeit those whom he foreknows will freely come), then there must be the provision of grace, sufficient to overcome the deadening effects of sin while not necessitating a believing response, in order for God to be said truly to know and to choose in eternity past those who would freely come. If there were to be either a lack of sufficient prevenient grace given to all (i.e., the absence of or insufficient distribution of prevenient grace as Arminians conceive it), or the presence of grace that necessarily brings about a saving response in the elect (i.e., the presence of irresistible grace as Calvinists conceive it), the doctrine of corporate election would fail along with the doctrine of prevenient grace.[9] An Arminian soteriology, then, depends greatly on its

---

7. Arminius states: "The third decree of God is that by which he has predetermined to administer the necessary, sufficient, and powerful means of repentance and faith, which administration occurs according to the wisdom of God, by which he knows what becomes his mercy and his severity, and according to his justice, by which he is prepared to follow what his wisdom has carried out" (quoted in ibid., 351–52).

8. It should be noted that even for the neo-Arminian position (called free-will theism by Pinnock and Rice [see Pinnock, *The Grace of God, the Will of Man*, chaps. 1, 6] in which God is said not to have exhaustive knowledge of the future and, therefore, cannot be said to elect those whom he knows will freely accept Christ), the doctrine of prevenient grace is essential. The neo-Arminian soteriology is still committed to the notion that God gives commonly to all a bestowal of grace that enables a positive response to revelation given, such that people either may or may not seek the salvation offered.

9. The point being made here is an instance of the valid type of argumentation called *modus tollens*, which argues as follows:
1. If A, then B
2. Not B
3. Therefore, not A

The point being made is that the doctrine of conditional election of classic Arminianism entails and depends on its doctrine of prevenient grace. So, if the doctrine of prevenient grace fails, likewise does its doctrine of conditional election. That is:
1. If conditional election, then prevenient grace
2. Not prevenient grace
3. Therefore, not conditional election

For a discussion of *modus tollens* and other valid forms of argumentation, see, e.g., Douglas N. Walton, *Informal Logic: A Handbook for Critical Argumentation* (Cambridge: Cambridge University Press, 1989), 108–33.

doctrine of prevenient grace, both as an explanation of how those dead in their sin exercise saving faith and of how God may rightly be said to know and to choose those who freely respond in saving faith.

Calvinist Soteriological Structure

For Calvinists, their complementary doctrines of God's unconditional election of those whom he will save and the effectual calling of the those elect ones through the provision of irresistible grace (i.e., the ECG doctrine) are closely related. In fact, even more so than with the corresponding Arminian doctrines, the Calvinist doctrines are mutually dependent and mutually entailing.

If God in eternity past has elected some to salvation, and this election is without respect to any qualities, actions, behavior, virtues, vices, or choices of those individuals themselves (i.e., God's election is not conditioned on their characteristics or actions),[10] then his calling of them to salvation must necessarily be effectual through the means of the bestowal of grace that is irresistible, bringing just those and no others to salvation whom he had in eternity past unconditionally elected to salvation. More simply put, an election that is unconditional requires God to be the one to bring to salvation those whom he has chosen through the means of effectual calling and irresistible grace. In a similar manner, if the ECG doctrine can be maintained, it follows that his effectual calling was of those and only those whom he previously and unconditionally chose to save.[11] Hence, the doctrine of unconditional election both entails and is entailed by the ECG doctrine.

The Outcome for Arminian and Calvinist Soteriologies

It should be evident that Arminian and Calvinist soteriologies stand or fall on their respective doctrines of saving grace. For the Arminian, the doctrine of prevenient grace is not an optional luxury that may be either included or

10. When Calvinists refer to God's election as unconditional, they have in mind conditions pertaining to the elect, not God. That is, God's election is unconditioned with respect to any and all qualities and behavior of elect persons in comparison to nonelect persons; but of course his election is conditioned on something in God: his wise counsel and perfect will resulting in the praise of the glory of his grace (Eph. 1:11–12). Therefore it is a caricature and a false representation of Calvinism to say that its doctrine of unconditional election requires that God's choice be arbitrary or capricious. For a recent enlightening treatment of this issue, see John Piper, *The Pleasures of God* (Portland, Ore.: Multnomah, 1991), 126–39.

11. See also John Calvin, *Institutes of the Christian Religion*, Library of Christian Classics, 2 vols., ed. John T. McNeill, trans. Ford Lewis Battles (Philadelphia: Westminster, 1960), 2.964 (3.24), where the chapter title reads, in part, "Election Is Confirmed By God's Call," and is followed by the section heading (3.24.1) that reads: "The call is dependent upon election and accordingly is solely a work of grace."

discarded; it is a necessary element without which an Arminian soteriology, and hence Arminianism, would collapse. Likewise, the ECG doctrine of Calvinism is a necessary complement to its doctrine of unconditional election, each of which entails and is entailed by the other, and both of which are necessary to its soteriology.

Given this understanding, it is important to see what Calvinists are claiming regarding Arminian and Calvinist soteriologies respectively. The reader must examine for himself or herself the biblical teaching and the argumentation presented on both sides of the issue, but we must be clear on what the Calvinist argumentation claims to yield. To see this, several comments are in order:

1. Calvinists claim that the Arminian doctrine of prevenient grace is not rightly supported by biblical teaching.[12]

2. Calvinists also claim that the Arminian doctrine of corporate election is unfounded.[13]

3. It is clear that if this Calvinist critique succeeds, an Arminian soteriology collapses.

4. The case against Arminianism is strengthened when positive support is forthcoming for both Calvinist soteriological doctrines of unconditional election and the ECG doctrine. Elsewhere in this work and beyond, Calvinists have endeavored to explain and to commend the biblical support for the doctrine of unconditional election.[14] If God's unconditional election of some to be saved can be successfully defended biblically, this doctrine not only supports a Calvinist soteriology, but also refutes its Arminian counterpart, because the two competing doctrines are mutually exclusive. Either God chooses those whom he knows will freely choose him (in which case the logical priority is given to human choice, and divine choice echoes human determination), or God chooses apart from external considerations those whom he will save (in which case the logical priority is given to God's choice, and human choosing reflects precisely what God previously and unconditionally determined). It cannot be both ways; one position is correct, or neither is correct, but both cannot be correct. It is the Calvinist contention that the doctrine of unconditional election reflects clear biblical teaching. As such, it supports a Calvinist soteriology while at the same time rendering impossible an Arminian soteriology.

---

12. See chapter 16 by Thomas R. Schreiner.

13. See chapter 4 by Thomas R. Schreiner; and see also John Piper, *The Justification of God* (Grand Rapids: Baker, ²1993).

14. See chapters 2, 3, and 7 by Robert Yarbrough, Donald J. Westblade, and S. M. Baugh. See also Paul K. Jewett, *Election and Predestination* (Grand Rapids: Eerdmans, 1985); C. Samuel Storms, *Chosen for Life* (Grand Rapids: Baker, 1987); R. C. Sproul, *Chosen by God* (Wheaton: Tyndale, 1986); and Piper, *Pleasures of God*, 123–58.

5. Likewise, the ECG doctrine of Calvinism is at direct odds with the Arminian doctrine of prevenient grace. They are mutually exclusive doctrines. Calvinists claim not only that the argumentation for prevenient grace is unconvincing, but also that the ECG doctrine is demanded by a careful understanding of biblical teaching. If the Calvinist ECG doctrine can be successfully argued, it then simultaneously supports Calvinism while it refutes Arminianism.

This summary explains the contribution that the ECG doctrine makes within a Calvinist soteriology. As the necessary complement and entailment of the doctrine of unconditional election, the ECG doctrine must be shown to be biblically and rationally supported if Calvinism is to succeed. And when support is given to establish the ECG doctrine as biblically correct, not only is a Calvinist soteriology supported but also its Arminian rival is rendered impossible. This leads us to examine the case for the ECG doctrine. Can it be successfully defended as a biblically correct doctrine?

Support for the ECG Doctrine

Preliminary Definitions and Distinctions

The means by which God brings sinners to saving faith involves his effectual calling through the word of the gospel and the provision of irresistible grace. What is meant by the terms *effectual calling* and *irresistible grace* as understood in a Calvinist soteriology?

The doctrine of effectual calling does not propose that each and every calling, by God to sinners, is effectual. In fact, Calvinists are careful to distinguish the general call from the effectual call. They make this distinction because they believe biblical teaching supports both kinds of calls. The *general call* (sometimes referred to as the *vocatio externa*) refers to God's revelation made known to all people, calling them to recognize that revelation as truth and to respond accordingly. There are, then, two expressions of the general call. The *vocatio realis,* the call from things (i.e., nature), is extended to all people through general revelation (expressed in the natural world and conscience), calling them to acknowledge and honor God as their Creator (Ps. 19:1–4; Acts 17:27; Rom. 1:19–21; 2:14–15). The *vocatio verbalis,* the call from words (i.e., the word of the gospel), is also extended throughout the world, through the proclamation of the gospel, telling all sinners everywhere that through faith in Christ they may receive forgiveness of their sins and have eternal life (Matt. 28:18–20; Acts 1:6–8; 26:16–23; Rom. 10:8–15;

1 Cor. 15:1–8).[15] But, because this call goes out to all people, and because not all are saved, clearly the general call is not effectual. That is, people may and do resist this twofold general call to honor God and to turn to Christ to be saved.

The doctrine of the *effectual call* (or the *vocatio interna*)[16] refers more specifically to God's inward and ultimately persuasive summons to repent of sin and to turn to Christ for salvation. Because it is always effectual or ultimately persuasive, and because not all are saved, not all are given this call; it is extended only to the elect, those whom God has unconditionally chosen to save (Rom. 8:28–30; 1 Cor. 1:22–24).[17]

In like manner, the doctrine of *irresistible grace* does not propose that each and every gracious work or influence of the Holy Spirit is irresistible. Clearly, there is biblical warrant for affirming a doctrine of resistible grace, if by this one means that people may resist certain gracious influences of the Spirit. The grieving and quenching of the Spirit (Eph. 4:30 and 1 Thess. 5:19 respectively) are examples of such resistance, as is the explicit statement by Stephen that the Jewish leaders "always resist[ed] the Holy Spirit," just as their fathers did (Acts 7:51). And when believers are admonished to "live by the Spirit, and you will not gratify the desires of the sinful nature" (Gal. 5:16), clearly the implication is that they may choose not to live by the Spirit's power, thus resisting the gracious and transforming work he wishes to accomplish in their lives. Not all grace, then, is irresistible.

When Calvinists refer to irresistible grace, they mean to say that the Holy Spirit is able, when he so chooses, to overcome all human resistance and so cause his gracious work to be utterly effective and ultimately irresistible. In soteriology, the doctrine of irresistible grace refers to the Spirit's work to overcome all sin-induced resistance and rebellion, opening blind eyes and enlivening hardened hearts so that sinners understand and embrace the gospel of salvation through faith in Christ (Acts 16:14; 2 Cor. 4:4–6; 2 Tim. 2:24–25). Such is the grace by which we are saved. May all honor and glory be given to God alone for such a wondrous salvation!

Biblical Support for the ECG Doctrine

In this section, I will endeavor to demonstrate how each of three central passages teaches the ECG doctrine, and how they form a strong cumulative

---

15. For the distinction between the *vocatio realis* and the *vocatio verbalis*, see Louis Berkhof, *Systematic Theology* (London: Banner of Truth, 1939), 457–58.

16. For the distinction between the *vocatio externa* and the *vocatio interna*, see Heinrich Heppe, *Reformed Dogmatics*, trans. G. T. Thomson (reprint, Grand Rapids: Baker, 1978), 512–13.

17. Discussion of these supporting biblical texts will be given shortly.

case for this Calvinist doctrine. Although each of these texts is discussed elsewhere in this work, special note is made of the particular implications they have toward the ECG doctrine.

John 6:22–65. In this text, we find Jesus in the midst of a striking confrontation with the multitudes, among whom were many disbelieving Jews. The multitudes had requested a sign from Jesus in order to believe in him, just as God in the past had performed the miracle of giving to ancient Israel manna out of heaven (6:30–31).[18] Jesus' response is startling. He claims that the Father is the one who gave bread out of heaven in the past, and now, in their very presence, he is again providing bread that gives life to the world. And when they ask that he give them this bread (6:34), Jesus declares, "I am the bread of life. He who comes to me will never go hungry, and he who believes in me will never be thirsty. But as I told you, you have seen me and still you do not believe" (6:35–36). In other words, God has indeed performed the sign that the multitudes were seeking. Jesus, the bread out of heaven, is here in their midst! All that is required of them is that they believe in him, and yet they remain in their unbelief.

It is here in the narrative that one of the main issues of the following section arises (that runs throughout 6:35–65). How is it that some, having seen the sign or revelation given by God, choose to believe in Christ and so gain eternal life, while others, presented with the same sign, continue in their disbelief, challenging Christ's claims and resisting the truth made known to them? Notice that both believers and unbelievers are presented with the same revelation, so the difference between the two groups cannot be a matter of requisite knowledge; both have seen the sign of Christ. What, then, accounts for belief by some and disbelief by others?

One might think at first blush that the answer to this question is found by appeal to differences in the respective groupings of people themselves. Some believe because they choose to believe, while others disbelieve because they choose to disbelieve. Despite its tautological structure, one might attempt to argue for the acceptance of this conclusion because it may appear that the text encourages it. After all, it is Jesus who says, "He who comes to me will never go hungry, and he who believes in me will never be thirsty" (6:35); "whoever comes to me I will never drive away" (6:37); "everyone who looks to the Son and believes in him shall have eternal life" (6:40); "he who believes has everlasting life" (6:47); and "I am the living bread that came down from heaven. If

---

18. This request is particularly difficult to account for in light of the immediately preceding miracle whereby Jesus fed the five thousand (presumably those of the multitude who ask for the sign were among this group—see Jesus' discussion with them about this earlier feeding [John 6:22–29]) from five loaves and two fish. In all likelihood this reveals the hardness of the sinful heart, that even after such a display of miraculous power, this same multitude wants to see a sign in order to believe.

anyone eats of this bread, he will live forever" (6:51). Surely, so the argument goes, these statements must indicate that anyone and everyone can believe. For indeed, what sense does it make to say generally to the multitudes that everyone who does believe may have eternal life unless everyone first is able so to believe? The "ought" of believing in Christ to be saved implies the "can" of common human ability to believe. Therefore, the answer to why some believe and others disbelieve is that some choose to believe while others choose to disbelieve. We are left with our tautology, but we are content in this, because of our conviction that ought implies can.

Our text devastates the logic of this position. The notion that the ought of believing to be saved implies the can of common human ability to believe is nowhere to be found in this text. Having said this, we must be clear on what is being argued. It is undeniable that the ought of believing to be saved is throughout this text. That is, Jesus explains in no uncertain terms that he is the bread of life, and that only as people believe in him will they have eternal life. All must believe in Christ to be saved; the ought or the necessity of belief in Christ for salvation is undeniable.

What is deniable is that this ought of belief implies the can of common human ability to believe. Our text never explicitly makes this logical inference upon which so much of Arminian soteriology rests, nor is it implied by anything said by Jesus here. What our text does tell us precludes the possibility of this ought-implies-can view.

Notice the development from 6:35–36 to 6:37. In 6:35–36 Jesus tells the multitudes that he is the bread of life and that anyone who believes in him will be saved. But, they do not so believe, although they have seen him. In Jesus' following statement we hear something of startling significance. He continues, "All that the Father gives me will come to me, and whoever comes to me I will never drive away" (6:37).[19] Jesus' point to the disbelieving multitudes might be paraphrased as follows: "Though you have seen me, the Father's sign of life-giving bread sent from heaven, even so you have not believed. But how different it is with those whom the Father gives me to save! All the Father gives to me, these, without fail, come to me. And because the Father gives them to me that I may save them, and because they, therefore, come to me to be saved, I certainly will not fail in my purpose to save them. Because all the Father gives me come, and because of your refusal to come

19. It should be noted that in John 6:35–37 "coming" to Christ and "believing" in Christ are synonymous and interchangeable concepts. This understanding is made especially clear in 6:35, where Christ says that those who come to him shall not hunger and those who believe in him shall not thirst. Just as hungering and thirsting are parallel expressions of the destitute and desperate condition of those outside of Christ, so too, coming to Christ and believing in Christ are parallel expressions of what such destitute sinners must do to be saved.

even though you have been shown the sign, it is evident that you have not been given to me by the Father."[20]

Implicit is the idea that only those given by the Father can come (an idea made explicit by Jesus), while explicit is the idea that all those given by the Father do come. The multitudes' disbelief is evidence that they are not among those given to Christ by the Father. They do not believe because they are not given to the Son.[21] As such, Jesus' teaching in John 6:35–37 parallels exactly his words to disbelieving Jews on another occasion: "But you do not believe because you are not my sheep" (John 10:26; cf. 8:47).[22] The point is not that they are not his sheep because of their disbelief, but their disbelief is owing to the fact they are not his sheep. Coming to Christ is causally linked by Jesus to having been given by the Father; all those who come do so precisely because the Father has given them to the Son.

And the point continues in 6:38–39. After making clear that he has come to do only the will of the Father, Jesus says, "And this is the will of him who sent me, that I shall lose none of all that he has given me, but raise them up at the last day" (6:39).[23] As if to make his point unmistakably clear, Jesus essentially repeats what he had just told the unbelieving multitudes: that he surely will save (i.e., raise up) all the Father gives him to save. That is, none that the Father gives to the Son will fail to come (6:37), and none that the Father gives the Son will be lost (6:37, 39).

What is the message to the unbelieving multitudes? Their disbelief indicates not only their personal rejection of the revelatory sign given from the Father (6:36), but even more profoundly, that they have not been given to the Son by the Father, because all of those that the Father gives the Son do not fail to come to him (6:37a), and all those given the Son, who then come,

20. See also D. A. Carson, *The Gospel According to John* (Grand Rapids: Eerdmans, 1991), 290, where he writes regarding 6:37: "The flow of the verse is then as follows: All that (a singular neuter is used to refer to the elect collectively) the Father gives to Jesus, as his gift to the Son, will surely come to him; and whoever in fact comes (by virtue of being given by the Father to the Son), Jesus undertakes to keep in, to preserve."

21. See Leon Morris, *The Gospel According to John* (Grand Rapids: Eerdmans, 1971), 367: "Before men can come to Christ it is necessary that the Father give them to Him. This is the explanation of the disconcerting fact that those who followed Jesus to hear Him, and who at the beginning wanted to make Him a king, were nevertheless not His followers in the true sense. They did not belong to the people of God. They were not among those whom God gives Him."

22. It is evident that John Calvin (*Commentary on the Gospel According to John*, vol. 1 [Grand Rapids: Eerdmans, 1948]) likewise saw this parallel. Commenting on John 6:37, he writes (251): "That their unbelief may not detract anything from his doctrine, he says, that the cause of so great obstinacy is, that they are reprobate, and do not belong to the flock of God."

23. Jesus' statement in 6:39 might be restated as: all the Father gives are saved. This being the case, this statement is a conflation of Jesus' previous statements, showing it to be their logical complement. Consider this sequence:
1. All the Father gives come (6:37a)
2. All who come are saved (6:35, 37b)
3. Therefore, all the Father gives are saved (6:39)

are saved (6:37b, 39b). Their ongoing disbelief is clear indication, for Jesus, that the Father has not given them to the Son to save. This seems the most compelling understanding of the meaning of Jesus' statements in 6:37–39 in light of his observation in 6:36 that the multitudes remain in disbelief though they have been faced with the Father's saving revelation in Jesus himself.

Thus far, we have seen that all the Father gives to the Son believe in him and are saved. The multitudes' disbelief is evidence, therefore, that they have not been given to the Son. Implicit in Jesus' understanding of their disbelief is the notion that only those given by the Father can come. But is there evidence that this notion, implicit in Jesus' teaching in John 6:35–39, is also explicitly taught? Is it possible for someone to come to the Son to be saved if the Father has not given that one to the Son? That is, it is one thing to claim (as Jesus explicitly does) that all those given by the Father come to the Son to be saved. But it is another question whether any not given by the Father may nonetheless come. Is it necessary, then, that one be given by the Father to the Son in order for that person to come to Christ and so be saved? Jesus addresses this question in his ongoing discussion with the disbelieving Jews (John 6:41–45).

In response to the Jews who grumbled over Jesus' claim to be the bread that came from heaven, Jesus answers, "Stop grumbling among yourselves. No one can come to me unless the Father who sent me draws him, and I will raise him up at the last day" (6:43–44). Here is Jesus' answer to the question of whether it is necessary that the Father gives to the Son those who will believe and so be saved. It is also Jesus' answer to the question of why some believe and others disbelieve. According to Jesus, those who come to him (i.e., believe in him) do so because they have previously been drawn by the Father to him. In other words, although all ought to believe in Christ, only those drawn by the Father can believe and be saved.

Of course, the nature of the drawing of the Father becomes the central concern. Those who insist on the ought-implies-can logic, and who accept the classic Reformation notion of total depravity affirmed also by Arminius, would be quick to assert that no people, in their deadened sinful state, are able on their own to believe in Christ. Anyone who comes must be drawn previously by the Father. All who come must have God's grace administered to their hearts, giving them the ability they otherwise would have lacked of believing in Christ. But, whether they believe or not is their doing, not God's. God must draw, to be sure; his drawing, however, only makes possible but not actual (or effectual) a believing response. This is the essence of the Arminian doctrine of prevenient grace. It affirms without question what the Pelagians and semi-Pelagians denied, namely, that as Christ himself says, "no one can come to me unless the Father who sent me draws him" (6:44a).

But, is the drawing of the Father (John 6:44) the type of drawing affirmed by Arminians? Is it an expression of prevenient grace, commonly distributed to all people, overcoming the effects of sin such that people can (but not must) believe in Christ? It will become clear that this cannot be the case, and that instead this text teaches that the drawing of the Father is both effectual (i.e., people not only are made able to believe, but also are drawn unfailingly and irresistibly to such belief) and selective (i.e., he draws those whom he chooses to give to the Son).[24] Notice the following points concerning John 6:44.

1. The drawing of the Father precedes the coming to Christ. When Christ says that no one can come (*dunatai elthein*) unless the Father draws him, it is clear that anyone's coming to Christ is preceded by being drawn by the Father. There is, then, a gracious and necessary drawing work of the Father without which no one is able to come to Christ.

2. The drawing of the Father results in the full and final salvation of those drawn. That is, the drawing of the Father does not result in the mere possibility of being saved, which possibility becomes an actuality only when the one drawn chooses to assent to that drawing; rather, it results in the actual salvation of all those drawn. This point is easily missed if 6:44a is permitted to stand without the remainder of Jesus' statement in 6:44b. Jesus' claim, "No one can come to me unless the Father who sent me draws him" (6:44a), is directly followed by, "and I will raise him up at the last day" (6:44b). It is clear that the one drawn is raised up on the last day; that is, the one drawn is saved.

3. Still, the question may arise whether being saved (or being raised up) is the result of the Father's drawing or of coming to Christ. That is, is Jesus saying that he will raise up all who come to him? Or is it that he will raise up all whom the Father draws? The answer is that both are true. As we observed, Jesus makes several references to the fact that everyone who comes to him or believes in him will be saved (see 6:35, 40, 47, 51). There is no doubt concerning this. But the question is, how do they come? Or, why do they believe?

Consider again the point of these statements: "All that the Father gives me will come to me, and whoever comes to me I will never drive away" (6:37); "And this is the will of him who sent me, that I shall lose none of all that he has given me, but raise them up at the last day" (6:39); and "Everyone who listens to the Father and learns from him comes to me" (6:45). As we saw, sinners come to be saved because they have been given to Christ by the Father. They believe because they are drawn, and all who are drawn, so believe.

---

24. Regarding John 6:44, Grant R. Osborne ("Soteriology in the Gospel of John," in Pinnock, *The Grace of God, the Will of Man*, 248–49) argues against the irresistibility of the drawing unto sure and certain salvation for all those drawn. He suggests that if the drawing here is irresistible, this leads to universalism, because in John 12:32 Jesus says he will draw all men to himself. It is not at all certain that the drawing of John 12:32 is universal. The context indicates it rather to be a drawing without distinction, not a drawing without exception (see Carson, *Gospel According to John*, 293, 444; and in this work, Schreiner, "Prevenient Grace," 377–78). Surely the individual contexts of the two passages must regulate the sort of drawing that is meant in each case. Putting John 12:32 aside, the issue we here are addressing is what is meant by the drawing of the Father in John 6:44 in light of its own context.

Therefore, it appears that it is true both that everyone who comes to Christ is saved and that all whom the Father draws are saved. In John 6:44, when Jesus says, "and I will raise him up at the last day," he has in mind the future salvation of all of those drawn to Christ by the Father, without which none would ever come.

The drawing of the Father has two results. First, it enables sinners to come to Christ (6:44a). Second, because of Christ's commitment to raise up those drawn (see 6:39 with 6:44), it ensures the final salvation of all those whom the Father has so drawn (6:44b).

4. Since the Father's drawing precedes belief in Christ, and since that drawing results in the salvation of those drawn, it follows that this drawing is effectual.[25] That this cannot be a general drawing merely making possible belief in Christ is evident in that the drawing produces both belief and actual salvation.

5. Because the drawing of the Father is effectual, it is clear that it cannot be a universal or commonly bestowed drawing to Christ, exerted on all people, but rather a selective drawing of those whom the Father chose to give to the Son.[26] Jesus spoke earlier in John's Gospel of the ultimate destinies of two peoples. For example, in John 5:27–29, Jesus referred to the day when the Son of man will exert his authority over all people, resulting in a resurrection of life for those who do good and a resurrection of judgment for those who do evil. Because it is clear that Jesus affirms the reality of heaven and hell and so denies the ultimate salvation of all people, the effectual drawing the Father performs must be selective. But of course, this is no surprise since Jesus has made clear throughout his discussion with the Jews in John 6 that all that the Father gives to him, he will not lose but will surely raise up at the last day (see 6:37, 39, 44–45, 65).

Jesus' statement in 6:45 ("Everyone who listens to the Father and learns from him comes to me") only reinforces his point in 6:44 by stating again its complementary truth. As 6:44 had stressed that no one can come apart from the drawing of the Father, 6:45 reaffirms the truth Jesus already presented in 6:37, namely, that all those given by the Father do come. As Augustine puts it:

> What is the meaning of "Every man who has heard and learned from the Father comes unto me" [John 6:45] except that there is none who hears from the Father,

---

25. Calvin, *John*, 257: "it follows that all are not drawn, but that God bestows this grace on those whom he has elected."

26. Carson, *Gospel According John*, 293, comments: "The thought of v[erse] 44 is the negative counterpart to v[erse] 37a. The latter tells us that all that the Father gives to the Son will come to him; here we are told that no-one can come to him unless the Father draws him. . . . The combination of v[erse] 37a and v[erse] 44 prove that this 'drawing' activity of the Father cannot be reduced to what theologians sometimes call 'prevenient grace' dispensed to every individual, for this 'drawing' is selective, or else the negative note in v[erse] 44 is meaningless."

and learns, who comes not to me? For if everyone who has heard from the Father, and has learned, comes, certainly everyone who does not come has not heard from the Father or learned; for if he had heard and learned, he would come. . . . [27]

These two truths (i.e., only those drawn can come, and all those drawn do come) serve together to require the ECG doctrine of Calvinism. Jesus' repeated affirmations of both truths, along with his rejection of universalism, make this doctrine undeniable.

Finally, Jesus' continued confrontation with these unbelievers comes to a climax in 6:60–65. Jesus acknowledges publicly the fact that some among his listeners do not believe, despite seeing and hearing all that has been presented to them (6:61–64). And then, as if to summarize again the reason why persistent disbelief continues on the part of these who have been with him, Jesus repeats and reinforces his earlier claim, saying, "This is why I told you that no one can come to me unless the Father has enabled him" (6:65). At this, we are told, many of those listening departed from Jesus and quit following him.

The substance of Jesus' response in the presence of persistent unbelief is significant.[28] He did not encourage these unbelievers to overcome the internal obstacles to belief in their own hearts as if it were up to them whether they would believe or not. Rather, Jesus' point here, just as it was in 6:44, is that the Father's enablement, the Father's drawing, is necessary for them to believe.

But what of the Arminian proposal that this drawing of the Father, although necessary, is in fact resistible? Could this be a reference to the common drawing that the Father exerts on all people, enabling but not rendering certain a response of saving faith? To the great detriment of an Arminian soteriology, this cannot be. If this enablement or drawing is distributed commonly to all, as Arminians hold, enabling any and all to believe, then Jesus' response makes no sense. In the Arminian view, what separates belief and unbelief is not the drawing of the Father; the Father draws all. Belief and unbelief, rather, is owing to what particular individuals (all of whom are drawn by the Father and so enabled to believe) freely choose to do. They may come, or they may refuse to come. God has drawn all, so it is up to them.

Jesus' analysis is quite different. When faced with persistent disbelief, Jesus affirms again unequivocally that only those drawn by the Father can come (6:65). But if all are drawn, what is the significance of this point to those re-

---

27. Augustine *On the Predestination of the Saints* 7.13, as quoted by Calvin, *Institutes*, 2.965 (3.24.1).

28. See also C. K. Barrett, *The Gospel According to St John* (London: SPCK, 1955), 252: "Because of the emergence of unbelief Jesus had explained the divine initiative which underlies faith. . . . There is no difference in meaning between the two clauses [v. 44 and v. 65] and they illuminate each other. Faith in Christ is not merely difficult; apart from God it is impossible (cf. Mark 10:27). Coming to Jesus is not a matter of free human decision."

maining in their disbelief? Clearly there would be no point to it, and it certainly would not prompt those listening to Jesus to depart permanently from him.

The Arminian view, that Jesus speaks in 6:65 (as he does also in 6:44) of God's prevenient grace, given to all, which is necessary for everyone to come but not rendering certain that any in fact comes, is akin to the following situation. Suppose a medical doctor diagnosed each of the members of a group of people as having the same disease. He prescribed two medications (call them RXA and RXB), both of which must be taken by each person in the group in order for each to get well. Some weeks later he meets with the group of patients and discovers that some remain sick while others are noticeably better. After inquiring further, he also discovers that all of the patients in the group have taken RXA but only those now doing better have taken, in addition, RXB. In response to this situation, the doctor declares to those still sick, "No one can get well without taking *RXA!*" While it is true that RXA is necessary to bring about these patients' healing (so the doctor is not technically incorrect in what he says), the doctor's response misses the point. Since all have been taking RXA, the necessity of their taking RXA is irrelevant. The doctor's statement, although it is true, does nothing to explain why some remain sick while others are now well.

The only point that Jesus can sensibly be making by his statement in 6:65 is that those resistant to him do not believe because they are not so drawn by the Father. He surely is not saying to people who are drawn by the Father that only those drawn by the Father can come. This would do nothing to explain what the context of this passage demands: why his opponents remain in their unbelief.[29] Rather, Jesus' point is this: no one can come who is not drawn by the Father (6:44, 65); all of those drawn by the Father do come (6:37, 45); those speaking with Jesus remain in their unbelief (6:36, 64); and therefore, the logical conclusion must be that their continued unbelief indicates that they are not drawn by the Father. That is, they do not believe because they are not drawn. The drawing of the Father, then, is both necessary and effectual.[30]

Let me bring the discussion on John 6 to a close by summarizing the main

---

29. Calvin, *John*, 276: "If this grace were bestowed on all without exception, it would have been unseasonable and inappropriate to have mentioned it in this passage; for we must understand that it was Christ's design to show that not many believe the Gospel, because faith proceeds only from the secret revelation of the Spirit."

30. The case for Arminianism is not made any easier by appealing to the fact that Jesus knew from the beginning who would believe and who would not (6:64), as if this is about the Arminian conception of foreknowledge, which somehow explains why some come and others do not. The point of 6:64 with 6:65 rather is this: because Jesus knew who would not believe, therefore this is why he had said to these unbelievers that no one can come unless the Father grants it. Jesus' knowledge of those who would not believe explains not why they remain unbelieving; rather, it explains why Jesus tells them (i.e., these particular disbelieving opponents) what he does: that only those whom the Father grants may in fact come. Because Jesus knew who the unbelievers were, he explains to them the reason for their continued disbelief despite the signs and revelation that has been presented to them.

ideas as they relate to our discussion.[31] In his dialogue with those persistent in their unbelief, Jesus makes two main points. Together, these points establish what the ECG doctrine affirms, namely, that God calls effectually and irresistibly his elect to saving faith in Christ.

First, all of those drawn to Christ by the Father do in fact come and are in fact saved (6:37, 39, 45). Second, only those drawn to Christ by the Father can in fact come (6:44, 65). Both of these points are derived directly from Jesus' own teaching within the context of continued unbelief (6:36, 64). Now, if all of those drawn do come (first point), the drawing that causes them to come must be effectual. If it were not effectual, Jesus could not rightly and explicitly say, as he does say, that all those drawn (i.e., given to the Son) come and that all those drawn will be raised up. Furthermore, if only those drawn can come (second point), then surely the drawing of God is selective. There is no point in telling disbelieving people who supposedly already are drawn by the Father that they must be drawn in order to come. Rather, to make sense of Jesus' analysis of the persistent disbelief surrounding him, his affirmations that only those drawn by the Father can come (6:44, 65) must signify the selective nature of the Father's drawing. Apart from this selective drawing, belief is impossible and the continued unbelief faced by Jesus is thereby explained. The calling of God on individuals' lives to salvation is effectual, thwarting all unbelieving resistance and drawing them irresistibly to belief in the Christ who will not fail to save them utterly.

1 Corinthians 1:18–31. First Corinthians 1:24 presents to us a powerful and God-honoring instance of God's calling that is at once effectual, irresistible, and selective. It reads: "but to those whom God has called, both Jews and Greeks, Christ the power of God and the wisdom of God." How does this text support the ECG doctrine?

Beginning in 1:17, Paul makes a temporary transition from discussing his own preaching of the gospel and baptism of others to centering on the nature of the gospel itself. That gospel or "message of the cross" (1:18), which he purposely refused to preach in clever, human wisdom (1:17), is, at one and the same time, God's power and wisdom for those being saved (1:18, 21, 24; cf. Rom. 1:16), while it is weakness and foolishness to those perishing (1:18, 23, 25). It is the same gospel in both cases, but some regard it as wise, powerful, and life-giving while others see it as mere folly.[32]

---

31. The theme of God's choosing and effectual drawing to saving belief continues through the rest of chapter 6, focusing now on the disciples themselves. In other words, Jesus' teachings more generally (6:22–65) are applied specifically with his own. See Carson, *Gospel According to John,* 303–4.

32. Notice the parallel thought in 2 Corinthians 2:15–16, where Paul likens the gospel to a fragrance or an aroma of Christ. To those being saved (2:15) it is an aroma of life (2:16); to those perishing (2:15), an aroma of death (2:16). The gospel, or aroma, is the same! The difference is in those smelling the fragrance and not in the fragrance itself.

The burning question, for our purposes, is why some consider it God's power and wisdom while others reject it as weakness and foolishness. That both responses to the same gospel occur is not disputed. What we must see is whether Paul gives any indication as to why such contrary responses occur.

Paul gives two answers to this question. First, he says that although the world in its wisdom did not come to know God, God was pleased to use the gospel to "save those who believe" (1:21). So what accounts for these two conflicting responses to the gospel? Answer: Some resist the message and some believe it. Paul affirms what Jesus had likewise taught in John 6 (see 6:35, 40, 47), namely, that all who believe the gospel of the Christ will be saved.

What must one believe to be saved? According to Paul, the object of a true and saving belief does not reside in a show of miraculous signs (1:22a; and note the parallel to Jesus' discussion with the disbelieving Jews in John 6:30–36), or in rhetorically wise human knowledge (1:22b), but is centered on the gospel affirmation of Christ crucified (1:23a). This is precisely why the gospel is for Jews a stumbling block and for Gentiles foolishness (1:23b). There is in the cross no outward display of the divinely spectacular or the humanly sagacious. And as such, there is no basis for human boasting when one's dependence is on the cross (see 1:29). The cross calls Jews and Greeks alike to humble acceptance of their own weakness and folly and of Christ crucified as the only true expression of real (i.e., God's!) power and wisdom (1:24) and hence as the only basis of their salvation.[33]

Still, the question lingers. When asked why the same gospel elicits two opposite responses, Paul says that the message preached saves those who believe. But, we wonder, is there any accounting for why some believe and others do not? By asking this question I am not suggesting that anything thus far presented by the apostle is wrong or misplaced. He is right to make clear that salvation comes to those who believe. So my question inquires whether he might be saying more than this, not something that would be corrective or contrary. And indeed, a close look at our text indicates that he offers another reason why some consider the message of the cross God's power and wisdom, while others reject it as weakness and foolishness.

Second, then, the gospel elicits conflicting responses because God calls some from among Jews and Gentiles who, as a group, reject the gospel, so that these (i.e., the called) accept the cross as God's power and wisdom while others (i.e., Jews and Gentiles generally, who are not called) remain in their prideful un-

---

33. See Gordon D. Fee, *The First Epistle to the Corinthians* (Grand Rapids: Eerdmans, 1987), 67, for a superb summary statement of 1:18–2:5: "[Paul] says in effect, 'So you think the gospel is a form of *sophia*? How foolish can you get? Look at its *message*: it is based on the story of a crucified Messiah. Who in the name of wisdom would have dreamed that up? Only God is so wise as to be so foolish' (1:18–25); 'Furthermore, look at its *recipients*. Yourselves! Who in the name of wisdom would have chosen you to be the new people of God?' (1:26–31); 'Finally, remember my *preaching*. Who in the name of wisdom would have come in such weakness? Yet look at its results' (2:1–5)."

belief and resistance. Look again for the development of thought in 1 Corinthians 1:23–24: "But we preach Christ crucified: a stumbling block to Jews and foolishness to Gentiles, but to those whom God has called, both Jews and Greeks, Christ the power of God and the wisdom of God." Consider the following paraphrase of these verses: "When Christ crucified is preached among Jews and Greeks generally, Jews stumble over it for its apparent weakness and ignobility while Gentiles ridicule it as the height of human folly. But amazingly, some among these very same Jews and Greeks, who otherwise flatly reject the gospel, are savingly called by God out of their resistant frame of mind regarding the gospel, to understand and embrace it now as God's marvelous good news! Here, they now see, in the cross, is found real power and wisdom. In Christ and Christ alone, they now understand, there resides the power of God and the wisdom of God that leads to salvation."

Why is it that the calling of 1 Corinthians 1:24 must be viewed as effectual (or, as stated in the preceding paraphrase, a "saving" call)? Or negatively, why cannot the call here be a call to all urging them to believe and so be saved? Consider the following two points:

1. The wording of 1:24 does not permit the notion of a general call given to all unbelieving Jews and Greeks, calling all to believe in Christ. Very specifically, Paul says, *autois de tois kletois, Ioudaiois te kai Hellesin*, literally, "but to those ones, to the called ones, both Jews and Greeks," or more naturally, "but to those who are the called, both Jews and Greeks" (NASB). The call is issued to a specific group, referred to here as *tois kletois*, the called ones, and it is clear that this group of the called ones comes out of the broader, general group of all the Jews and Gentiles. Therefore, the wording of the text precludes the notion that this is a call to all; it is a call to some from among all the Jews and Gentiles, to "the called."

2. It makes no sense to contrast Jews and Greeks generally with those Jews and Greeks who are called (as 1:23–24 does) if the difference between believing Jews and Greeks and disbelieving Jews and Greeks is in their respective choices only. In such a case, all are called, and some choose to believe while some disbelieve. It is true that other texts speak clearly of the gospel going to all so that whoever believes may come and be saved (e.g., Rom. 10:12–13), but this clearly cannot be what our present text is about.

The contrast is made between those called from disbelieving Jews and Greeks and, by implication, those not called, making up the general class of Jews and Greeks who regard the gospel as weakness and folly. The point is that Jews and Greeks generally reject the gospel. But God intervenes, and toward some of these otherwise disbelieving Jews and Gentiles, he extends his saving call. This cannot be a call to all; it must be a call to some.

The Arminian view of the general call extended with prevenient grace will not work here. Again, similarly to John 6:65, it makes no sense to say regarding Jews and Greeks, if all are called (as Arminians claim), that God called from Jews and

Greeks those who were then saved. A calling in such a case does not explain the contrary responses to the gospel. Consider again the illustration of the two medications. To explain why some are still sick and others well, it will not do to appeal to the medication they take in common. So, if 1:24 refers to the general call, it is then irrelevant to why some believe and others reject the gospel, since by definition both groups received in common the benefit of the call.

Furthermore, this cannot be a resistible call, making merely possible but not certain a saving response. Why must the call here be seen as irresistible? Because the called are not described as those who hear and may (or may not) believe, but as those who hear and do believe. That is, the called actually see and believe in Christ as God's power and wisdom. It results in their actual salvation.[34] In short, then, the call of 1 Corinthians 1:24 is, of necessity, selective, effectual, and ultimately irresistible against all previous rejection and disbelief.

The remaining verses (1:26–31) only serve to strengthen the conclusion just arrived at by providing for us the reason God's call to salvation must be seen as his work of effectually bringing sinners to salvation. Paul states two reasons in the following verses, which actually merge into one comprehensive and glorious divine purpose for our salvation. First, since any and all are saved, not because of their wisdom or power but because God has chosen them (note: this is stated three times in 1:27–28) out of their weakness, impotence, and baseness (1:26–28), it follows that "no one may boast before him" (1:29). And second, because those who are saved are in Christ "because of him" (1:30), it follows that any who boast must boast solely "in the Lord" (1:31). That God has so called us to see Christ as his wisdom and power that leads to salvation means, then, that all human boasting is deemed utterly unfounded and that rightful boasting belongs only in the Lord. To God alone belongs all honor and glory![35]

---

34. Fee, *First Epistle to the Corinthians*, 76–77: "Those who are 'being saved' (v. 18), the 'believing ones' (v. 21), are so because of God's prior action; they are 'those whom God has called' (see 1:1–2, 9). For them the preaching of 'Christ crucified' is effectual. . . . Paul's concern here is not so much on their being able to *perceive* the cross as wisdom . . . , but on the actual *effective work* of the cross in the world."

35. This insistence, that all glory be given to God alone for our salvation, leads many Calvinists to demean and reject the Arminian notion that, ultimately, we are responsible for whether we are saved or not. Yes, for the Arminian, God provides in Christ a substitute sacrifice for our sins, and yes, he gives prevenient grace enabling belief; but ultimately it is up to us whether to believe or not. That is, God does all he can do, commonly and universally, so the difference between those who believe and those who do not rests in what we humans do, not in what God does. How, then, can the Arminian contend all the credit for our salvation is owing to God alone? Consider these words from Loraine Boettner, *The Reformed Doctrine of Predestination* (Grand Rapids: Eerdmans, [7]1951), 170: "[Arminianism] has insisted upon 'free will,' 'the power of contrary choice,' etc., and has taught that ultimately the sinner determines his own destiny. In its more consistent forms it makes man a co-savior with Christ, as if the glory in redemption was to be divided between the grace of Christ and the will of man, the latter dividing the spoils with the former."

Notice that the point is not that God deserves such honor because he provided Christ as the way of salvation, or because he commissioned the proclamation of the gospel to all the world, or because he extends the offer of salvation generally to any who will believe. These are all good and right bases for giving honor to God, but they are not, either individually or collectively, the basis for honoring God stated in our text. Rather, God alone is to be honored because he chose the foolish, the weak, and the lowly (1:26–28), and it is because of him that we are in Christ (1:30). In other words, the basis for boasting in the Lord is not that he made our salvation possible but that he saved us by his calling (1:24, 26) and his choosing (1:27–28, 30). Therefore any and all human basis for boasting is eliminated (1:29), and all honor and glory is owing solely to him (1:31)!

One final point. Notice Paul's use of "calling" to link his more general discussion of God's salvation of unnamed Jews and Greeks (1:18–25) with his very personal references to God's salvation of these particular Corinthian Christians (1:26–31). Verse 26 provides the link when it says, "Brothers, think of what you were when you were called" (lit., "consider your calling"). The point is this: what Paul taught generally in 1:24 about God's calling of otherwise disbelieving Jews and Greeks to see in Christ God's wisdom and power, he now, in 1:26, applies to the Corinthians themselves.[36] Just as Jews and Greeks as a general class reject the gospel, so that God must call some out of their hardness and resistance to see and to embrace the glory of the cross of Christ, in like manner he has called you! The calling of 1:24, which we argued can only rightly be seen as effectual, must likewise, in 1:26, refer to the effectual calling to salvation of these weak and lowly Corinthians. Only then is the usage of "calling" in 1:24 and 1:26 parallel, as it surely must be, and only then does the emphasis in the following verses (1:27–31) on God's glory owing to his choosing and saving make good sense and rightly follow.

The word of the cross is repulsive to sinners. It rebukes our humanly crafted idols of wisdom and power, and it calls us to bow humbly and destitute before a cross on which hangs one who is himself destitute, beaten, bleeding, and dying. But why do this? Why exchange the pinnacles of human glory for this cross, this symbol of sheer impotence and utter folly? Indeed, it makes no sense, until—until, that is, God opens eyes blinded to the beauty and glory of the truth and softens hearts hardened with prideful and sinful resistance. Among the hosts of these blind and resistant, God calls! And when that call is extended, a transformation occurs (not that it may occur, but it does occur). That ignoble cross now is seen as the most magnificent

---

36. For the relation of "call" in 1:24 and 1:26, see Fee, *First Epistle to the Corinthians*, 79; and John Calvin, *Commentary on the Epistles of Paul the Apostle to the Corinthians*, vol. 1 (Grand Rapids: Eerdmans, 1948), 90.

symbol of glory! Here, and here alone, is the epitome of true power and wisdom! Here, and here alone, is God's saving grace manifest. May praise, therefore, be given to God *alone*, not only for the provision of Christ, and not only for the proclamation of the gospel, but also for his saving and effectual calling by which we now see Christ for who he is, nothing less than the power of God and the wisdom of God. To offer such humble and solitary praise to God is to give living expression to the command of 1 Corinthians 1:31: "Let him who boasts boast in the Lord"!

Romans 8:28–30. We come now to the last, and perhaps the most straightforward, expression of God's effectual call we will examine in this chapter. The statement of greatest importance for our present concerns is found in 8:30: "those he predestined, he also called; those he called, he also justified; those he justified, he also glorified." We might paraphrase it in this way: "All[37] of those whom God has predestined to become conformed to the likeness of Christ (from 8:29), to all of these so predestined, he extends his call. And just as all the predestined are also called, so too all those whom he calls heed the call to believe and so are justified. And just as all the predestined are called and all the called are justified, so too all those justified are also glorified."

The calling spoken of here cannot be the general gospel call to repent and believe in Christ to be saved.[38] Rather, the calling of 8:30 must refer to God's effectual call, that is, a call that cannot fail to lead people to exercise saving faith and so be justified. Why is this? The general call is extended to everyone indiscriminately, some of whom believe and others of whom disbelieve. There are two categories of people who receive the general call: those who hear and accept the gospel and those who hear and reject it. But such is not the case with those spoken of as "called" in 8:30.

One category of people is described in 8:29–30. Those foreknown[39] are the same individuals as those predestined, those predestined are the same as those called, those called the same as those justified, and those justified the same as those glorified. That is, all the individuals spoken of in 8:29–30 are foreknown,

---

37. That it is precisely the same people who are predestined as are called, justified, and glorified, see Douglas J. Moo, *Romans 1–8*, WEC (Chicago: Moody, 1991), 572: "The exact correspondence between those who are the objects of predestining and those who experience this calling is emphasized by the demonstrative pronoun (*toutous*, "these"): 'it was precisely those who were predestined who also (*kai*) were called.'"

38. Regarding *ekalesen* of 8:30, see James D. G. Dunn, *Romans 1–8* (Dallas: Word, 1988), 485: "The thought is not of an invitation which might be rejected; God does not leave his purpose to chance but puts it into effect himself. Paul looks at the whole process from the perspective of its successful outcome, where the redeemed gladly affirm that their coming to faith was wholly God's doing."

39. On "foreknowledge" here as expressive of God's prior loving and elective purposes, see chapters 7, 13, and 21 by S. M. Baugh, Thomas J. Nettles, and Paul Helm. And for a careful and thorough discussion of "foreknowledge" in Romans 8:29, see Moo, *Romans 1–8*, 568–71.

predestined, called, justified, and glorified. None is foreknown that is not predestined. None is predestined that is not called. And none is called that is not both justified and glorified. So then, if in Romans 8:30 all those called are justified and glorified, but if many who hear God's general gospel call to believe instead resist and so are neither justified nor glorified, then it follows that the "call" of 8:30 is the effectual call (which effects the justification of all those so called) and not the general call (which does not effect the justification of all those so called because it can be—and is—resisted).

Of what benefit is this teaching to those who are the called of God? In the flow of thought of Romans 8, verses 29–30 are meant to provide the theological basis or undergirding for the promise articulated in verse 28. God works in all things for the good of those who love him, those who are called according to his purpose. What relation does being called by God have to this stated assurance of God working good? Simply this: since all whom God calls he also justifies and glorifies, it is clear that God will permit nothing to hinder his ultimate and good purposes for his called ones from coming to fruition. It is a sovereign God who saves sinners, and the same sovereign God works all things for the good of his own—those whom he has called and who, then, love him—guaranteeing their salvation now as well as their future glory and joy! Because God calls to salvation, and because God's calling is effectual to save both now and forever, we can be confident that nothing can hinder God's good purposes. He will fulfill them, for his own, to the end.

Conclusion

If a Calvinist soteriology is to commend itself as coherent, viable, and sound, establishing the ECG doctrine is essential. As the necessary complement and entailment of the doctrine of unconditional election, the case for the ECG doctrine must succeed. Furthermore, if a Calvinist soteriology is to commend itself to those committed fully and unreservedly to biblical authority, the ECG doctrine must be shown to be expressive of clear biblical teaching. For the purposes of this study, it is hoped that sufficient biblical warrant has been offered for concluding that the ECG doctrine of Calvinism is scripturally justified and that, therefore, the case for the ECG doctrine succeeds.

In addition, to the extent that the case for the ECG doctrine of Calvinism succeeds, its Arminian rival doctrine of prevenient grace falters. Since evidence for the ECG doctrine is evidence against the doctrine of prevenient grace, we conclude as well that an Arminian soteriology is correspondingly harmed.

The focus of this chapter has been, of necessity, on one significant aspect of a Calvinist soteriology. Not everything for Calvinism or against Arminianism can here be shown. But when the case for the ECG doctrine is put alongside the case against the doctrine of prevenient grace (as demonstrated elsewhere in this work), one gains a fuller picture of the relative strengths and weaknesses of the two rival soteriologies. Furthermore, one's ability in such an evaluation is again enlarged when the case for unconditional election is set alongside the case against conditional (or corporate) election (which are also dealt with in this work). The result of this cumulative case must be judged by each thoughtful Christian. The judgment of this writer is that, when all is considered, the evidence overwhelmingly supports a Calvinist soteriology while rendering its Arminian counterpart untenable.

Although the case made here for the ECG doctrine is only part of a much bigger picture, the result has been to show the place effectual calling and irresistible grace have in a broader Calvinist soteriology. Everything about this doctrine elicits our humble amazement at a gracious God who would call undeserving and blind sinners out of darkness into his marvelous light. To God alone belongs all glory and honor! Praise be to his great and gracious name!

16

Does Scripture Teach Prevenient Grace in the Wesleyan Sense?

Thomas R. Schreiner

The Nature of Fallen Humanity

This chapter explores whether the Wesleyan concept of prevenient grace can be supported from the Scriptures. Before examining this question, I want to emphasize that there is a significant area of common ground between Wesleyans and Calvinists. The disagreements that we have in some areas can cause us to overlook the extent to which we agree on major doctrines. In one arena of theology, namely, anthropology, the harmony between Wesleyans and Calvinists is of the utmost importance and our harmony in this area should be celebrated. Both camps acknowledge that fallen human beings are born with a corrupt nature that is in bondage to sin, and that human beings can do no good apart from the grace of God.

To sketch in the biblical data on the human condition since the fall is helpful. Thereby we will see the extent to which Wesleyans and Calvinists agree, and the gulf that the Wesleyan understanding of prevenient grace creates between Arminians and Calvinists will also be illuminated. Paul teaches that all human beings are born with a corrupt nature inherited from Adam (Rom. 5:12–19). Without specifying the precise connection between Adam's sin and our condemnation—which is itself the subject of a long theological controversy—it is clear from the text that we are sinners because of Adam's sin.[1] Through Adam's sin we died (Rom. 5:15, 17), are condemned (Rom. 5:16, 18), and are constituted as sinners (Rom. 5:19).[2]

Harmonizing with this portrait of humanity in Romans 5 is Ephesians 2:3, which says we are by nature "objects of wrath." Human beings by nature (*physei*) are deserving of wrath, indicating that they are all born with a nature that is sinful. The near context in Ephesians 2 confirms the depth of human depravity. Human beings are "dead in transgressions and sins" (Eph. 2:1; cf. 2:5 and Col. 2:13). The deadness of fallen humanity indicates that we are devoid of life upon our entrance into the world. We have no inclination toward genuine righteousness or goodness. Paul proceeds to say in Ephesians 2:2–3 that we lived under the sway of the world, the devil, and the flesh before conversion.

What is in the consciousness of those who are under the control of the "flesh"? There is not necessarily a conscious awareness of rebellion against God. Life in the flesh consists in "gratifying the cravings of our sinful nature and following its desires and thoughts" (Eph. 2:3). The desires of people who are "by nature objects of wrath" are naturally and instinctively sinful desires. In other words, unregenerate people sin by merely doing what they wish to do, by carrying out the motivations that are in their hearts. Sinful desires dominate those who are in the flesh.

Is there biblical warrant for saying that the desires of the unregenerate are dominated by sin? Ephesians 2:3 suggests such a conclusion in saying that people are dead in trespasses and sins and that they are "by nature objects of wrath." The trespasses and sins flow from a nature that is sinful and warrants God's wrath. Titus 3:3 confirms such a conclusion. "At one time we too were foolish, disobedient, deceived and enslaved by all kinds of passions and pleasures. We lived in malice and envy, being hated and hating one another." Note here that Paul says that we were "*enslaved* by all kinds of passions and pleasures" (italics added). It is fair to conclude that people who are enslaved by their own desires are under the domination and tyranny of sin. This kind of tyranny is not externally coerced. People do what they want to do, in that they pursue their own pleasures and desires. Nonetheless, to describe this pursuit of their own desires as slavery because they have no desire, inclination, or aspiration to do good is appropriate.

The bondage of the will, then, is a slavery to our own desires. Unregenerate human beings are captivated by what they want to do! Jesus himself diagnosed sinning as an indication of slavery. "Everyone who sins is a slave to sin" (John

---

1. For two insightful treatments of this text see Douglas J. Moo, *Romans 1–8,* WEC (Chicago: Moody, 1991), 325–59; C. E. B. Cranfield, *A Critical and Exegetical Commentary on the Epistle to the Romans,* 2 vols., ICC (Edinburgh: T. and T. Clark, 1975, 1979), 269–91.

2. Arthur Skevington Wood ("The Contribution of John Wesley to the Theology of Grace," in *Grace Unlimited,* ed. Clark H. Pinnock [Minneapolis: Bethany Fellowship, 1975], 212) demonstrates that Wesley interpreted our participation in Adam's sin similarly.

8:34; cf. 2 Pet. 2:19). Paul confirms that unregenerate people are slaves of sin. He reminds the Romans that "you are slaves to sin" (Rom. 6:17) and speaks of the time "when you were slaves to sin" (Rom. 6:20). They had presented "the parts of [their] bod[ies] in slavery to impurity and ever-increasing wickedness" (Rom. 6:19). Believers have been crucified with Christ "so that the body of sin might be done away with, that we should no longer be slaves to sin" (Rom. 6:6). If Christ died so that we should no longer be slaves to sin, the clear implication is that we were formerly slaves to sin. Sin is described in Romans 6 as a power that holds its captives in thralldom. Unbelievers are enslaved to sin in the sense that all they want to do is sin. They are free to do what is good in the sense that they have opportunities to do so. They fail to avail themselves of these opportunities, however, because they do not desire to do what is good. The captivity of sin is so powerful that they always desire to sin.

Do unregenerate human beings always sin? Is there not some good in their lives? We are not saying that they are as evil as they can possibly be. Jesus says, ". . . you then, though you are evil, know how to give good gifts to your children" (Luke 11:13). If people were as evil as they possibly could be, they would not desire to give good things to their children. They would presumably find ways to inflict only evil upon their children. Unbelieving parents often love their children and their friends (cf. Matt. 5:46–47). They also may do much that is good for society. It should be noted that Jesus still says that they are evil. Evil people still give good gifts to their children and do kind things for other people.

If people are not as sinful as they can possibly be, then in what sense are they slaves to sin? It is crucial to establish a biblical definition of sin. Of course, sin consists in disobeying the law (1 John 3:4). But the root of sin is much deeper than this. Romans 1:21–25 clarifies that the heart of sin is failing to glorify God as God. The heart of sin is a belittling of God and a scorning of his glory, which involves a failure to glorify and thank him (Rom. 1:21). As Romans 3:23 says, "All have sinned and fall short of the glory of God." Sinners do not give God the supreme place in their lives but exchange "the glory of the immortal God for images made to look like mortal man and birds and animals and reptiles" (Rom. 1:23). In other words, people "served created things rather than the Creator" (Rom. 1:25). Sin is not first and foremost the practice of evil deeds but an attitude that gives glory to something other than God. People may be loving to their children and kind to their neighbors and never give a thought to God. The essence of sin is self-worship rather than God-worship. The serpent persuaded Eve and Adam to eat the fruit of the tree by promising them that they would "be like God" (Gen. 3:5). They could dispense with God and worship themselves; they would worship the creature rather than the Creator.

Such a conception of sin helps us understand how people can perform actions that externally conform with righteousness yet remain slaves of sin. These actions are not motivated by a desire to honor and glorify God as God.

They are not done out of an attitude of faith, which brings glory to God (Rom. 4:20). Faith brings glory to God because he is seen to be the all-powerful one who supplies our every good, and thus is deserving of praise and honor. Actions that externally conform with righteousness may still be sin, in that they are not done for God's glory and by faith. The necessity of faith is underscored by Romans 14:23, where Paul notes that "everything that does not come from faith is sin." Slavery to sin does not mean that people always engage in reprehensible behavior. It means that the unregenerate never desire to bring glory to God, but are passionately committed to upholding their own glory and honor.

Of course, the power of sin is such that all have fallen short of conformity with God's law (Rom. 1:18–3:20). No one has perfectly done all that the law requires. The extent of our slavery to sin is, however, even deeper than this. It is not merely that the "sinful mind is hostile to God" (Rom. 8:7). It is also true that it "does not submit to God's law, nor can it do so" (Rom. 8:7). Those in the flesh have an intense hatred of God burning within them, whether they are conscious of this or not. Moreover, they have no ability to keep God's law. Paul is not saying that there is no opportunity to keep the law. Nor is he saying that people want to keep the law, but God prevents them from keeping it. His point is that those in the flesh have no moral ability to keep the law perfectly or to glorify God. The power of sin is so great that they "cannot please God" (Rom. 8:8) and do his will. They are slaves to sin.

The Wesleyan View of Fallen Humanity

It is notable that John Wesley would agree with the preceding diagnosis. He writes,

> I believe that Adam, before his fall, had such freedom of will, that he might choose either good or evil; but that, since the fall, no child of man has a natural power to choose anything that is truly good. Yet I know (and who does not?) that man has still freedom of will in things of indifferent nature.[3]

Human beings since the fall are so enmeshed in the power of sin that apart from divine grace they cannot choose what is spiritually good.[4] This point is

---

3. *The Works of John Wesley*, ed. T. Jackson, 14 vols. (1831; reprint, Grand Rapids: Baker, 1979), 10:350. Hereafter designated as *Works*.

4. Wesleyan theology differs from that of Charles Finney in that Finney believed that all people possess the ability, apart from grace, to choose what is good. Contrary to Wesleyans he rejects the idea that people are born morally depraved because of Adam's sin. Thus, it is not surprising to learn that Finney repudiated the doctrine of prevenient grace. See J. E. Smith, "The Theology of Charles Finney: A System of Self-Reformation," *Trin J* 13 (1992): 75–77, 82–84.

often acknowledged by Wesley scholars.[5] Harald Lindström rightly remarks that "Wesley maintains that natural man is totally corrupt."[6] He is "sinful through and through, has no knowledge of God and no power to turn to him of his own free will."[7] Robert V. Rakestraw says that in Wesley's theology "men and women are born in sin and unable in themselves to make the least move toward God."[8] Colin W. Williams affirms the same point: "Because of original sin, the natural man is 'dead to God' and unable to move toward God or respond to him."[9] Leo G. Cox says, "By nature man receives nothing that is good. . . . He is free but free only to do evil and to follow on in the way of sin."[10] Wesley did not believe that the will of fallen humanity was free. He says, "Such is the freedom of the will; free only to evil; free to 'drink iniquity like water;' to wander farther and farther from the living God, and do more 'despite to the Spirit of grace!'"[11] The Wesleyan analysis of the human condition does not differ fundamentally from the Calvinistic one.[12] Indeed, in 1745 John Wesley said that his theology was "within a hair's breadth" of Calvinism "(1) In ascribing all good to the free grace of God. (2) *In denying all natural free-will*, and all power antecedent to grace. And, (3) In excluding all merit from man; even for what he has or does by the grace of God."[13] Wesley's analysis of the human condition and his bold proclamation of divine grace should warm the heart of any evangelical Calvinist.

Prevenient Grace in the Wesleyan System

If Wesleyans and Calvinists concur on the human condition, wherein do they differ? One major place that Wesleyans break with Calvinists is through their doctrine of prevenient grace. Elton Hendricks says that this doctrine "played a more important role in Wesley's theological thought

5. See Wood, "Theology of Grace," 212–13; Charles A. Rogers, *The Concept of Prevenient Grace in the Theology of John Wesley* (Ph.D. dissertation, Duke University, 1967), 107–13, 156–58, 194–98, 200–2.
6. Harald Lindström, *Wesley and Sanctification: A Study in the Doctrine of Salvation* (London: Epworth, 1950), 45.
7. Ibid.
8. Robert V. Rakestraw, "John Wesley as a Theologian of Grace," *JETS* 27 (1984): 196.
9. Colin W. Williams, *John Wesley's Theology Today* (Nashville: Abingdon, 1960), 41.
10. Leo G. Cox, "Prevenient Grace—A Wesleyan View," *JETS* 12 (1969): 147.
11. *Works*, 5:104.
12. So also Melvin E. Dieter, "The Wesleyan Perspective," in *Five Views on Sanctification* (Grand Rapids: Zondervan, 1987), 21–23; M. Elton Hendricks, "John Wesley and Natural Theology," *Wesley Th J* 18 (1983): 9; J. Weldon Smith III, "Some Notes on Wesley's Doctrine of Prevenient Grace," *Religion in Life* 34 (1964–65): 70–74. The extent of the agreement should be qualified, according to H. Orton Wiley, *Christian Theology* (Kansas City, Mo.: Beacon Hill, 1952), 2:353.
13. *Works*, 8:284–85. Italics added.

than in that of any other Protestant theologian."[14] Williams affirms that it "has very great significance in his theology."[15] Even though Calvinists and Arminians hold much in common, H. Ray Dunning rightly says that "the truth that holds them but a hair's breadth apart at the point of the watershed is the doctrine of *prevenient grace*."[16] The differences between Calvinists and Arminians on this point should not be minimized. William Ragsdale Cannon is correct in saying that "though Wesleyanism and Calvinism come in this instance so close together, they are in reality worlds apart."[17] How crucial is prevenient grace to the Wesleyan system? Wesleyans themselves seem to concur that their theology hinges on the doctrine. Robert E. Chiles says that "without it, the Calvinist logic is irrefutable."[18] Williams asserts that Wesley's theology of prevenient grace "broke the chain of logical necessity by which the Calvinist doctrine of predestination seems to flow from the doctrine of original sin."[19] It seems fair to conclude that if prevenient grace is not taught in Scripture, then the credibility of Wesleyan theology is seriously undermined.

Before probing to see whether Scripture teaches prevenient grace, it is necessary to explore what Wesleyans mean by the term. We need to recall that Wesley himself was not a systematic theologian but a pastoral theologian who developed his theology in the course of his ministry. Thus, no systematic treatment of the theme of prevenient grace is found in his writings.[20] In Wesleyan theology there are various conceptions of prevenient grace that we do not need to specify here since, as we shall see, there is common ground within the various positions on the issue that concerns us.[21]

---

14. Hendricks, "Natural Theology," 8.

15. Williams, *Wesley's Theology*, 41.

16. H. Ray Dunning, *Grace, Faith, and Holiness: A Wesleyan Systematic Theology* (Kansas City, Mo.: Beacon Hill, 1988), 49.

17. William Ragsdale Cannon, *The Theology of John Wesley: With Special Reference to the Doctrine of Justification* (New York: University Press of America, 1974), 102.

18. Robert E. Chiles, *Theological Transition in American Methodism: 1790–1935* (Nashville: Abingdon, 1965), 50.

19. Williams, *Wesley's Theology*, 44. See also his comments on 46. In agreement with Williams are Rakestraw ("John Wesley," 197) and Wood ("Theology of Grace," 215).

20. For a survey of the positions of Wesley and John Fletcher see Mark Royster, *John Wesley's Doctrine of Prevenient Grace in Missiological Perspective* (D.Miss. dissertation, Asbury Theological Seminary, 1989), 30–72.

21. Rogers in his dissertation (see n. 5) has provided the most comprehensive analysis of Wesley's doctrine. See particularly his distinction between the early (*Prevenient Grace*, 127–35) and later Wesley (159–263) on prevenient grace. For the purposes of this chapter only Wesley's later theology of prevenient grace is in view. Rogers also includes a survey (5–16) of Wesleyan scholarship on prevenient grace; see also Royster (*Missiological Perspective*, 73–93). For three different understandings of prevenient grace in the Wesleyan tradition see Thomas A. Langford, *Practical Divinity: Theology in the Wesleyan Tradition* (Nashville: Abingdon, 1983), 33. Chiles (*American Methodism*, 150–51) specifies two strands of prevenient grace among Wesleyans.

In some respects Wesleyans use the term *prevenient grace* in a way that matches with the Calvinist term *common grace*.[22] The conscience, according to Wesley, is to be ascribed to prevenient grace.[23] It is not to be understood as a natural gift but is supernaturally given by God.[24] In addition, some moral excellence and virtue in the world exists even among those who are unregenerate.[25] Prevenient grace is responsible for the goodness that is present to some extent in every society, even in cultures that are largely non-Christian.[26] We are not surprised to learn, then, that the relationship between prevenient grace and natural theology has been explored by some, with a close connection being suggested.[27]

The Wesleyan understanding of prevenient grace differs from the Calvinistic conception of common grace in one important area. In the Calvinistic scheme common grace does not and cannot lead to salvation. It functions to restrain evil in the world but does not lead unbelievers to faith. For Wesleyans, prevenient grace may lead one to salvation. Cox rightly says, "The Wesleyan teaches that the prevenient grace leads on to saving grace, prepares for it, enables a person to enter into it."[28] Indeed, in Wesley's theology it seems that a proper response to prevenient grace could lead to the salvation of those who have not heard the gospel.[29] What we are interested in exploring, however, is not how prevenient grace affects those who have never heard the gospel. The distinctive aspect of prevenient grace that is relevant for our discussion is that it provides the ability to choose salvation, an ability that was surrendered by Adam's sin. Wesley describes it as follows:

> Salvation begins with what is usually termed (and very properly) *preventing grace;* including the first wish to please God, the first dawn of light concerning his will, and the first slight transient conviction of having sinned against him. All these imply some tendency toward life; some degree of salvation; the beginning of a deliverance from a blind, unfeeling heart, quite insensible of God and the things of God.[30]

22. So Dunning, *Grace, Faith, and Holiness*, 296; cf. Cox, "Prevenient Grace," 143–44. In fact, Wiley (*Christian Theology*, 2:357) thinks that the Wesleyan conception of prevenient grace precludes any need for "common grace."

23. *Works*, 7:187–88. For Wesley's understanding of the role of prevenient grace in relationship to the conscience see Rogers, *Prevenient Grace*, 184–89.

24. So Rakestraw, "John Wesley," 197; Lindström, *Wesley and Sanctification*, 48. Wesley (*Works*, 7:187; see also 6:512) specifically says it is "a supernatural gift."

25. Wesley, *Works*, 7:345; see also 7:374.

26. So John Miley, *Systematic Theology* (New York: Eaton and Mains, 1894), 2:244, 246.

27. See Hendricks, "Natural Theology," 7–17; Smith, "Prevenient Grace," 77–80; Lindström, *Wesley and Sanctification*, 46–47.

28. Cox, "Prevenient Grace," 144.

29. See Dunning (*Grace, Faith, and Holiness*, 161–70) for a helpful discussion. See also Rogers, *Prevenient Grace*, 243–47.

30. *Works*, 6:509.

What separates Calvinists from Wesleyans is that the former see electing grace as given only to some (the elect) and insist that this grace cannot ultimately be resisted. The latter argue that prevenient grace is given to all people and that it can be resisted. What is common in all Wesleyan theories of prevenient grace is that the freedom, which was lost in Adam's sin, is sufficiently restored to enable people to choose salvation.[31] Prevenient grace provides people with the ability to choose or reject God. As sinners born in Adam, they had no ability to do good or to choose what is right. But as recipients of prevenient grace they can once again choose the good. Wesley said, "Natural free-will, in the present state of mankind, I do not understand: I only assert, that

31. The description of prevenient grace in this paragraph is supported by Langford, *Practical Divinity*, 33; Dunning, *Grace, Faith, and Holiness*, 339; Rakestraw, "John Wesley," 196; Williams, *Wesley's Theology*, 41, 46; Chiles, *American Methodism*, 149; Cox, "Prevenient Grace," 147–49; Lindström, *Wesley and Sanctification*, 45–46; Hendricks, "Natural Theology," 9–11; Smith, "Prevenient Grace," 75; Henry C. Thiessen, *Lectures in Systematic Theology*, rev. Vernon D. Doerksen (Grand Rapids: Eerdmans, 1979), 106, 259; William B. Pope, *A Compendium of Christian Theology* (London: Wesleyan Conference Office, 1880), 2:358–67.

Rogers's own conclusions regarding Wesley's understanding of prevenient grace, on first glance, seem to be radically different from that suggested by the other scholars. Further analysis, however, reveals that the difference is one of degree, not one of kind. Rogers argues (*Prevenient Grace*, 217–19) that prevenient grace, according to Wesley, does not provide people with the ability to choose salvation. Prevenient grace in Wesley's thought is a gift given, not a gift that is offered and can be rejected. People are passive in the reception of faith, and there is no emphasis on the role of human decision in receiving faith. Thus faith is irresistible at the moment given. Rogers's explanation may lead one to think that Wesley was a Calvinist! But this is not the whole story. Rogers contends that prevenient grace (*Prevenient Grace*, 228–30, 237, 271, 282–83, 288) in Wesley's thought plays a decisive role before one comes to faith. Prevenient grace operates through the law and conscience to bring conviction of sin and despair of ever pleasing God. People have the freedom to resist the conviction of sin that comes from the law and conscience. If they do not respond appropriately to the conviction of sin mediated by the law and conscience, then they will not be saved. Prevenient grace leads one to the very brink of salvation if one responds positively to the "means of grace" that precede saving faith. Thus, prevenient grace is irresistible at the moment one exercises faith, but long before one receives faith the grace of God can be resisted. Only those who satisfactorily respond to prevenient grace come to the point where saving faith can be exercised. It seems that Rogers is in harmony with other Wesleyans in his conception of prevenient grace, for the grace God gives can still be resisted. Human beings may choose to respond to or resist the influence of the law and conscience. The final and ultimate determination lies with human choice. Rogers differs from other Wesleyans in locating the point of resistance in another place in Wesley's theology, namely, one's response to the means of grace before conversion.

For views that are quite similar to Rogers's see Royster (*Missiological Perspective*, 90–91) and Robert E. Cushman, "Salvation for All: Wesley and Calvinism," in *Methodism*, ed. W. K. Anderson (Nashville: Methodist Publishing House, 1947). It is clear from Royster's concluding definition that ability to choose what is good is included in his understanding of prevenient grace, for he says (92) that prevenient grace provides "the freedom/power to respond positively to subsequent directions from God."

there is a measure of free-will supernaturally restored to every man, together with that supernatural light which 'enlightens every man that cometh into the world.'"[32] Prevenient grace does not guarantee that the good will be chosen. It simply provides the opportunity or liberty to choose salvation. People may stifle the grace given and turn away from God, or they may respond to God's grace and turn to him in order to be saved.

Obviously, prevenient grace fixes a large gulf between Calvinism and Wesleyanism. Calvinists contend that the unregenerate have no ability or desire to choose God. God's election of some is what brings them from darkness to light, from Satan's kingdom to God's. Wesleyans believe that God has given prevenient grace to all people. As descendants of Adam they were born with no ability or desire to choose God, but God has counteracted this inability by the gift of prevenient grace. Now all people have the ability to choose God. The ultimate determination of salvation is the human decision to say no or yes to God.[33]

Wesleyan Arguments in Favor of Prevenient Grace

For all Bible-believing Christians, the most important question in matters of doctrinal dispute is this: what is the Bible's teaching as it pertains to the issue at hand? Calvinists and Arminians likewise must turn to the Bible. The critical question is whether or not the doctrine of prevenient grace is supported by Scripture. We cannot examine this issue until we see the arguments that are put forward to defend the doctrine. Wesleyans use at least four arguments to support the idea that prevenient grace is a doctrine rooted in Scripture.

First, the Scripture text that is appealed to quite often is John 1:9.[34] "The true light that gives light to every man was coming into the world." The meaning of this text is not analyzed in detail by Wesleyan scholars, but their understanding seems clear enough. The coming of Jesus Christ into the world brought enough light to all people so that they are now able to reject or accept the message of the gospel. The illumination *(phōtizei)* refers to the granting of grace that overcomes the darkness that penetrated human hearts as a result of Adam's sin. This illumination does not guarantee salvation; it simply makes it possible for men and women to choose salvation.

---

32. *Works*, 10:229–30.
33. Rakestraw ("John Wesley," 199) rightly says that in Wesley's theology "that one is ultimately the determining factor in the decision of his or her justification. Faith is offered as God's free gift, but the sinner must then actively respond to that offer and reach out with the arms of true repentance to receive the gift."
34. E.g., Wesley, *Works*, 10:230, 7:188; Lindström, *Wesley and Sanctification*, 45.

Such an understanding of the verse may be confirmed in the subsequent context. Some rejected the light and "did not receive him" (John 1:11), while others responded to the light and "received him" (John 1:12). It should also be noted that this illumination is not restricted to a few. It is granted to "every person" *(panta anthrōpon)*. This would support the Wesleyan view that prevenient grace is given to all people.

A second argument employed by Wesleyans is that prevenient grace is granted in the atonement of Christ (e.g., Tit. 2:11; John 12:32).[35] This argument is bound up with the universality of Christ's atonement. His death for all necessarily implies that grace is given to some extent to all. The argument is that Christ would not die for all unless all were granted the opportunity to accept or reject him. John 12:32 can be understood as supporting this theory. Jesus says, "But I, when I am lifted up from the earth, will draw all men to myself." Henry Thiessen says about this verse, "There issues a power from the cross of Christ that goes out to all men, though many continue to resist that power."[36] In the death of Christ grace is operative so that all people are "drawn" *(helkuō)* to him. The drawing does not guarantee salvation but makes it possible,[37] supporting the idea that grace is given in the atonement that reverses the total inability of people to choose God. In addition, it should be pointed out that John 12:32 refers to "all people" *(pantas)*. The grace given in the atonement is not limited to some but is universally distributed, giving all people everywhere the opportunity to respond or reject it.

The third Wesleyan argument in favor of prevenient grace has a theological cast. God must have granted the power to choose him because otherwise the warnings, invitations, and commands in Scripture are meaningless.[38] Why would God give commands to people if they are unable to put them into practice? There are numerous texts in Scripture in which commands, invitation, and warnings are employed. Perhaps Romans 2:4 is a particularly appropriate verse to cite in support.[39] "Or do you show contempt for the riches of his kindness, tolerance and patience, not realizing that God's kindness leads you toward repentance?" God would not command people to repent and be waiting for them to repent if he knew that they could not do so. His kindness is such that he has provided the means

35. So, e.g., Miley, *Systematic Theology*, 2:247; Wiley, *Christian Theology*, 2:353; Adam Clarke, *Christian Theology* (New York: Eaton and Mains, 1835), 117; Wood, "Theology of Grace," 216; Langford, *Practical Divinity*, 34; Smith, "Prevenient Grace," 75; Lindström, *Wesley and Sanctification*, 49; Dunning, *Grace, Faith, and Holiness*, 339.

36. Thiessen, *Systematic Theology*, 261.

37. Cf. Grant R. Osborne, "Soteriology in the Gospel of John," in *The Grace of God, the Will of Man: A Case for Arminianism*, ed. Clark H. Pinnock (Grand Rapids: Zondervan, 1989), 249.

38. Cf. Clarke, *Christian Theology*, 130, 132; Miley, *Systematic Theology*, 2:245–46.

39. Cf. Thiessen, *Systematic Theology*, 106.

for every person to repent if they would only avail themselves of that means.

Fourth, prevenient grace is supported by the very nature of God.[40] A God of mercy, wisdom, justice, and love would not leave human beings without an opportunity to repent and choose salvation. A God of love and mercy who desires all to be saved (1 Tim. 2:4) would see to it that all have the chance to partake of salvation. If God elects only a few, he is guilty of partiality.[41]

A Critique of the Wesleyan Arguments for Prevenient Grace

We now proceed to analyze the four arguments for prevenient grace advanced by Wesleyans. I will argue that their case is unpersuasive and that their doctrine of prevenient grace is not found in Scripture. Wesleyans, however, advance some exegetical and theological arguments in defense of prevenient grace that will be considered here.

We turn first of all to John 1:9. The crucial phrase for our purposes is *phōtizei panta anthrōpon* (enlightens every person), which enlightening is ascribed to "the true light." Wesleyans understand this enlightenment to refer to prevenient grace, which is given to all people, but there are serious reasons for doubting that this is the meaning of the verse. In fact, the verse can be understood in three other ways that do not yield the Wesleyan interpretation. First, the illumination could refer to general revelation, which is granted to all people through the created order.[42] This shifts the debate to different ground, for some argue that general revelation is sufficient for salvation.[43] Such a view is unpersuasive given Paul's estimation of general revelation in Romans 1:18–32.[44] In any case, D. A. Carson is correct in dismissing a reference to general revelation since this would have been more appropriately dealt with earlier in the prologue (i.e., John 1:3–4).[45] The

---

40. So Wesley, *Works*, 10:36ff; Wood, "Theology of Grace," 211–12; Lindström, *Wesley and Sanctification*, 46.

41. Cf. Thiessen, *Systematic Theology*, 260.

42. So Leon Morris, *The Gospel According to John*, NICNT (Grand Rapids: Eerdmans, 1971), 95.

43. In fact, in Wesleyan theology there is not a clear line of demarcation between general revelation and special revelation with respect to prevenient grace. See 371.

44. See Moo's (*Romans 1–8*, 91–124) thorough exegesis in defense of this conclusion. Neither does Romans 2:14–15 suggest the possibility of salvation through obeying one's conscience. See Thomas R. Schreiner, "Does Paul Believe in Justification by Works? Another Look at Romans 2," *The Bulletin for Biblical Research* 3 (1993): 131–58. Wesley believed that this passage taught the doctrine of prevenient grace. See John Wesley, *Explanatory Notes Upon the New Testament*, 2 vols. (reprint, Grand Rapids: Baker, 1981), comment on Romans 2:14 in volume 2.

45. D. A. Carson, *The Gospel According to John* (Grand Rapids: Eerdmans, 1991), 123.

specific context is not general revelation but the response of people to the incarnate Word of God, Jesus Christ.

Second, the illumination may refer to an inward illumination that leads to conversion.[46] In this case, John would not be saying that illumination is given to all people "without exception" but to all "without distinction."[47] The light is not confined to the Jews, but also has an effect among the Gentiles. Other sheep that are not of the fold of the Jews will be brought in (John 10:16). Jesus died not only for the Jews but also for the children of God scattered throughout the world (John 11:51–52).

The context of John 1:9–13, however, suggests that another interpretation is the most probable.[48] The word *enlighten (phōtizō)* refers not to inward illumination but to the exposure that comes when light is shed upon something. Some are shown to be evil because they did not know or receive Jesus (John 1:10–11), while others are revealed to be righteous because they have received Jesus and have been born of God (John 1:12–13). John 3:19–21 confirms this interpretation. Those who are evil shrink from coming to the light because they do want their works to be exposed (v. 20). But those who practice the truth gladly come to the light so that it might be manifest that their works are wrought in God (v. 21). The light that enlightens every person does not entail the bestowment of grace, nor does it refer to the inward illumination of the heart by the Spirit of God. Rather, the light exposes and reveals the moral and spiritual state of one's heart. C. K. Barrett rightly says that "the light shines upon every man for judgement, to reveal what he is."[49] Or, as Carson remarks, "Inner illumination is then not in view" but "the objective revelation" that occurs at the coming of the "true light."[50] John 1:9 is not, therefore, suggesting that through Christ's coming each person is given the ability to choose salvation. The purpose of the verse is to say that the coming of the true light exposes and reveals where people are in their relationship to God.[51]

46. The word *phōtizō* has the meaning of inward illumination in, e.g., Psalm 18:9 (LXX); Ephesians 1:18; 3:9.

47. So Carson, *John*, 123.

48. For the interpretation suggested here see C. K. Barrett, *The Gospel According to St. John* (Philadelphia: Westminster, ²1978), 161; Carson, *John*, 124.

49. Barrett, *John*, 161.

50. Carson, *John*, 124.

51. John emphasizes that the light, Jesus, has come into the world so that people might believe in him (1:6–8; 12:35–36) or follow him (8:12). The call to believe in the light, though, is a far cry from saying that all have been given the ability to do so. Indeed, John, speaking of those who did not believe, says they "could not believe" because God "has blinded their eyes" (12:39–40). This judicial hardening by God does not lessen human responsibility in John's eyes (cf. 12:43). Jesus has come into the world as light so that people would believe in him and they should do so! For some wise comments on how God's judicial hardening is compatible with other biblical themes see Carson, *John*, 448–49.

Wesleyans appeal to grace given in the atonement and Christ's death for all as an indication of prevenient grace. I shall not examine the question of the extent of the atonement since that is treated elsewhere in this work.[52] Indeed, Calvinists have typically seen grace as bestowed upon the elect in the atonement, but in this case the grace bestowed is effective and guarantees salvation. The question is whether in the atonement of Christ the Wesleyan conception of prevenient grace is taught; that is, does Scripture teach that people are given the ability to choose or to reject God by virtue of the atonement? Doubtless grace is manifested in the atonement. For instance, Titus 2:11 says that "the grace of God that brings salvation has appeared to all men." Calvinists usually argue that this text teaches that the atonement secures and accomplishes redemption for the elect. It is not my purpose to defend or refute that interpretation. Even if the text were suggesting that salvation is potentially available for all people (cf. 1 Tim. 4:10), that is a far cry from saying that through the atonement God has counteracted the effects of Adam's sin so that all people have the opportunity to accept or reject him. Titus 2:11 says that God's grace has been manifested through Christ's work on the cross, but it does not say that God has thereby supplied the ability to believe to all people. Wesleyans conclude from the atonement effected by Christ that enough grace has been imparted to all people so that they can now choose whether or not to believe. But it is precisely this point that is not taught explicitly in the verse. It does not necessarily follow that since grace was manifested in the death of Christ that all people as a result have the ability to believe in him. Specific exegetical support for this conclusion is lacking.

A text that might lead to the Wesleyan conclusion is John 12:32. But this involves a misreading of the text. In John 6:37 Jesus says, "All that the Father gives me will come to me, and whoever comes to me I will never drive away." Note that this text specifically teaches that only some will come to Jesus, namely, those who have been given by the Father to the Son. In other words, the Father has not given all to the Son; he has selected only some, and it is they who will come to the Son and believe in him (cf. John 6:35).[53] The teaching of John 6:37 is reaffirmed in 6:44. "No one can come to me unless the Father who sent me draws him, and I will raise him at the last day." The word *draw (helkuō)*, which is used in John 12:32, is also used in John 6:37. The point of John 6:44 is that the Father does not draw all people, only some. Carson rightly remarks, "The combination of v[erse] 37a

---

52. See chapter 18 by J. I. Packer.

53. For more detailed support of divine election in John see Robert W. Yarbrough, "Divine Election in the Gospel of John," in chapter 2 of this work; see also D. A. Carson, *Divine Sovereignty and Human Responsibility: Biblical Perspectives in Tension* (Atlanta: John Knox, 1981), 125–98.

and v[erse] 44 prove that this 'drawing' activity of the Father cannot be reduced to what theologians sometimes call 'prevenient grace' dispensed to every individual, for this 'drawing' is selective, or else the negative note of v[erse] 44 is meaningless."[54] The Johannine conception of drawing is not that it makes salvation possible, but that it makes salvation effectual. Those who are drawn will come to Jesus and believe in him.

Does this definition of drawing mean that John teaches universalism, since 12:32 says that Jesus will draw all to himself by virtue of the cross? The context of John 12:20–33 helps us answer that question. Greeks, that is, Gentiles, approached Philip because they wanted to see Jesus (vv. 20–23). Jesus ignores the request and instead speaks of the need for a grain of wheat to die in order to bear fruit (vv. 24–26), and of his commitment to carry out his commission (vv. 27–28). Jesus' death is the means by which God's judgment of the world and his triumph over Satan will be accomplished (v. 31). He concludes by saying that if he is lifted up he will draw all people to himself (v. 32).

The context is of paramount importance for understanding John 12:32. Jesus appears to ignore the request from his disciples to meet with the Greeks who wanted to see him. But the point Jesus makes is that the only way Gentiles will come to him is through his death. He must die in order to bear much fruit and bring Gentiles to himself. The power of Satan as the ruler of the world will be broken only by the cross. Thus, when Jesus speaks of drawing all people to himself by virtue of the cross, the issue in the context is how Gentiles can come to Jesus. The drawing of all does not refer to all people individually but the means by which Gentiles will be included in the people of God. Carson again rightly interprets the verse. "Here 'all men' reminds the reader of what triggered these statements, [namely,] the arrival of the Greeks, and means 'all people without distinction, Jews and Gentiles alike', not all individuals without exception."[55] The Wesleyan theory that prevenient grace is provided in the atonement so that people are given ability to choose salvation cannot be supported from the context of John 12.

The third Wesleyan argument for prevenient grace is probably the most powerful one. Why would God give commands unless people were given some ability to obey them? Romans 2:4 says that his kindness is intended to lead people to repentance. Does this not imply that people have the ability to repent if they would only choose to do so?

It should be acknowledged that Wesleyan logic is coherent here, and one can see why Wesleyans would deduce human ability from the giving of commands. Nonetheless, even though their logic is impeccable, it does not necessarily follow that their conclusion is true. An argument may be logically co-

54. Carson, *John*, 293.
55. Ibid., 444.

herent and not fit with the state of affairs in the world because the answer given is not comprehensive. To put it another way, one of the premises in the Wesleyan argument is not in accord with the reality of life as it is portrayed in the Scriptures. They are incorrect in deducing that God would not give commands without giving the moral ability to obey them. The distinction between physical and moral ability is crucial.[56] For instance, human beings are physically able (in most cases) to walk up steps, but they are physically unable to jump over houses. In a similar way, God gives commands to unbelievers that they can physically obey; that is, they could observe his commandments if they desired to do so. Unbelievers are morally unable to keep God's commands in the sense that they have no desire to obey all of his commandments. God commands all people (Gal. 3:10; Rom. 1:18–3:20) to obey his law perfectly, but no one is morally able to do this. Because all people are born with a sin nature inherited from Adam, they will inevitably sin. Even though people cannot morally obey God's commands, biblical authors assume that they should keep his commandments. They should keep his commandments because they are right and good (Rom. 7:12) and are not physically impossible to keep. People could observe the commandments if they wanted to do so. The biblical view, however, is that unbelievers as slaves of sin have no desire to keep God's law.[57]

The state of affairs that obtains under the law remains when Christ comes. That is, all people should come to Jesus in order to have life (John 5:40). Jesus upbraids those who do not believe despite all his works (Matt. 11:20–24), and he invites all to come to him (Matt. 11:28–30). Yet he also teaches that no one can come to him unless drawn by the Father (John 6:44), and only those to whom the Father and Son reveal themselves will come to know him (Matt. 11:25–27). All people are summoned to believe in Jesus and are censured for not believing. Nonetheless, the Scriptures also teach that they have no moral ability to believe, and that the only way they will believe is if they are given by the Father to the Son. This revelation is not vouchsafed to all people but only to the elect. Jesus commands believers to be perfect (Matt. 5:48), but the need for forgiveness (Matt. 6:14–15) demonstrates that perfection is impossible to attain.

The problem with Wesleyanism at this point is that it is guided by human logic and rationality rather than the Scriptures. Their view that commands would not be given that people could not morally obey is certainly attractive. But our counterargument is that such a notion is not taught in the Scriptures. The doctrine of original sin and human inability is

---

56. For a recent explanation of this distinction which is a model of clarity see David M. Ciocchi, "Understanding Our Ability to Endure Temptation: A Theological Watershed," *JETS* 35 (1992): 463–68.

57. It should be pointed out that Adam was created with both physical and moral ability to obey God's commands. We cannot here pursue the difficult question as to why Adam sinned.

an offense to reason.[58] This is not to say that it is irrational. The distinction between physical and moral ability goes a long way toward resolving the difficulties. Nonetheless, not all the difficulties are resolved by the Calvinist view, for ultimately we do not fully understand how people can be responsible for sin when they are born with an inclination that will inevitably lead them to sin.

An example from another area of life might help. Robert Wright in an article on alcoholism was musing on the theory that it might be determined by one's genes.[59] If so, could we conclude that people are not responsible for alcoholism? Wright correctly says no. If we draw this conclusion, then the reality of human responsibility will be slowly whittled away as we discover the impact of genetics on human behavior. Even if alcoholism is determined genetically, people are still responsible for their behavior.[60] We may not fully understand how both determinism and human responsibility can be true, but both are necessary to account for the nature of humanity and genetic research. So too, sinners who have inherited a sin nature from Adam and who have no moral ability to obey God's law and no inclination to respond to him are still responsible for their failure to respond to God's grace.

The preceding comments prepare us for understanding Romans 2:4. The wording of this text should be taken seriously, but our own philosophical presuppositions should not be read into it. It is the case that the kindness of God should lead people to repentance.[61] God's kindness is not a charade but is profoundly present in that he spares people and does not immediately destroy them for their sin. The kindness and patience of God should induce people to seek him and to confess their sin. But this text does not say that people have the moral ability to repent and turn to God. It simply says that they should repent and turn to him. Wesleyans read into this verse their theology of prevenient grace, thereby squeezing more out of the verse than it says.[62]

---

58. This is the title of Bernard Ramm's book on original sin, *Offense to Reason* (New York: Harper and Row, 1985).

59. Robert Wright, "Alcohol and Free Will: The Supreme Court Reopens an Old Question," *The New Republic* 197, 24 (14 December 1987): 14–16.

60. Wright himself seems to fall prey to rationalism insofar as he subordinates human responsibility to determinism. Nonetheless, he insists that life will not make sense unless we hold people to be responsible.

61. The present indicative *agei* is understood here as conative. So C. F. D. Moule, *An Idiom Book of New Testament Greek*, 2d ed. (Cambridge: Cambridge University Press, 1959), 8. *Agei* should not be pressed as a present indicative to say that God's kindness is actually leading the Jews to repent. The point of the verse is that God's kindness should lead them to repent.

62. Another text that could be used to support prevenient grace is Acts 7:51, where Stephen says to his adversaries, "you always resist the Holy Spirit." It is true that there is a work of the Spirit that is resisted by unbelievers. This should be distinguished, however, from saying that God has granted all people the ability to respond to his grace. In fact, the text seems to suggest the opposite. People resist the Holy Spirit because of their bondage to sin. Scripture teaches that for the elect God graciously overcomes their resistance and brings them to repentance (2 Tim. 2:25–26).

What we have said about Romans 2:4 leads us naturally to the fourth argument used for prevenient grace, that is, the justice, wisdom, mercy, and love of God. What I have been arguing is that the fundamental problem with the Wesleyan understanding of prevenient grace is that it is not taught in the Scriptures. It is a philosophical imposition of a certain world view upon the Scriptures. This world view is attractive because it neatly solves, to some extent, issues such as the problem of evil and why human beings are held responsible for sin. But the Scriptures do not yield such neat solutions.[63] God is wholly just in condemning sinners who have no ability to obey his law (Rom. 8:7–8). They fail to keep the law because they do not want to obey it. In sinning they carry out the desires of their hearts. God is merciful and loving in not destroying them immediately and offering them salvation. It is a mistake, however, to say that God's love and mercy will provide every person an equal chance to believe. God would be just in sending all to hell since all have sinned. The love and mercy extended to the elect is undeserved. God is obligated to save no one, but out of a heart of mercy he saves some (Eph. 2:4–7). Those who believe that God must extend mercy equally to all are subtly falling into the trap of believing that God would not be good without showing mercy equally to all. This comes perilously close to the conclusion that God should show mercy to all to the same extent, and that such mercy is obligatory. But if God should show equal mercy to all, then mercy is no longer viewed as undeserved. In this view mercy extended to all is demanded by justice. This kind of reasoning should be rejected because the Scriptures make it clear that no one deserves to be saved, that all people could be justly sent to hell, and that God's mercy is so stunning because it is undeserved.

The scandal of the Calvinist system is that ultimately the logical problems posed cannot be fully resolved. The final resolution of the problem of human responsibility and divine justice is beyond our rational capacity. The doctrine of prevenient grace in the Wesleyan sense is read into the Scriptures because it solves so many logical problems and attempts to clarify how God is just and loving. Calvinists also affirm God's mercy, wisdom, justice, and love. We trust that he is good, and that no one will perish who does not deserve judgment. There is significant evidence to vindicate the justice, mercy, and love of God. Nonetheless, we cannot comprehensively explain how these attributes of God fit the reality portrayed in the Scriptures. There are finally some mysteries that we cannot unravel.

63. For a semipopular treatment that is a more detailed explanation of the biblical view see D. A. Carson, *How Long O Lord? Reflections on Suffering and Evil* (Grand Rapids: Baker, 1990).

Conclusion

The doctrine of prevenient grace should be accepted only if it can be sustained from a careful exegesis of the Scriptures. What was most striking to me in my research was how little scriptural exegesis has been done by Wesleyans in defense of prevenient grace. It is vital to their system of theology, for even Wesleyans admit that without it "Calvinist logic is irrefutable."[64] Nonetheless, not much exegetical work has been done in support of the doctrine. This is particularly astonishing when one compares the biblical data for prevenient grace to Calvinist texts that support unconditional election. The Calvinist case has been promulgated, rightly or wrongly, via a detailed exegesis of numerous texts. The plight of humanity due to Adam's sin (which we investigated) is reversed only by the electing grace of God, according to the Calvinist. Wesleyans contend that prevenient grace counteracts the inability of humanity due to Adam's sin, but firm biblical evidence seems to be lacking. One can be pardoned, then, for wondering whether this theory is based on scriptural exegesis. Millard Erickson rightly says about it, "The problem is that there is no clear and adequate basis in Scripture for this concept of universal enablement. The theory, appealing though it is in many ways, simply is not taught explicitly in the Bible."[65]

Prevenient grace is attractive because it solves so many problems, but it should be rejected because it cannot be exegetically vindicated. But if prevenient grace is rejected, then all people are in bondage to sin. They will never turn to God because they are so enslaved by sin that they will never desire to turn to him. How then can any be saved? The Scriptures teach that the effectual calling of God is what persuades those who are chosen to turn to him. God's grace effectively works in the heart of the elect so that they see the beauty and glory of Christ and put their faith in him (2 Cor. 4:6). Because God's choice lies behind our salvation, we cannot boast before him that we were noble or wise enough to choose him. We can only boast in the Lord who chose us to be his own (1 Cor. 1:29, 31).

64. See note 18.
65. Millard J. Erickson, *Christian Theology* (Grand Rapids: Baker, 1985), 925.

17

Reflections on Assurance

D. A. CARSON

Introduction

So far as I know, there has been no English-language, full-scale treatment of the biblical theology of Christian assurance for more than fifty years. There have been numerous dictionary articles and the like, along with occasional discussions in journals. There have also been sophisticated studies of assurance as found in the theology of some notable Christian thinker or period, such as the book by Arthur S. Yates that examines assurance with special reference to John Wesley,[1] or the discussion of assurance that pervades R. T. Kendall's treatment of the move from Calvin to English Calvinism,[2] or the dissertation by Joel R. Beeke that studies personal assurance from Westminster to Alexander Comrie.[3] There have been countless studies of related biblical themes: perseverance, apostasy, the nature of covenant, the nature of faith, justification, and much more—too many to itemize; and there have

From D. A. Carson, "Reflections on Christian Assurance," *WTJ* 54 (1992): 1–29. Reprinted by permission. This chapter includes some minor changes from the original.

1. Arthur S. Yates, *The Doctrine of Assurance with Special Reference to John Wesley* (London: Epworth, 1952).

2. R. T. Kendall, *Calvin and English Calvinism to 1649* (Oxford: Oxford University Press, 1979). Similarly, there is more limited but still important discussion of the theme in Alan C. Clifford, *Atonement and Justification: English Evangelical Theology 1640–1790—An Evaluation* (Oxford: Oxford University Press, 1990).

3. Joel R. Beeke, "Personal Assurance of Faith: English Puritanism and the Dutch 'Nadere Reformatie': From Westminster to Alexander Comrie (1640–1760)" (Ph.D. dissertation, Westminster Theological Seminary, 1988).

been numerous popular treatments of Christian assurance. But although at one time assurance was not only a question of pressing pastoral importance but in certain respects a test of theological systems, in recent decades it has not received the attention it deserves.

This chapter makes no pretensions of redressing the balance. My aim is far more modest. First, I shall identify a number of tendencies in contemporary literature that bear on Christian assurance. Then I shall offer a number of biblical and theological reflections—really not much more than pump-priming—designed to set out the contours in which a biblical theology of Christian assurance might be constructed.

Some Contemporary Tendencies

By "Christian assurance," I refer to a Christian believer's confidence that he or she is already in a right standing with God, and that this will issue in ultimate salvation. This definition of assurance maintains the future orientation that has dominated much of the discussion in past centuries, but there are two entailments: (1) This is a far narrower definition than might have been deployed. For instance, the Epistle to the Hebrews speaks of the boldness Christians enjoy in coming before God, now that their high priest has entered into the heavenly tabernacle to intercede on their behalf. John writes of the confidence believers enjoy when they approach God in prayer. These, too, are dimensions of Christian assurance, important dimensions—but not the assurance that is the focal point of this study. (2) It should be immediately obvious that no single word gives us access to the theme. Some studies have begun by analyzing *pistis* or *parrēsia* or some other word, but questions about Christian assurance rise from the pages of the New Testament wherever believers are promised consummated salvation, or are warned of apostasy, or are assured of eternal life conditional on some factor; and so we must probe, however superficially, a representative number of such themes and passages. Ideally, we should begin with inductive study of each corpus; pragmatically, the limitations of this study dictate that we attempt no more than brief explorations.

Before embarking on such explorations, however, it is important to grasp the dominant parameters of the discussion today. What, then, are some of the more important tendencies in contemporary biblical and theological literature that bear on the subject? I begin with the most narrowly academic tendencies, and work down to the most popular.

Not only is there a tendency to stress the diverse emphases in many biblical texts, but there are even more diverse interpretations of them. Certainly the question of Christian assurance is raised by what appear to be tensions within the biblical documents themselves. On the one hand, Paul insists that all those who are foreknown, predestined, called, and justified will one day be glorified (Rom. 8:30); on the other, he tells the Corinthians to examine themselves to see if they are in the faith (2 Cor. 13:5). Christians are given "very great and precious promises" (2 Pet. 1:4), but such promises properly function to enable them to make their calling and election sure (1:10). If the fourth Gospel repeatedly assures us that Jesus, and then the Father himself, preserve all those the Father has given to the Son (e.g., John 6:37–40; 17:6–17), Jesus' interlocutors nevertheless are told that only those who hold to his teaching are truly his disciples (8:31). On the face of it, passages such as Hebrews 6:4–6 envisage the possibility of apostasy from which there is no reprieve. If so, how can believers be finally certain that they will not fall into such abysmal loss? John writes his first epistle in order that those who believe in the name of the Son of God might know that they have eternal life: this certainly sounds as if it is possible to believe in the name of the Son of God without knowing that one has eternal life.

Many scholars attempt no synthesis; indeed, they judge any attempt at synthesis to be illegitimate. But even among less skeptical scholars, these and many more passages are variously interpreted. One need only read the published form of I. Howard Marshall's dissertation,[4] and the recent dissertation by Judith M. Gundry Volf,[5] to appreciate how differently many of the same texts can be read. Meanwhile, the voluminous writings of E. P. Sanders,[6] and the growing number of responses to them, have shifted the center of discussion on Paul from justification and freedom from law to "covenantal nomism," thereby giving rise to notions of "getting in" and "staying in" that are quite different from those historically assumed by much of Protestantism, especially Lutheran Protestantism. At the risk of simplification, "getting in" turns on God's grace; "staying in" turns on the believer's obedience. The texts that can be lined up to defend this reading of Paul are substantial. If they are accepted without qualification, the implications for Christian assurance are stunning: Christian assurance becomes entirely hostage to Christian obedience, and is not established as a constituent element of saving faith itself.

4. I. Howard Marshall, *Kept by the Power of God: A Study of Perseverance and Falling Away* (Minneapolis: Bethany, 1975). See also his essay, "The Problem of Apostasy in New Testament Theology," now most accessible in his recently published book of essays, *Jesus the Saviour: Studies in New Testament Theology* (London: SPCK, 1990), 306–24.

5. Judith M. Gundry Volf, *Paul and Perseverance: Staying In and Falling Away*, WUNT 37 (Tübingen: J. C. B. Mohr [Paul Siebeck], 1990).

6. Especially *Paul and Palestinian Judaism: A Comparison of Patterns of Religion* (Philadelphia: Fortress, 1977); idem, *Paul, the Law, and the Jewish People* (Philadelphia: Fortress, 1983).

Or again, one need only compare Protestant and Catholic commentaries on 1 John to observe a chasm between their approaches. With but rare exceptions, the former treat 1 John as a treatise that provides criteria or tests (understood and arranged rather differently from commentator to commentator) to foster assurance among believers; the latter largely bypass the theme of assurance and see in this book a depiction of proper Christian communal life.

A major reexamination of relevant Reformation arguments is currently underway. Although some pre-Reformation Christian thinkers had treated the possibility of Christian assurance (e.g., Augustine, Duns Scotus), the consensus in the period leading up to the Reformation treated such assurance as conjectural, since knowledge of God's saving grace depended on good works and penance that "tied forgiveness to ecclesiastical authority."[7] Not only did the Reformation, by emphasizing Scripture, reduce the intermediary authority of the church, and therefore its role in binding and loosing the Christian conscience—its virulent emphasis on *sola fide* led Luther to see assurance as an element of saving faith. If one truly trusts Christ for the forgiveness of sins and full justification, so far also is one assured of his forgiveness. The same connection can be found in Calvin (*Institutes* 3.2.7); ultimately, he grounds assurance on Christ himself (*Institutes* 3.24.5). It is disputed just what place Calvin allows for works in Christian assurance; certainly in his thought they do not enjoy more than a subsidiary role. By contrast, the English Puritans, greatly dependent on the transitional figure of William Perkins,[8] himself deeply indebted to Beza and others, placed much more emphasis on the role of a transformed life in lending assurance to the Christian mind and conscience.[9]

Most scholars would not demur from this potted history. Debate has become heated, however, owing to the work of Kendall and those who have rushed to support him or to detract from his argument that English Calvinism owes far less to Calvin and far more to Beza than is commonly recognized, and to the work of M. Charles Bell, who argues that

---

7. R. W. A. Letham, "Assurance," in *New Dictionary of Theology*, ed. Sinclair B. Ferguson et al. (Leicester: InterVarsity, 1988), 51.

8. Cf. especially Ian Breward, ed., *The Work of William Perkins* (Abingdon: Marcham, 1970).

9. Despite the best efforts of R. M. Hawkes ("The Logic of Assurance in English Puritan Theology," *WTJ* 52 [1990]: 247–61) to minimize the conceptual distance between the magisterial reformers and the English Puritans on the matter of assurance, his own evidence admits more of a distance than he acknowledges. For instance, he argues that for Thomas Brooks "assurance is, somehow, a necessary part of faith" (250). The authenticating citation from Brooks reads, "Faith, in time, will of its own accord raise and advance itself to assurance" (*Heaven on Earth* [1654; reprint, London: Banner of Truth, 1961], 21). But that is simply another way of saying that *mature* ("in time") faith brings with it assurance. The issue is whether saving faith entails assurance in all who at any time are exercising such faith.

whereas Calvin taught that faith is fundamentally passive in nature, is centred in the mind or understanding, is primarily to be viewed in terms of certain knowledge, such that assurance of salvation is of the essence of faith, and is grounded *extra nos,* that is, outside ourselves in the person and work of Jesus Christ, Scottish theology, on the other hand, gradually came to teach that faith is primarily active, centred within the will or heart, and that assurance is *not* of the essence of faith, but is a fruit of faith, and is to be gathered through self-examination and syllogistic deduction, thereby placing the grounds of assurance *intra nos,* within ourselves.[10]

For Kendall, the challenge is not merely one of naming the right heroes, but of returning to the pristine Calvinism of Calvin, over against what he judges to be the scholastic Calvinism of many of his successors. There are important (and disputed) entailments in Kendall's study for the doctrine of definite atonement—and for understanding Christian assurance. Positions are sufficiently entrenched, and the topic sufficiently current, that in the second volume of the biography of Martyn Lloyd-Jones, Iain Murray devotes six pages to refuting Kendall.[11] Murray concludes that if Kendall is right and "full assurance" inheres in saving faith, there are "devastating practical consequences":

> If it were true then it would follow: (1) that anyone lacking "full assurance" has to be treated as not being a Christian at all; (2) that all converts can be told that their assurance is complete, contrary to the New Testament directions to converts to press on to fuller assurance (Hebrews 6:11; 2 Peter 1:5–10; 1 John 1:4); and (3) that if faith means full assurance then the many warnings of Scripture on the need to observe that true faith is always accompanied by holiness of life become needless.[12]

Of course, Kendall might well reply that Murray makes assurance dependent not on justification but on sanctification (understanding the latter term in its use in Reformed dogmatics, not in its more flexible use in the Pauline corpus), and ultimately fosters an unhealthy introspection that functions not unlike Arminianism or semi-Pelagianism. For his part, Beeke[13] argues that the differences between Calvin and the (later) Calvinists on the relations between faith and assurance are largely quantitative, not qualitative. Faced with changing pastoral contexts, Beeke argues, Calvinists allotted greater sensitivity to the degree of assurance that a Christian might experience, but nevertheless in their "meticulous argumentation" adhered to the fundamen-

---

10. M. Charles Bell, *Calvin and Scottish Theology: The Doctrine of Assurance* (Edinburgh: Handsel, 1985), 8.
11. Iain H. Murray, *D. Martyn Lloyd-Jones,* vol. 2, *The Fight of Faith: 1939–1981* (Edinburgh: Banner of Truth, 1990), 721–26.
12. Ibid., 726.
13. "Personal Assurance of Faith."

tal principles of the early Reformation. Within this framework they could argue that assurance of faith has more complex grounds than a simple resting on God's objective promises. On the whole, Beeke is correct for the notable figures he treats. Unfortunately, he writes history as if the "Annales" school of historiography had never developed, and makes no attempt either to limit his conclusions to those he studies or to probe how faith and assurance were handled in the lives of ordinary Christians in both English Puritanism and the Calvinist infiltration of the Dutch Reformation.

Certainly both sides of this essentially historical debate have full arsenals by which to take on the other's positions. For our purposes, however, it is worth observing that both sides recognize that the debate is not merely a historical one—What did Calvin (or Beza, or Perkins, or Comrie) actually teach?—but a doctrinal one with substantial theological and pastoral implications. We may range from the experience of many Scottish highlanders who habitually refuse to receive the communion elements on the ground that they lack personal assurance (and this lack stems from their own estimate of unsatisfactory evidences of grace in their lives), to the wretched "easy believism" of many in the western world who, having professed faith, feel no pull toward holiness and no shame when they take the elements. A thousand variations of experience dot the landscape between these two extremes.

In America, the basis of Christian assurance has erupted as the distinguishing banner of a small but vociferous segment of evangelicalism. The movement is strong enough to have formed its own organization, the Grace Evangelical Society, complete with its own journal.[14] All of the publications that have emerged so far are at the popular or semipopular level; but that ensures wider circulation, not less. Doubtless the most influential of these writings is a book by Zane Hodges, *The Gospel under Siege.*[15] The popular preacher John F. MacArthur Jr. has responded at about the same level,[16] but with so large a number of unguarded statements or overstatements that his work has spawned more controversy than healing.[17]

The concern of Hodges and his colleagues is to make Christian assurance absolutely certain. To accomplish this, they tie assurance exclusively to saving faith and divorce it from any support in a transformed life. The countless passages that tie genuine discipleship to obedience are handled by making a

14. *Journal of the Grace Evangelical Society.*
15. Zane C. Hodges, *The Gospel under Siege: A Study on Faith and Works* (Dallas: Redencion Viva, 1981). See also his *Grace in Eclipse* (Dallas: Redencion Viva, 1985), and his *Absolutely Free* (Dallas: Redencion Viva; Grand Rapids: Zondervan, 1989).
16. John F. MacArthur Jr., *The Gospel according to Jesus* (Grand Rapids: Zondervan, 1988).
17. One of the better reviews is by Darrell F. Bock, "A Review of *The Gospel according to Jesus,*" *BibSac* 141 (1989): 21–40.

disjunction between "discipleship" passages and those that promise eternal life. Eternal life turns on faith in the saving Son of God; discipleship turns on obedience; and Christian assurance is tied only to the former. To link assurance in any way to the latter, it is argued, is to corrupt a salvation of free grace and turn it into a salvation partly dependent on works. If my salvation depends only on free grace, then the basis of my assurance is as steadfast as the freedom of that grace. But if my assurance depends on observing certain changes in conduct in my life, themselves the fruit of obedience, then implicitly I am saying that, since I cannot be assured of salvation without seeing obedience, salvation itself depends on some mixture of faith plus obedience—and free grace is thereby destroyed. Hence the name of this new evangelical society. Its members are persuaded that the purity of the gospel of grace is at stake.

There are numerous entailments to this analysis. Those who disagree with them are dismissed as supporters of "lordship salvation," understood to mean that these opponents insist that part of the requirement for becoming a Christian, for receiving salvation, is the confession of Jesus as Lord. In the view of Hodges and his colleagues, trusting Jesus as Savior is all that is required for salvation. "Repentance," in their view, must be understood in a narrowly etymological sense: it is the mental "change of mind" that accepts Jesus as the Savior, but entails no necessary sorrow over sin or turning away from it. That is the fruit of confessing Jesus as Lord; it is the fruit of obedience, and properly emerges from the confidence of knowing that one's sins are already forgiven. In some of the writings of this camp, this analysis is justified by referring to 1 Corinthians 3 and Paul's division of the race into the natural man, the carnal man, and the spiritual man. The natural man is unredeemed; the carnal man enjoys salvation, but lives like the world, and is finally saved "only as one escaping through the flames" (3:15), while his works are burned up. The spiritual man knows Jesus as Lord and is walking in growing obedience.

Hodges would feel offended to have his view branded as "easy believism" or "cheap grace" or "greasy grace" or the like. He insists that Christians who do not constantly commit themselves to obedience pay high prices for their rebellion. But the price, he says, is never loss of salvation, nor (assuming the initial trust was genuine) a post facto discovery that the initial trust was not genuine, for that would tie assurance, and therefore salvation itself, to works.

Apart from these movements, there is a tendency to say very little about Christian assurance in most of our churches. Indeed, one might reasonably argue that a major reason why so many aberrant views are being so widely circulated is that there is a vacuum that cries out to be filled. I have not conducted a scientific poll to establish changing patterns over the last few decades. My impression, however, is that in many churches Christian assurance is not a major topic for sermons or discussion groups, largely because popular eschatology has become so realized that there is very little futurist element left, except at the merely creedal level. If we do not long for the consummation of our salvation in the new heaven and the new earth, for the *visio Dei* that is the believer's inheritance, then there is little point in talking about our assurance of gaining it.

In what follows, I shall sometimes engage one or more of these tendencies directly; but my principal aim is to offer some biblical and theological observations that may help us to cut a swath through the debates and refocus them a little. For instance, whatever the rights and wrongs of the historical arguments over the influence of Calvin, it is arguable that some of the lines of the debate are seriously askew because they too quickly press toward atemporal *dogmatic* questions without pausing adequately to reflect on *redemptive-historical* matters lodged in Scripture itself. I shall also argue that one major biblical-theological motif has largely been overlooked in these debates, a motif that has the potential for orienting the discussions, both academic and popular, in fresh directions.

Biblical and Theological Reflections

The New Testament writers admit no qualitative, absolute disjunction between genuine believers who display obedience to Jesus in their lives, and genuine believers who do not. Limitations of time and space require that I restrict my comments to one passage and one theme.

1 Corinthians 3. All of 1 Corinthians 1:10–4:20 is devoted to Paul's handling of the divisiveness of the Corinthians (see esp. 1:10–11; 3:5–6, 21–23; 4:6ff.), itself tied to their conviction that they are preeminently wise and spiritual (see 1:18ff.; 2:6ff.; 3:18ff.). Meanwhile, their thinking and their conduct are so spiritually immature—they are "mere infants in Christ" (3:1)—that Paul could not address them as "spiritual" *(pneumatikos),* as they thought themselves to be, but as "worldly." This last word is perhaps better rendered more literally as "fleshly" *(sarkinos),* that is, made of flesh. The charge has extra bite, since the Corinthians think themselves so "spiritual" that they are not even sure there is a resurrection body still to be gained (1 Cor. 15). They were certainly "fleshly," "made of flesh," when Paul was among them (v. 1); the tragedy is that they are still "fleshly" (v. 3): here Paul changes to *(sarkikos)* (in the best reading), that is, having the characteristics of flesh, clearly with ethical overtones.[18] They are "acting like mere men"

---

18. So, rightly, Gordon D. Fee, *The First Epistle to the Corinthians,* NICNT (Grand Rapids: Eerdmans, 1987), 123–24.

(*anthrōpoi*, v. 3). The evidence for this is found in their "jealousy and quarreling," in their determination to lionize this or that human leader.

The crucial question, then, is whether Paul is introducing a new ontological level of Christian existence. He does not place the Corinthians among all whom he dismisses as *psychikoi* (2:14), those who are "natural" and therefore without the Spirit. Not only has he already noted their spiritual endowments (1:4–9), but Paul elsewhere repeatedly insists that one cannot be utterly devoid of the Spirit and be a Christian (Rom. 8:9; Gal. 3:2–3; Tit. 3:5–7). Yet by saying that the Corinthians are acting and thinking not like "spiritual" but "fleshly" people, like "mere men," he is charging them with the thoughts and conduct of those who do not have the Spirit. The tension is palpable, and the result is centuries of debate and misunderstanding. But the most obvious way to take Paul's words is that he is using strong language to force his readers to face up to the inherent inconsistency of their position. They have the Spirit, but at this junction they are neither thinking nor acting as if they do.

This is a more believable approach than those that suppose Paul himself is introducing an ontological distinction in the congregation. That is surely intrinsically unlikely, given the concern of the first four chapters to establish unity. Others try to find a shift in meaning in *pneumatikos* (spiritual) from chapter 2 to chapter 3,[19] or base a massive tripartite division of humankind (natural/carnal [KJV]/spiritual) on these verses. But apart from the fact that the same division cannot be found clearly drawn out elsewhere in Paul, such a reading flies in the face of one of the principal emphases in Pauline ethics, namely, the appeal "to be what you are."

Thus, when Paul says that he could not address the Corinthians as "spiritual," there is a sense in which he is admitting that there are "unspiritual" believers. He does not mean the Corinthian believers do not have the Spirit—there are no "unspiritual" believers in that sense—but that they are displaying a great deal of "unspiritual" behavior, which must stop.

Three observations must be entered. (1) If this is a fair reading of the passage, nothing here introduces an absolute, qualitative disjunction between those who are "fleshly" ("carnal" if you prefer) and those who are spiritual. All apart from perfectionists will admit that at the level of behavior, all Christians, insofar as they too participate in jealousy and quarreling, are sometimes "carnal." There is no attempt to tie the distinctions here to a theoretical disjunction between those who accept Jesus as Savior and those who accept him as Lord. (2) The sins in view are not of the sort that make us think the Corinthians are distancing themselves from their baptismal vows. This is not the case of someone who made a profession of faith at an evangelistic rally, followed

19. E.g., P. J. Du Plessis, ΤΕΛΕΙΟΣ: *The Idea of Perfection in the New Testament* (Kampen: Kok, 1959), 183–85.

391

D. A. Carson

the way of Christ for a few months, and then lived in a manner indistinguishable from that of any pagan for the next fifteen years, despite conscientious pastoral interest. Nor is it the case of a person who indulges in gross sexual immorality and who will not repent, like the man described in 1 Corinthians 5, of whose spiritual state not even the apostle seems to be sure, let alone confident. This is not to minimize the sins of jealousy and quarreling; it is to place them within the context of Christians who at many levels do display the presence and power of the Spirit (1:3–8), even though in this regard they are thinking and acting in ways that are out of step with the Spirit. (3) Above all, there is nothing in this chapter to connect these "carnal" Christians to the person described in verses 14–15. To justify this point, we must press on to the contribution of the next two paragraphs in the text.

Because the Corinthians' carnality is displayed in their propensity to form parties attached to particular leaders, Paul finds it necessary to explain the limited contribution such leaders have made. He develops two extended metaphors. The first is agricultural (3:5–9): Paul planted the seed, Apollos watered it, but God alone made it grow. Both the sower and the one who waters the seed have one purpose. Each "will be rewarded according to his own labor" (3:8). In this metaphor, the Corinthians do not figure as laborers. Paul and Apollos are "God's fellow workers"; the Corinthians are "God's field" (v. 9).

Then the metaphor changes, but with the same distinctions firmly in place. The Corinthians are "God's building" (v. 9); Paul is the contractor who has laid the foundation, Jesus Christ himself, with others building on the foundation that he laid. Within the constraints of this metaphor, it is the *builder* whose work will be shown up for what it is on the last day; the fire will test the quality of each *builder's* work.[20] "If what he has *built* survives, he will receive his reward. If it is burned up, he will suffer loss; he himself will be saved, but only as one escaping through the flames" (3:14–15). It is slightly misfocused to conclude, with Hans Conzelmann and many other commentators, that "unsatisfactory works performed by the Christian *as a Christian* do not cause his damnation."[21] Doubtless there is some sense in which that is true, but Paul's concern in this context is not to make application to the ordinary Christian, and certainly not to those whom he thinks are still "mere infants" (3:1), but to raise a standard that holds Christian leaders to account. In short, we are not here dealing with perennial backsliding or utter moral indifference, but shoddy workmanship among those who are accounted the leaders of the Christian church.

20. We need not decide here if this "work" is the Christian church, or professing Christians, or some abstraction of the builder's labor. That question is important in its own right, but irrelevant to our present concerns.
21. Hans Conzelmann, *1 Corinthians*, Hermeneia (Philadelphia: Fortress, 1975), 77.

Only in verses 16–17 is there a hint of a broader application, and it is no more than a hint. Maintaining the metaphor drawn from the building industry, Paul specifies that the Corinthians are not merely a building, but God's temple, his dwelling. If "anyone destroys God's temple, God will destroy him; for God's temple is sacred, and you are that temple." It is possible to read these verses as nothing more than a forceful reiteration of the lesson drawn in verses 10–15. Nevertheless, because Paul now speaks of "anyone" and not simply the builders, it suggests, in the context of the first four chapters, that those given to division, jealousy, and quarreling in the church are also in danger of doing damage to the church, God's temple. Since they are that temple, they are simultaneously doing damage to themselves and courting God's judgment.

It appears, then, that in this chapter Paul acknowledges that Christians do not always live up to what they are called to be, that every such failure is a serious breech, that those who do damage to the church are particularly threatened by God's judgment, and that some who are viewed as leaders in the church, although they will themselves be saved on the day of judgment, will have nothing to show for their labor. It does not encourage us to think that it is possible to accept Jesus as Savior, and thus be promoted from the "natural" to the "carnal" level, in transit, as it were, to the "spiritual" stage, at which point one has accepted Jesus as Lord. Still less does it encourage us to think of the "carnal" Christian as someone who once made a profession of faith and who now lives in every respect like the surrounding pagan world.

The new covenant. New covenant language is fairly pervasive in the New Testament, its themes far more so. Both Luke (Luke 22:20) and Paul (1 Cor. 11:25) report that Jesus, on the night he was betrayed, took such language on his own lips and tied the theme to his impending death. If Matthew and Mark omit "new," the implication is present anyway, since it is difficult to discover any sense in which Jesus' impending death signaled or ratified the old covenant. Hebrews 8 and 10 specifically tie the prophecy of Jeremiah 31:31–34 to the substance of Christian faith; 2 Corinthians 3 and Galatians 4 are no less insistent on setting forth the significance of the (new) covenant. Beyond such explicit language lies a large array of New Testament themes that presuppose the Old Testament promises of the new covenant (e.g., Jer. 31:29ff.; 32:36–41; Ezek. 36:25–27; Mal. 3:1), not least the "new birth" language of John 3.[22]

The point to be observed is that these Old Testament promises foresee a time when God's law is written on the heart of his people. Teachers will no longer say, "Know the Lord," for they will all know him (Jer. 31): the outlook is not of a time when there will be no teachers, but no *mediating* teach-

---

22. See D. A. Carson, *The Gospel according to John* (Grand Rapids: Eerdmans, 1991), 185–203.

ers, no *mediators*, whose very office ensures them that they have an endowment not enjoyed by others. The new covenant will not be like the tribal covenant associated with Moses' name, when the fathers ate sour grapes and their children's teeth were set on edge. Rather, it is characterized by the removal of the heart of stone among all of God's covenantal people.[23] To use the language of Ezekiel 36, the new covenant will be characterized by cleansing (sprinkling with water) and spiritual renewal (a new heart and a new spirit).

Add to this the many Old Testament passages that anticipate the time when God's Spirit is poured out on his people (e.g., Isa. 44:3–5; Ezek. 11:19–20; 36:25–27; Joel 2:28–32), along with the fulfillment of these passages in the New Testament, and another important part of what is characteristic of the new covenant age is dropped into place. The Spirit is bequeathed by the glorified Christ (John's Gospel), the Spirit is given as the *arrabōn* of the ultimate inheritance (Paul), the Spirit vivifies, empowers, and directs the church (Acts). The period between Pentecost and Christ's return is supremely the age of the Spirit, the powerful Spirit who renews, convicts, cleanses, empowers. Doubtless we "groan inwardly as we wait eagerly for our adoption as sons, the redemption of our bodies" (Rom. 8:23), but meanwhile God has sent his own Son in the likeness of sinful man, "in order that the righteous requirements of the law might be fully met in us, who do not live according to the sinful nature but according to the Spirit" (Rom. 8:4).

It appears that a great deal of the debate over assurance has been controlled by forensic categories associated with justification and faith, but has largely ignored the categories of power and transformation associated with the Spirit and new covenant. A fundamental component of such themes is that the people of the new covenant are *by definition* granted a new heart and empowered by the Spirit to walk in holiness, to love righteousness, to prove pleasing to the Lord. This means that, insofar as the writers of the New Testament thought of themselves as new covenant heirs, they could not think of themselves as other than Spirit-endowed, regenerate, transformed. The New Testament does not preserve the old covenant distinction between the locus of the covenant community and the locus of the remnant, or between the locus of the covenant community and the locus of the leaders on whom special endowment had fallen. It is of the essence of the new covenant that those who are in it have been given a new heart, have been cleansed, have received the Holy Spirit. Moreover, this theme cannot rightly be divorced from the entailments of justification and of salvation through faith. The gift of the Spirit is tied to justification (Rom. 5–8); salvation by grace through faith (Eph.

___
23. Thus the explicit eschatological focus of Jeremiah's use of the "sour grapes" proverb makes it function rather differently from the formal parallel in Ezekiel 18:2. Cf. Robert P. Carroll, *Jeremiah: A Commentary* (Philadelphia: Westminster, 1986), 608–9.

2:8), "not by works so that no one can boast" (Eph. 2:9), is tied to the fact that we are "God's workmanship, created in Christ Jesus to do good works, which God prepared in advance for us to do" (Eph. 2:10).

One must not conclude from this line of reasoning that new covenant believers are anywhere promised moral and spiritual perfection this side of the new heaven and the new earth. Nevertheless, both the Old Testament prophecies regarding the new covenant and the age of the Spirit, and the New Testament claims regarding their fulfillment, lead us to expect transformed lives. Indeed, it is precisely this unequivocal expectation that authorizes Paul to set up the tension we have already noted: the exhortations to live up to what we are in Christ are predicated on the assumption that what we are in Christ *necessarily* brings transformation, so that moral failure is *theologically* shocking, however pragmatically realistic it may be. Indeed, it might be argued that this accounts for some of the tension in 1 John. The setting that calls forth that epistle I shall briefly discuss a little farther on. For the moment, it is worth recalling John's insistence that believers do sin, and people who claim they do not are liars, self-deluded, and guilty of charging God with falsehood (1 John 1:6–10). At the same time, he repeatedly insists that sinning is not done among Christians. Various explanations have been advanced, but the most obvious is still the best: although both our experience and our location between the "already" and the "not yet" teach us that we do sin and we will sin, yet every single instance of sin is shocking, inexcusable, forbidden, appalling, out of line with what we are as Christians.[24]

It would take too much space to treat all the passages that are adduced to justify the counterclaim, or to demonstrate the methodological flaws inherent in Hodges' treatment of repentance. But even on the basis of the brief probings here, especially into the nature of the new covenant, it appears justified to claim that the New Testament writers nowhere admit an absolute, qualitative disjunction between genuine believers who in their conduct display obedience to the Lord Jesus and genuine believers who do not. This at least raises the possibility that some forms of Christian assurance might be validly based on observably transformed conduct, without in any way suggesting that such conduct wins or earns or gains salvation. How that might be related to other themes—the grounding of Christian assurance in the object of faith, Jesus Christ himself—is still to be explored. But ignoring the covenantal aspects of Christianity in favor of narrowly forensic categories has been one of the chief reasons for confusion in this area.

24. On Paul's view of some of the tensions experienced by Christians living under the aegis of the kingdom while still living in the old creation, see David Wenham, "The Christian Life: A Life of Tension? A Consideration of the Nature of Christian Experience in Paul," in *Pauline Studies: Essays Presented to Professor F. F. Bruce on His Seventieth Birthday*, ed. Donald A. Hagner and Murray J. Harris (Exeter: Paternoster, 1980), 80–94.

Several New Testament writers recognize the existence of spurious or transitory faith, and this recognition must be factored into any responsible doctrine of Christian assurance. This subject is exceedingly complex, for it is tied to the nature of apostasy and to protracted debates over the security of the believer in the New Testament. For the sake of clarity, I shall proceed in seven steps.

1. Discussion of a figure like Judas Iscariot is extremely problematic. Frequently comparisons and contrasts are drawn between his "defection" and that of Peter (I use "defection" in an attempt to find a word that can reasonably refer to the actions of both men). But quite apart from the intrinsic value of the exercise, it is doubtful if the apostasy of Judas is to be construed as apostasy from full-blown Christian faith. To put the matter another way, the experiences of "coming to faith" of men and women in the four Gospels is in certain respects unique, unrepeatable in any generation after the resurrection and Pentecost. Their coming to faith required the lapse of time until the One they came to confess as Messiah was crucified and rose again. Doubtless they struggled with doubts and sins and selfishness, and therefore in certain respects they may serve as paradigms for our own spiritual pilgrimages. Nevertheless, none of us today, in our own coming to faith, had to wait for the next major redemptive-historical appointment, the death and resurrection of God's Son, before our fledgling faith could become fully Christian. Nor did we have to tarry in Jerusalem until the day of Pentecost had come.[25] But if the first disciples' coming to faith was not exactly like ours, then Judas Iscariot's apostasy from whatever level he had attained before the crucifixion was not exactly like apostasy in Hebrews 6 or 10. This is not to minimize his sin in the slightest; it is to argue that no substantial view of what apostasy might mean under the new covenant can begin with Iscariot, still less with, say, Korah.

2. Little help on the nature of apostasy is to be gained by simple word studies. The word *apostasia,* for instance, occurs only twice in the New Testament, once to refer to turning away from Moses on the part of Jews (Acts 21:21), the other to refer to the great rebellion that takes place when the man of lawlessness is revealed (2 Thess. 2:3).

We may perhaps adopt a working definition of "apostasy," independent of any Greek word, along such lines as these: it is the decisive turning away from a religious position and stance once firmly held. It differs from ordinary unbelief in that it involves turning away from a position of belief; it differs from backsliding in that it is calculated, decisive, and irrevocable; it differs from merely changing one's mind over some relatively minor theological point in that it involves the rejection of an entire position and stance.

---

25. Incidentally, this is one of the reasons why studies that seek to use the Gospels as first and foremost guides to the nature of Christian discipleship, on the basis of the first followers' experiences and reactions, are deeply flawed.

3. It is disputed how many passages in the New Testament describe or refer to such apostasy. Was Demas an apostate (2 Tim. 4:10)? Did the immoral man of 1 Corinthians 5 die an apostate? But however many or few, some passages cannot easily be circumvented. It must be strenuously insisted that attempts to reduce the shock and power of severe warnings like those in Hebrews 6:4–6 and 2 Corinthians 13:5, by arguing that the warnings are merely hypothetical, or that the turning aside of those described in Hebrews 6:4–6 and 1 John 2:19 is from useful service but not from salvation, are desperate expedients that responsible exegesis will happily avoid.

4. The real question is whether, with Marshall[26] and others who follow him, we shall say that in these instances genuine believers have fallen away, or that although they were believers in some sense they were not genuine believers at all. There are genuine difficulties both ways.

One of the most competent treatments of some of the issues is the study by Volf, which examines the theme of perseverance in the seven Pauline Epistles over which there is least dispute as to their authenticity.[27] In the first section, she describes what it is like to "stay in." "A continuity in the divine work of salvation emerges in which a particular aspect of salvation is seen to imply the succeeding ones."[28] Paul repeatedly draws attention to the "eternal divine initiatives in salvation: divine election, foreknowledge and predestination"[29] (Rom. 8:23, 29–30; 2 Cor. 1:22; 5:5; Phil. 1:6; 1 Thess. 5:9; 2 Thess. 2:13–14). On the other hand, for Paul "the process of consummating the work of salvation is more like an obstacle course than a downhill ride to the finishline"[30] (Rom. 5:1–11; 8:28, 31–39; 1 Cor. 1:8–9; 10:13; 1 Thess. 5:23–24; 2 Thess. 3:3). God's faithfulness is manifested in strengthening and protecting and preserving his people.

> Paul gives clear and ample evidence of his view that Christians' salvation is certain to reach completion. This thought is integral to his understanding of individual salvation. Though threats to the consummation of Christians' salvation may and will appear, they cannot successfully challenge it. God's faithfulness and love make divine triumph the unquestionable outcome. For Paul, certainty of final salvation rests on God's continued intervention to that end.[31]

In the second section of her book, Volf examines an array of passages (Rom. 14:1–23; 1 Cor. 5:1–5; 6:9–11; 8:7–13; 10:12; 11:27–34; Gal. 5:9–11) to argue that for Paul "continuity in salvation does not make Christian

---

26. *Kept by the Power of God;* "The Problem of Apostasy."
27. *Paul and Perseverance.*
28. Ibid., 80.
29. Ibid.
30. Ibid., 81.
31. Ibid., 82.

conduct irrelevant."[32] Against Sanders, Volf argues that although morality and integrity and obedience matter enormously to Paul, and although Paul envisages punishment falling on some believers who disobey, "Paul does not make Christians' final salvation dependent on their
repentance from post-conversion sins."[33] Then she makes one of the few
false steps in her book: she argues that it is possible to lose one's mem-
bership in the "in-group" by "falsifying one's Christian profession by
one's behavior. . . . But when this happens, continuity in actual salvation
is not interrupted."[34] In other words, at this point she agrees with Sanders that staying in the "in-group" is conditional on good behavior, but
she qualifies Sanders by arguing that this is not the same as remaining in
salvation. Her exegesis is to be questioned at a number of points, and
she has not adequately come to grips with the significance of what belonging to the new covenant community entails; for as we have seen, the
nature of the new covenant drives us to the conclusion that there is a certain sense in which *extra ecclesiam nulla salus.*

In part 3, Volf examines Romans 9–11, 2 Corinthians 13:5; and Galatians
5:1–4 in order to discover what unbelief signifies among those who profess
to be Christians. In 2 Corinthians 13:5, for instance, she argues that Paul
cannot be warning against loss of salvation, since the context "shows that
ἀδόκιμος can only mean rejection as a nonconvert, and that the exhortation
to self-testing has the main purpose of pointing out Paul's own provenness
as an apostle and possibly the subordinate purpose of exposing some Corinthians to be falsely professing Christians."[35] She holds that the election of Israel does not entail automatic participation in salvation *"apart from faith in
Christ."*[36] She might have done a little more work on the diverse ways Paul
thinks of "election"; but that is perhaps a picky point. In her final section,
Volf examines Paul's reflections on the final outcome of his own apostolic
mission (1 Cor. 9:23–27; 15:2; 2 Cor. 6:1; Gal. 2:2; 4:11; 1 Thess. 3:5; Phil.
2:16). If he fears that his labor might prove to be "in vain" (Phil. 2:16;
1 Thess. 3:5; Gal. 2:2; 4:11), it can only be because he fears that some of "his
seeming converts would have no salvation. Whether failure in the eschatological test should be traced to his converts' false profession or their apostasy
from salvation is a question not answered by Paul in these texts."[37] But Volf
notes that Paul, while distrusting his own success, seems to give way to confidence "when he views the situation from the perspective of God's faithful-

---

32. Ibid., 155.
33. Ibid., 157.
34. Ibid.
35. Ibid., 226.
36. Ibid.
37. Ibid., 282.

ness to professing Christians in whom he sees the divine work of salvation taking place."[38] I shall argue that this is an extremely important observation.

5. Apart from points of exegetical detail, the methodological difference between those who hold that genuine believers fall away and those who hold that those who fall away are not genuine believers seems to turn on two issues.

How strong are the passages that seem to affirm the ultimate preservation and perseverance of God's people? This is something that Marshall, for instance, does not directly address. He fairly expounds some of the passages that affirm that God's people continue in salvation to the end, but then diminishes their weight by setting over against them those passages that emphasize human responsibility to persevere, or those passages that refer to apostasy (however defined). The resulting formulation always makes the preservation of God's people unto consummated salvation absolutely contingent: God is the one who faithfully preserves his people, provided they do not defect. But what warrants such diminution of the apparent weight of the perseverance passages?

For example, John refers to the elect as all that the Father gives Jesus (John 6:37a), and by a litotes insists that Jesus will keep in or preserve all of these people (i.e., he will not drive them away, 6:37b),[39] on the ground that the Son came to do his Father's will, which is none other than that he should preserve all those whom the Father has given him (6:38–40). It is exceedingly difficult to diminish the finality of this statement without implying that Jesus proves unwilling to preserve or incapable of preserving all those the Father has given him. Most Christians would be aghast to use texts that affirm or assume Jesus' humanity to diminish those that affirm his deity, and vice versa. We have come to accept some mystery in our christological formulations; we seek interpretations that allow complementary texts to have their full vigor without permitting diminution of their most obvious meaning by some form of mutual annihilation. Can a case be mounted that in this area, too, there is a definable mystery that should not be allowed to be diminished by such mutual annihilation? I shall shortly argue that there is. But meanwhile, it seems that the strong New Testament emphases on the security of the believer should not be qualified by mere subtraction, unless there is the strongest exegetical warrant for doing so.

More positively, is there warrant for thinking the New Testament writers have categories for transitory faith, spurious faith—in short, for faith that seems like saving faith, but which proves to be spurious? If there is, then the

---

38. Ibid.

39. The litotes cannot possibly mean that Jesus will welcome in those who come to him. In context it must mean that he will keep in those who have been given to him. See Carson, *John*, 290.

passages that speak of falling away do not force us to conclude that the defection is from *genuine* faith.

In fact, in every major New Testament corpus, there are numerous warnings against or descriptions of spurious faith. For instance, in Matthew Jesus envisages that some who have addressed him as "Lord, Lord," and who have prophesied in his name and driven out demons in his name and performed many miracles in his name, will be excluded from the kingdom of heaven: "I will tell them plainly, 'I never knew you. Away from me, you evildoers!'" (Matt. 7:21–23). The one who enters the kingdom is "he who does the will of my Father who is in heaven" (7:21). John (2:23–25) testifies that when Jesus attended the first Passover feast of his ministry, "many people saw the miraculous signs he was doing and believed in his name,"[40] but Jesus would not entrust himself to them: he knew what was in their heart. A little later (John 8:31), to "the Jews who had believed him,"[41] Jesus gives a criterion that establishes who are genuine disciples: "If you hold to my teaching, you are really my disciples." The same stance is reflected in 1 John 2:19. Those who have seceded from the church are described in telling terms: "They went out from us, but they did not really belong to us. For if they had belonged to us, they would have remained with us; but their going showed that none of them belonged to us." In other words, genuine faith, by definition, perseveres; where there is no perseverance, by definition the faith cannot be genuine. Again, "anyone who runs ahead and does not continue in the teaching of Christ does not have God; whoever continues in the teaching has both the Father and the Son" (2 John 9). Paul says as much: he informs the Colossians that God has reconciled them by Christ's physical body through death, to present them holy in his sight, without blemish and free from accusation— "if," he writes, "you continue in your faith, established and firm, not moved from the hope held out in the gospel" (Col. 1:22-23). In short, genuine faith is tied to perseverance; transitory faith is spurious. We find similar emphases in 2 Peter 1:10–11. Before we come across the "apostasy" passages in the Epistle to the Hebrews, we read (in Heb. 3:14), "We have come to share in Christ if we hold firmly till the end the confidence we had at first" (see also 3:6; 4:14; 6:11; etc.).

40. It is important to recognize that the expression here is *pisteuō eis* plus the accusative, thereby providing a critical counterexample to those who think this expression always signals saving faith in the Fourth Gospel, while *pisteuō* plus the dative denotes unreliable faith. In reality, the small variation in form is typical of the Fourth Evangelist, who is well known for his slight variations without clear-cut semantic distinction.

41. Because the expression in 8:31 is *pisteuō* plus the dative, while in 8:30 *pisteuō eis* plus the accusative lies behind "those who put their faith in him," some have argued that the Jews in 8:31 constitute a separate group with distinguishably inferior faith. This is wholly unlikely; see note 40.

The range and diversity of these sorts of passages (I have cited only a small percentage of them) utterly preclude the possibility that they all refer to persevering in discipleship that goes beyond "mere" salvation. Whereas a few of these passages, taken alone, might suggest that continuing in salvation to the end depends absolutely on our own efforts at perseverance, responsible biblical theology must seek to integrate them with the promises of God's preserving initiative, not less rich in each major New Testament corpus, and with the passages in this list that make perseverance a criterion of genuine faith. For example, those who had seceded had once belonged to the church (1 John 2:19); otherwise John could not say that "they went out from us."[42] To all observers, for all practical purposes, the seceders were once baptized members of the church, fully accepted as Christians. Nevertheless, John insists, they were never really "of us," for if they had been "they would have remained with us." In other words, John presupposes that spurious faith is possible, but that genuine faith, by definition, perseveres.

In short, the methodological point of division between the two principal interpretations—the one that argues genuine believers can fall away, and the one that argues that those who fall away are necessarily spurious or transitory believers—turns on the two issues I have just defined.

6. If the tack I have taken is largely correct, the doctrinal area where we must become a little more sophisticated is in the theology of conversion. The question could be put several ways, but perhaps this will do: Is there New Testament warrant for thinking that there is some third alternative to being clearly "in" or "out"? To simplify the discussion, let us grant that God knows precisely who is "in" or "out." The question then becomes, Is there New Testament warrant for thinking that, as far as Christian observers are concerned, some people are not clearly either "in" or "out," that the step of conversion is not always luminously clear?

Implicitly, of course, we have already answered this question by listing a few of the New Testament passages where apparent conversions proved spurious (e.g., 1 John 2:19), or where the genuineness of the profession is irrefragably tied to perseverance (thereby implying that transitory faith is under a cloud). The parable of the sower—or, better, of the soils (Mark 4 par.)—illustrates the same point. In addition to the receptive soil that enables the seed to produce fruit in varying measure, there are three other kinds. The hard pathway stops the seed from embedding itself in dirt, and the birds of the air eat it: the picture is of people who hear the word of God, but from whom it is snatched away by Satan before it can germinate. The seed that falls "on rocky places" lodges in a thin layer of topsoil that covers limestone bedrock.

---

42. The attempt to avoid this by Hodges (*Gospel under Siege,* 54), who rather implausibly takes the "us" to refer to the apostolic communion, or perhaps the initial Palestinian church, does not solve the problem, but merely changes the location of the church.

Because it is so shallow, this topsoil heats up quickly, encourages the seed to germinate, and therefore initially produces what seems to be the most promising crop. Unfortunately, as the sun burns throughout the long, hot summer, these plants are scorched: their roots search for moisture, but come up against the bedrock, and the plant dies. The explanation tells us that this pictures those who receive the word with joy. Sadly, because they have no root, "they last only a short time." When trouble or persecution comes, they fall away. And finally, some seed falls on thorny ground. Here, too, the seed germinates and sends up tendrils, but the competition exerted by the more robust thorns chokes the young plants, so that they bear no grain. Here we are to think of those who hear the word, but whose hearing faces the competition of worries, the deceitfulness of wealth, and desires for other things. These distractions "choke the word, making it unfruitful."

The important thing to observe is that two of the three fruitless soils sprout life, but do not bear fruit This is not bleeding the parable for more than it is worth: recall that in the case of the seed that falls on rocky soil, the interpretation of the parable provided in the text itself describes the reality pictured by the parable as people who "hear the word and at once receive it with joy," but who "last only a short time." To all observers save God himself, this seed promises the best harvest, but this spiritual life proves transitory.

Several popular interpreters associated with the Grace Evangelical Society find this so uncomfortable that they reinterpret the parable. They say that instead of having three soils that are viewed negatively and one that is viewed positively, the alignment should go another way: there are two soils that are viewed negatively (the pathway and the thorns), and two that produce life (the rocky soil and the good soil), one of which also produces fruit. This will not do: the seed scattered on thorny soil also produces plants, but these plants never bear grain (Mark 4:7): the thorns choke the plants, not the ungerminated seeds. I suppose they could respond by suggesting that there is only one soil treated negatively (the pathway), and three treated positively, only one of which bears fruit. But the narrative parable does not read that way: such an interpretation is being imported from an alien theological structure; it would be strange in the context of a Gospel tradition that repeatedly insists people are known by their fruit, not by their life without fruit; and in its context the parable of the soils, especially in Mark and Matthew, joins other parables in elucidating the nature of the kingdom that has already dawned but is not yet consummated. Its purpose is to show that the kingdom is not now dawning with apocalyptic suddenness and clarity, but in the lives of those who hear the gospel of the kingdom and produce fruit. To argue that it is also introducing a category for spiritual life that is nevertheless fruitless is simply alien to the concerns of the chapter, and contrary to one of the driving motifs of all three synoptic Gospels.

Ideally, it would be helpful at this point to offer a detailed exegesis of Hebrews 6:4–6, and of similar passages in the New Testament, but we must limit ourselves to some focal observations. Too often the challenge raised by Hebrews 6 is cast in a simple alternative: Are those who are so warned Christians or not? If one argues for the "not," one is hard-pressed to explain the string of descriptions: "those who have once been enlightened, who have tasted the Holy Spirit, who have tasted the goodness of the word of God and the powers of the coming age." If one argues they are Christians, the dominant alternatives in the commentaries are that the warning is merely hypothetical—which is utterly at odds with the driving repetition of the theme in the book, and the seriousness with which it is presented; that the falling away is not from salvation—which simply will not square with 6:6 and especially with 10:26ff.; or that genuine believers may lose their salvation—which resurrects the problems of reconciling this view with the many passages that urge us to trust the certain, preserving work of the grace of God, not least in this epistle, where God offers comfort and incentive to his people by promising, "Never will I leave you; never will I forsake you" (13:5).

But there is a better alternative, once we have recognized that our theology of conversion is too simplistic. We have already seen that three chapters earlier Hebrews virtually defines true believers as those who hold firmly to the end the confidence they had at first (3:6, 14). In other words, like other New Testament books the Epistle to the Hebrews allows for a kind of transitory faith, a form of conversion which, like the seed sown on rocky soil, has all the signs of life, but which does not persevere. The Spirit brings initial enlightenment; the person enjoys the word of God (like the one in Mark 4 who hears the word and immediately receives it with joy), and tastes something of the power of the coming age: perhaps old habits fall away, and a new love for holiness and for God and his reign emerge. But according to the description of genuine Christianity already provided by the book, none of this is enough: there must also be perseverance.

Against the background of the theology of the epistle, the reasons for such warnings are clear enough. The incarnate Son of God is God's last word to humankind (1:1–4). Therefore those who neglect the great salvation that only he brings cannot escape (2:1ff.). The sacrifice the Son offered was "once for all." There is therefore no more offering for sin (10:18, 26), still less a repetition of this one sacrifice (9:25–28). This one sacrifice, offered once for all, is forever entirely sufficient for all of God's people (10:10–14). Therefore any who taste of its fruit, recognize its origin, ally themselves with its significance, and then deliberately reject this gospel, have no place left to turn: there is no more forgiveness of sins. This is apostasy: it is turning away from a religious position and stance once firmly held. But that is still shy of saying that the faith so exercised was necessarily saving faith in some ultimate sense, if part of the definition of saving faith includes the criterion of perseverance.

403

7. What is the essence of the difference, then, so far as assurance is concerned, between the person who holds that all genuine believers will be preserved to the end, and that those who fall away from apparent faith only enjoy spurious, transitory faith, and the person who holds that genuine believers may fall away? Marshall's analysis, using "Calvinist" and "non-Calvinist" to denote the two groups respectively, runs like this:

> If a person is in the former group, he has still to heed the warning: only by so doing can he show that he is one of the elect. In other words, the Calvinist 'believer' cannot fall away from 'true' faith, but he can 'fall away' from what proves in the end to be only seeming faith. The possibility of falling away remains. But in neither case does the person know for certain whether he is a true or a seeming disciple. All that he knows is that Christ alone can save and that he must trust in Christ, and that he sees signs in his life which may give him some assurance that he is a true disciple. But these signs may be misleading.
>
> It comes down to a question of assurance. Whoever said, 'The Calvinist knows that he cannot fall from salvation but does not know whether he has got it', had it summed up nicely. But this can be counterfeit and misleading. The non-Calvinist knows that he has salvation—because he trusts in the promises of God—but is aware that, left to himself, he could lose it. So he holds to Christ. It seems to me the practical effect is the same.[43]

At a merely mechanistic level, I think this analysis is largely correct. But three caveats must be added. Even if at certain levels the practical effect is the same, that does not mean the underlying structures are the same. One must still decide which approach is most faithful to most texts. In my view, Marshall does not adequately handle the numerous passages and themes that do promise the security of the believer. Psychologically, the focus is not the same. Historically, of course, it is a commonplace that some branches of Calvinism have developed their own forms of introversion, believers constantly examining themselves to see if they were displaying sufficient fruit to justify their conclusion that they were among the elect—thus strangely mirroring their Arminian counterparts who sometimes gave themselves to worrying if they were truly holding on to the promises of God. Thus at their worst, the two approaches meet in strange and sad ways. But at their best, the focus of the two systems is nonetheless quite different. Despite Marshall's salutary emphasis on the promises of God, at the end of the day the security of the believer finally rests with the believer. For those from the opposite camp, the security of the believer finally rests with God—and that, I suggest, rightly taught and applied, draws the believer back to God himself, to trust in God, to renewed faith that is of a piece with trusting him in the first place. In any case, this analysis entirely neglects to wrestle with the way we are to think of

43. Marshall, "The Problem of Apostasy," 313.

God's sovereign preservation of his people, and our responsibility to persevere; and so to that subject we now turn.

The biblical writers either presuppose or explicitly teach what might be called compatibilism, and this has an important, and neglected, bearing on the subject of Christian assurance. I have written on this subject at some length elsewhere,[44] and must restrict myself to a few potted explanations. Compatibilism is the view that the following two statements are, despite superficial evidence to the contrary, mutually compatible: God is absolutely sovereign but his sovereignty does not in any way mitigate human responsibility; human beings are responsible creatures (i.e., they choose, decide, obey, disobey, believe, rebel, and so forth), but their responsibility never serves to make God absolutely contingent.

The compatibilist, then, believes that both of these statements are true, that they are mutually compatible. That does not mean compatibilists claim they can show exactly how both of these statements can be simultaneously true. Rather, if they are rigorous thinkers, they think that there is enough reasonable evidence to demonstrate that nothing proves the pair of statements incompatible. Therefore other evidence that seems to justify the statements individually cannot be ruled out of court on the grounds that the two statements contradict each other.

My contention is that the biblical writers, insofar as they reveal themselves on this subject, are without exception compatibilists. When Joseph responds to his brothers' alarm by saying that when they sold him to the Midianites they meant it for evil, while God meant it for good (Gen. 50:19–20), the thinking is compatibilistic. Joseph does not say that God had initiated a lovely plan to send Joseph down to Egypt by first-class chariot, but the brothers corrupted the plan by their evil machinations. Nor does he say that the brothers hatched an evil plot, but God rushed in to the rescue by turning their evil into good (though some passages portray God in precisely such categories). Rather, in one and the same event, God and the brothers were working, the one with good intent, the others with evil intent. God's sovereign, unseen sway does not mitigate the brothers' evil; their malice does not catch God by surprise and make him utterly contingent.

In the same way, the Assyrians can be described as mere tools in Yahweh's hands as he disciplines his people (Isa. 10:5ff.). But that does not reduce their responsibility. In their foolish pride they think they are achieving these military victories on their own. Therefore God will hold them accountable for

44. D. A. Carson, *Divine Sovereignty and Human Responsibility: Biblical Themes in Tension* (Atlanta: John Knox, 1981); idem, *How Long, O Lord? Reflection on Suffering and Evil* (Grand Rapids: Baker, 1991), chaps. 11 and 12.

their arrogance, and, after using them the way a workman wields a saw or an axe, will turn again to rend them.

When the Philippians are told to work out their own salvation with fear and trembling,[45] on the ground that it is God who is working in them both to will and to act according to his good purpose, it is important to observe what is not said. The Philippians are not told to work out their salvation since God has done his bit and now it is their turn; nor are they told that they should simply "let go and let God," since after all salvation is all of grace. Rather, they are encouraged to work out their salvation precisely because it is God who is at work in them, both at the level of their wills and at the level of their actions. God's sovereignty functions as an incentive to work, not a disincentive. Similarly, when in a night vision the Lord encourages Paul to preach on in Corinth (Acts 18:9–10), the ground is that the Lord has many people in this place. In other words, election here functions as an incentive to evangelism, not a disincentive.

Nowhere, perhaps, are such compatibilistic tendencies more starkly pre-supposed than in Acts 4, when the church turns to prayer after the first whiff of persecution. The Christians invoke the "Sovereign Lord" who made the heaven and earth, and cite Psalm 2 as they remember that all the rage and plotting of the nations against the Lord and against his anointed One are fu-tile: the Lord will have them in derision. Small wonder these believers saw the deepest fulfillment of Psalm 2 in the death of their Master: "Indeed Herod and Pontius Pilate met together with the Gentiles and the people of Israel in this city to conspire against your holy servant Jesus, whom you anointed" (4:27). Then they add, "They did what your power and will had decided beforehand should happen" (4:28).

A moment's reflection discloses that anything other than a compatibilist approach to these events destroys the gospel itself. Christians cannot possibly believe that the cross began as a nasty conspiracy by wicked politicians, with God riding in on a white charger at the last moment to turn their evil into good: that would mean that the plan of redemption was not a plan after all. Nor can they believe that God's sovereign control of the events excused all the human players: if Herod, Judas, Pontius Pilate, and other leaders were not involved in a conspiracy of which they were wretchedly culpable, it is hard to imagine how any human being in God's world could be thought cul-pable of anything—and in that case, why offer an atoning sacrifice for ac-tions for which there could be no guilt?

45. I do not accept the interpretations of these verses advanced by O. Glombitza ("Mit Furcht und Zittern. Zum Verständnis von Phil.2.12," *NovT* 3 [1959]: 100–106) and R. P. Mar-tin (*Philippians,* NCB [London: Oliphants, 1976], 102–3) respectively, but detailed discussion would be out of place here. Cf. now Peter T. O'Brien, *The Epistle to the Philippians: A Com-mentary on the Greek Text,* NIGTC (Grand Rapids: Eerdmans, 1991).

Before turning to the bearing of compatibilism on Christian assurance, it is necessary to take three steps.

1. If we accept, on the admittedly scanty evidence marshalled here, that biblical writers in every major corpus espouse compatibilism, we should perhaps pause to allay suspicions that compatibilism surreptitiously embraces sheer logical contradiction, and should forthwith be abandoned, regardless of what biblical writers think.[46] Modern compatibilists, I have said, do not try to show exactly how the two crucial propositions hold together. Rather, they elucidate the considerable unknowns that nullify most of the counterarguments. In particular: We do not know how an eternal God operates in time. We scarcely know what time is; it is not at all clear what eternity is (Does God know sequence?), still less how he relates to our time. The question is critical in debates over foreordination and predestination. Similarly, we do not know how a sovereign God operates through secondary agents who nevertheless are held accountable for their deeds. The definition of freedom that enters almost all discussions of human responsibility is far more problematic than people think. If freedom entails absolute power to contrary, then God is necessarily contingent, and compatibilism is destroyed. But if, for instance, freedom turns on voluntarism, that is, human beings are responsible and accountable because they do what they want to do, there is no necessary infringement on the sovereignty of God—as Jonathan Edwards demonstrated more than two centuries ago. Above all, we have almost no idea how God can be simultaneously sovereign and personal—yet the Scriptures insist on both. Virtually all of the elements that go into our thinking as to what personal relationships are about are based on our experience of relations with other human beings—and we are finite. We talk with one another, ask questions, hear answers, respond with love or wrath, cherish friendships, and so forth—and all of these elements demand the passage of time and presuppose finite actors. Similarly, in Scripture God can be portrayed asking questions, hearing answers, responding with love or wrath, cherishing friendships, and so forth; yet other texts insist he is also sovereign, the one "who works out everything in conformity with the purpose of his will" (Eph. 1:11). I have no idea how to conceptualize a God who is both sovereign and personal, but I perceive that if both are not simultaneously true, the God of the Bible disappears, and Christianity, indeed theism itself, is destroyed. In short, the mystery of compatibilism is traceable to the mystery of God, to what we do not know about God.

2. Along with the Bible's insistence on compatibilism is its insistence on the goodness of God. Elsewhere I have argued at length[47] that the enormous biblical evidence for this duality leads to an unavoidable conclusion: al-

46. Many philosophers adopt exactly that stance. Nevertheless, compatibilism enjoys respectable support in some philosophical circles. See the bibliography in the works already cited.
47. *How Long, O Lord?*

though God, by virtue of the fact that he is sovereign, stands behind both good and evil (e.g., God can be portrayed as the one who incites David to number the people, the one who sends a strong delusion so that people will believe the lie, the one who sends nations to war, the one of whom Romans 8:28 is predicated), he stands behind good and evil asymmetrically. He stands behind evil in such a way that none of it takes place outside the limits of his sovereign sway, but so that no evil is chargeable to him; he stands behind good in such a way that all of it is credited to him. Do not ask me to explain *how* this can be so: these are components of the biblical "givens," perspectives that the biblical writers teach or assume.

3. This means that we are locked into mystery. That should not be surprising: we are thinking about God. If there were nothing mysterious about him, I suppose he would not be God: he would be too small, too easily tamed, too domesticated. But if we respect the mystery of compatibilism, precisely because it is tied to what we do not know about God himself, then the most important thing we can do to foster personal and corporate fidelity to the portrait of God disclosed in Scripture, is to observe how the complementary truths of compatibilism *function in Scripture, and insist that in our hands they will function in the same ways, and in no other.*

For example, election, an element in the biblical portrayal of God's sovereignty, never functions so as to destroy human responsibility, to limit the urgency of preaching the gospel, to foster fatalism, or the like. It frequently functions to tie salvation to grace and to engender humility (Rom. 9), to encourage evangelism (Acts 18:9–10), and much more. Invitations to believe or to obey the gospel never function to make God absolutely contingent; rather, they function to bring people to saving faith, increase human responsibility, magnify the forbearance of God, and so forth. If we allow the components of compatibilism to function in ways much removed from the biblical constraints, we will end up implicitly disowning the compatibilism that is everywhere assumed, and is, finally, nothing more than a corollary of the doctrine of God. We will end up tarnishing the biblical witness to who God is and what he is like.

Most Christians have become used to other facets of Christian doctrine that involve mystery, and if they are reasonably informed they will be fairly careful both to locate the mystery in the right place and not to destroy the mystery by drawing inferences that destroy some essential component elsewhere in the structure. Perhaps the best example is Christology. Most of us want to be careful enough about our affirmation of Jesus' deity that we do not unwittingly derogate his humanity, and vice versa. We acknowledge the mystery, and we take some pains, along with believers in every era, to try to incorporate all the biblical evidence on this subject into the formulations of our doctrinal affirmations. We may not be completely successful; but that is our commitment. In the area of compatibilism, however, too few have adequately recognized that there is a mystery at stake, and that laying profane hands on the biblical evidence too quickly, without recognizing the nature and location of the mystery, ends up with tragic loss to the doctrine of God. For example, if human responsibility is made to depend on a definition of freedom that involves absolute power to contrary, then God becomes absolutely contingent. One of the poles of combatibilism is destroyed; we are left, not with mystery, but with logical contradiction.

Clearly, compatibilism touches many subjects: election, the problem of suffering, the nature of prayer, and much else. What is not often recognized is that it bears directly on the nature of Christian assurance. For, on the one hand, we are dealing with a plethora of texts that promise God's sovereign commitment to preserve his own elect; on the other, believers are enjoined to persevere in faithfulness to the new covenant and the Lord of the covenant, to the calling by which they were called. This is nothing other than God's sovereignty and human responsibility dressed up in another form.

So we will always have some mystery. The important thing will be to locate the mystery in the right place. It will not do to affirm God's sovereign protection of his elect, and then make such preservation absolutely contingent on human faithfulness: that is not mystery, but logical contradiction. But if our articulation of the doctrine of assurance leaves no loose ends, there is every reason to think that we have denied compatibilism somewhere—in exactly the same way that some treatments of election remove all difficulties but leave the texts behind. Moreover, the same safeguard that we apply in other areas where mystery intrudes into Christian doctrine must be applied here: let the various passages relevant to Christian assurance function in our lives and theological systems the way they do in Scripture. Do warnings against apostasy function to annul the promises of God? Of course not. They are designed to promote perseverance. Do the promises of God serve to engender lethargy? Of course not. They are designed to promote zeal, gratitude, and appreciation of God's fidelity.

But this discussion of function leads us to the final reflection.

The biblical writers do not deal with only one sort of doubt, and therefore they do not mete out only one kind of assurance. This rather obvious fact is sometimes overlooked. The magisterial Reformers rebelled against the sale of indulgences, the location of absolution within the hands of a priestly minority, the loss of confidence in the finished work of Christ, the lack of Christian assurance. By tying assurance to justification, they successfully met this challenge, prompting the Tridentine standards to pronounce the *anathema sit* on those who claimed such assurance.[48]

---

48. See the excellent discussion by Klaas Runia, "Justification and Roman Catholicism," in *Right with God: Justification in the Bible and the World*, ed. D. A. Carson (Exeter: Paternoster; Grand Rapids: Baker, 1992).

But there are many different kinds of doubt. Even if we narrowly focus on those elements of doubt that can jeopardize the Christian's assurance that the salvation now begun will finally be brought to victorious consummation, the diversity is nevertheless remarkable. Doubtless the solution to much of it is to focus attention on the exclusive finality of Christ and his death and resurrection on our behalf, to magnify God's unfailing promises and his love (e.g., John 5:24; 6:37ff.; 10 passim; Rom. 8:15–17, 29–30, 38–39; Phil. 1:6; 2 Tim. 1:12). But lack of assurance may be prompted by secret sin. Worse, a Christian may stumble into prolonged sin and not feel any lack of assurance—just like the Israelites in Deuteronomy and elsewhere who are warned against relying on election and feel no fear or shame when they sin. In that case, James 2 may call into question the reality of the "faith" that is exercised, if it is not accompanied by works; for the assumption in the New Testament is that saving faith, tied as it is to the new covenant and the power of the Spirit, necessarily issues in good works. Although works cannot save and cannot be the primary ground of one's assurance (that, surely, is Christ and his work and promises), they may serve as corroborating evidence. More accurately, in James 2 and 2 Corinthians 13:10, the lack of corroborating evidence may call in question the reality of the putative faith; in 2 Peter 1:10 the desirability of persevering corroboration functions as an incentive to enduring fidelity and fruitfulness. Here, then, the English Puritans have some justification for their emphases, if not always for their overemphases.

Still more interesting is the argument of 1 John. Many Protestant commentators follow the classic treatment of Robert Law in detecting "tests of life" in this epistle. These are usually thought to be three, sometimes four: appropriate allegiance to certain truth, in this case the confession that the Christ, the Son of God, is Jesus; principial obedience; love for other believers; and, in some analyses, the witness of the Spirit (though some think this witness is not a private experience but a way of summarizing the other "tests").

But a more refined analysis is possible if we observe more carefully the likely background and observable function of these so-called tests. Despite many counterproposals, I remain persuaded that John is confronting a crisis precipitated by the secession of some members who have been powerfully influenced by some form of protognosticism. Their departure left behind believers who were, spiritually speaking, badly bruised. The raw triumphalism of most forms of gnosticism dented the confidence of those who refused to go along with the movement. In this light, the so-called tests are not primarily given to exclude certain people on the grounds that they failed to meet the challenges, but to reassure believers that their fidelity to the gospel, along the lines indicated, was itself reason enough to enable them to regain their quiet Christian assurance. The very places where the seceders failed or made outrageous counterclaims, thereby threatening the Christians and jolting their assurance, were the places where the Christians were proving faithful and reliable—in doctrine, obedience, and love. Such faithfulness and reliability constituted evidence of God's work in their lives, and therefore could legitimately be taken by those who believed in the name of the Son of God as corroborating grounds that they truly enjoyed eternal life. Such restored confidence before God had other practical ramifications: in particular, it also issued in renewed confidence in prayer (3:21–22; 5:14–16).[49]

What we learn from these observations is that there is a pastoral dimension to the biblical witness on Christian assurance. We should have known it all along. No one can long serve as a pastor without coming across, say, a young woman who doubts that she is good enough to be forgiven by Christ, an aging man who wonders if he will be transported to glory when he dies, a church member who is having doubts about his salvation and who (it is discovered) is sleeping with his secretary, some nominal believers who display nothing of the promised fruit of the new covenant but who are convinced by the slogan "Once saved, always saved" that they are in no danger, and a gaggle of young people who are unsure of their spiritual status because they have been confronted by those who claim to have the "full gospel." Anyone who applies exactly the same spiritual remedy to these diverse ailments ought to have his license as a spiritual physician immediately rescinded.

Some Conclusions

If we appreciate the undergirding mystery that stands behind the Christian assurance, we will let the various complementary biblical statements stand in their naked power and function without endless reductionism.[50]

Close observation of the functions of the various biblical statements in their immediate and canonical contexts will do much to safeguard our theology against dangerous reductionism and pastoral malpractice. Zane Hodges is happy to speak of Christians ceasing to name the name of Christ and denying the faith completely, even though (he insists) God keeps such people "saved," that is, in the faith. From a pastoral point of view, what is one to say to these unbelieving believers, these Christ-denying Christians? If the way

49. Of course, virtually everything I have said about 1 John is disputed. I shall seek to offer detailed defense of these judgments in a forthcoming commentary (NIGTC).

50. I should point out that in many classic treatments on assurance there is a threefold focus: the objective work of Christ grounded in the plan of God, the demonstrable transformation of the believer that is the new birth's inevitable result, and the inner witness of the Spirit (so, for instance, Richard Sibbes: see the discussion in Mark E. Dever, "Richard Sibbes and the 'Truly Evangelicall Church of England': A Study in Reformed Divinity and Early Stuart Conformity" [Ph.D. dissertation, Cambridge University, 1992]). This third leg, tied to such passages as Romans 8:15–17, I have not discussed here, but it needs and deserves serious reflection. It is connected in important ways to the subject of revival. All three legs must be set out in biblical array and pastorally wise proportion in any comprehensive treatment of assurance.

the Scriptures function in such cases is borne in mind, both our theology and our counsel will grow in maturity and biblical balance.

The sort of approach that makes absolute, epistemologically tight, Christian assurance the sine qua non of theological systems and proceeds to engage in a massive rereading of the rest of Scripture, rereadings that are too clever by half, in order to justify this a priori, are ill-conceived. Indeed, granted the proper location of the underlying tension between God's sovereignty and human responsibility, they are as methodologically ill-conceived as, say, J. A. T. Robinson's attempt to develop a Christology grounded exclusively in Jesus' humanity, that humanity serving as a grid that filters out complementary evidence.[51]

Because every part of Christian doctrine is tied, one way or another, to every other part, doubtless a case can be made for beginning with the doctrine of assurance. It is odd, however, that a few contemporary studies have made personal assurance, or some peculiar understanding of it, the touchstone for the entire structure of Christian theology. The result has been truly astonishing distortions. On balance, this is a strange place to begin and end the study of theology. One might have begun with God, with Christ, with redemption, with revelation.

It is important to insist that the view of perseverance and assurance outlined in this chapter does not make perseverance the basis of assurance—as if to say that no one is entitled to any form of assurance until ultimate perseverance has been demonstrated. I have not argued that perseverance is the basis for assurance; rather, I have argued that failure to persevere serves to undermine assurance. The basis of assurance is Christ and his work and its entailments.

In short, the biblical writers offer believers all the assurance they could ever want, grounding such assurance in the character of God, the nature of the new covenant, the finality of election, the love of God, and much more beside. But they never allow such assurance to become a sop for spiritual indifference; indeed, the same vision is what drives them to insist that the God who has called them to his new covenant works powerfully in them to conform them to the likeness of his Son, to the fruitfulness the Spirit empowers us to produce. This becomes both an incentive to press on to the mark of the upward call in Christ Jesus, and an implicit challenge to those who cry "Lord, Lord" but do not do what he commands.

51. *The Human Face of God* (London: SCM, 1973).

412

18

The Love of God:
Universal and Particular

J. I. PACKER

On Knowing Love

It was, I think, Voltaire who first observed that ever since God made man in his own image man has been trying to return the compliment. Whoever said it, it is true, and many theological mistakes have been made through likening the God of infinite power, holiness, goodness, and wisdom to finite and fallen humanity.

The KISS formula—"keep it simple, stupid!"—is current wisecracking wisdom. But the idea behind the formula, namely, that the notion that seems simplest will always be soundest, has been around in theology since at least the third century, when Sabellians and Arians "simplified" the truth of the Trinity in a way that actually denied it (the former turning God into a quick-change artist playing three roles, the latter turning the divine Son and Spirit into two high-class creatures). Many more theological mistakes have come from embracing simplistic naiveties that at the time felt comfortable to the mind.

The idea of the grace of God that prompts this chapter seems to involve error of both kinds, as we shall see. Since however my goal here is positive exposition with the minimum of controversy, I focus first not on disputable opinions, but on basic questions of definition and method.

My title affirms that God's love is a reality. All Christian teaching says this. But what is love? Asking that question must be our starting point, for

413

"love," both as a noun and as a verb, is among the most misused words in the English language. And although God's love is our prime concern we must begin by noting how modern Westerners use the word of each other, for it is here that the worst confusions arise.

"Love" is a term that, because of its historic Christian associations, still carries in what was once Christendom glowing overtones of nobility and grandeur. Certainly, the mutual devotion of lovers, and the self-sacrificing paths of parenthood and friendship, can be noble indeed. But in current use "love" has become virtually synonymous with liking and wanting something or someone, and there is nothing necessarily noble or grand about that. "I love chocolate," "I love sunsets," "I love jazz," "I love redheads," "I love sex"—such states of liking and wanting are so many egocentric highroads to self-gratifying self-indulgence. When persons are the objects of our likes and wants, then manipulation, exploitation, and abuse are likely to result, alternating with unprincipled indulgence of the other person's whims on the principle, it seems, of doing to others as you would like them to do to you. Parents "loving" their children by giving them everything they ever want is an obvious example. Thus, what we call our love for people often does them harm. Sometimes it is assumed that God's love, if real, would itself take the form of unprincipled indulgence of our whims, and then the fact that comforts we pray for are not always given is treated as proving a lack either of love or of power on God's part. Such are the confusions that have to be sorted out.

In *The Four Loves* C. S. Lewis distinguished *agape* (the New Testament Greek word for God's love and Christian love) from *storge* (the feeling of affection or fondness); *eros* (the feeling of desire and need for some person or thing that is felt to be attractive, especially in sexual or aesthetic contexts); and *philia* (the attitude of friendliness to one who is friendly to you). Each of these three is a blend of animal instinct, personal taste, appreciative awareness, and self-gratifying impulse, and in this all three differ radically from *agape*.

What is *agape*? Human *agape* is a way (1 Cor. 13:1)—that is, a path of action—of which four things are true. First, it is a purpose of doing good to others, and so in some sense making those others great. *Agape* Godward, triggered by gratitude for grace, makes God great by exalting him in praise, thanksgiving, and obedience. *Agape* manward, neighbor love as Scripture calls it, makes fellow humans great by serving not their professed wants, but their observed real needs. Thus, marital *agape* seeks fulfillment for the spouse and parental *agape* seeks maturity for the children. Second, *agape* is measured not by sweetness of talk or strength of feeling, but by what it does, and more specifically by what of its own it gives, for the fulfilling of its purpose. Third, *agape* does not wait to be courted, nor does it limit itself to those who at once appreciate it, but it takes the initiative in giving help where help is required, and finds its joy in bringing others benefit. The question of who deserves to be helped is not raised; *agape* means doing good to the needy, not to the meritorious, and to the needy however undeserving they might be. Fourth, *agape* is precise about its object. The famous *Peanuts* quote, "I love the human race—it's people I can't stand," is precisely not *agape*. *Agape* focuses on particular people with particular needs, and prays and works to deliver them from evil. In all of this it is directly modeled on the love of God revealed in the gospel.

Knowing God's Love: The Method

Basic to Christianity is the conviction that we learn what love is from watching God in action—supremely, from watching God in the person of the Father's incarnate Son, Jesus Christ, as he lives, gives, suffers, and dies to achieve our redemption. We do the watching through Bible study, following the narratives of the Gospels and the explanations in the Epistles. The point is often made that before Christianity arrived the *agape* word-group was unspecific, was rarely used, and signified no more than contentment with something, so that by defining it in terms of the love shown forth in Christ the apostles made it a new thing—love of a kind that the world never dreamed of before. This is right, and we must never let ourselves think of *agape* in any terms not validated by the redemptive work of Jesus.

But to understand correctly what the New Testament says about this love of God we must set it in the frame of the total biblical witness to God, and that means observing the following perspectival guidelines.

Remember *the sovereignty of the divine Creator*. Older Reformed theology, organizing the teaching of the canonical Scriptures, called the different aspects of God's being his attributes, some communicable and others incommunicable. The former, so called because in our sanctification they begin to be reproduced in us, were commonly listed as wisdom, truth, goodness (meaning grace, mercy, and longsuffering love), holiness, and righteousness; highlighting God's personhood, they together answered the question How does God behave? The latter, commonly listed as self-existence (aseity), immutability, infinity, eternity, and simplicity (meaning inner integration), highlighted God's transcendence; combining as an answer to the question How does God exist? They underlined at every point the contrast between the majestic self-sustaining omnipotence of the divine life and the creaturely dependence, weakness, and sinful disorder of ours. God's sovereignty, in which the perfection of his powers operates to express the perfection of his moral character, straddles this classification, for it is essentially personal action on an altogether transcendent plane. God "rules in the world and his will is the final cause of all things, including specifically creation and preservation (Ps. 95:6; Rev. 4:11), human government (Pr. 21:1; Dn. 4:35), the salvation of God's people (Rom. 8:29f.; Eph. 1:4, 11), the sufferings of Christ (Lk. 22:42; Acts 2:23), man's life and destiny (Acts 18:21; Rom. 15:32), and even the smallest details of life (Mt. 10:29). God reigns in his universe. . . ."[1] The love of God is thus sovereign love, and must always be acknowledged as such.

Remember *the triunity of the divine Lord*. Within the one God's complex being are three personal centers ("centers" is not perhaps an ideal word, but we have none better). Each is "I" to himself and "you" to the other two. By God's own naming they are the Father, the Son, and the Holy Spirit. God is a society, a community of mutual love, and a team: he is they and they are he, if such language may be allowed. (See Matt. 28:19; John 14:15–26; 2 Cor. 13:14; Eph. 1:3–14; 2:18–22; Rev. 1:4–5; etc. Though the apostles developed no trinitarian vocabulary, trinitarian thinking pervades the entire New Testament.) Speaking epistemologically, the truth of the Trinity became known only through the life and words of the incarnate Son who came from the Father and prayed to the Father, and who when returning to the Father promised that the Spirit would be sent as his deputy; but speaking ontologically, the fact of God's triunity is eternal. The love of God is thus triune love, and should always be thought of in that way.

Remember *the unity of the divine character*. God in Scripture regularly uses the word *holy* with a global meaning, to bring together and hold together in our minds both the metaphysical perfections and the moral glories characterizing the triune Lord, who in all his words and deeds is unchangeably wise, just, pure, good, and true. Every time he says he is holy or calls himself the Holy One of Israel, the adjective carries this full weight of meaning. In this broad sense, therefore, holiness is the attribute displayed in all God's attributes; and thus the love of God is holy love, and must ever be viewed so, in explicit relation to the other aspects of God's being.

Remember *the analogy of the divine self-description*. This point follows from the last. God who gave us language prompted his penmen in Scripture to speak of him in nouns, verbs, and adjectives taken from the common human stock of language, just as he did himself when speaking through the prophets and through his Son, Jesus Christ. But because all these words ordinarily refer to finite and fallen human beings, when they are used of God they must be partially redefined: the core of the meaning will remain, but all associations or implications that suggest human finitude and fallenness must be eliminated, and the core meaning must be set in the frame of God's perfection and purity. It is evident that the Bible writers were mentally doing this all the time, in a way that had become second nature to them, and in interpreting their writings we must follow this out. So the love of God is not identical with, but analogous to, what is noblest in human love, and the precise

1. Bruce Milne, *Know the Truth* (Downers Grove: InterVarsity, 1982), 66.

terms of the analogical adjustment our minds must make at this point have to be learned from the rest of the teaching about God that the Bible gives. What was said about *agape* has already alerted us to the major difference there is between God's love and man's.

Remember *the epistemology of the divine instruction.* God through his Spirit interprets the Bible to us, that is, enables us to understand the writers' meaning and apply their points to ourselves, and so to apprehend what he, the divine Author, wishes to teach us from the inspired text. But the Bible is a set of more or less occasional writings, in which things dealt with in detail are clearer than those to which only passing reference is made. Knowing that sin has twisted our minds, just as it has twisted our moral sensibilities, and both at a deeper level than we can track, we should not let ourselves speculate beyond what Scripture clearly teaches, and should be willing to settle for ignorance (*docta ignorantia,* well-taught ignorance, as it has been called) rather than indulge our theological fancies.

Also, we should take "what Scripture clearly teaches" to mean "what exegesis shows that the Bible writers wanted their readers to gather from their words"—not what those words might seem to be saying when recontextualized in a latter-day dogmatic frame. So our understanding of the love of God must be limited by what the Bible's homiletical flowings of thought actually yield. We should confine ourselves to this, and eschew extrapolations beyond it.

A model of this kind of conscientious theological discretion, and one that bears directly on our present subject, is Anglican Article 17 (1571), "Of Predestination and Election." In Reformation days, as since, treatments of God's love in election were often given shape, overshadowed, and indeed preempted by wrangles of an abstract sort about God's sovereignty in reprobation. But in the New Testament, most notably in Romans 8:28–11:36 and Ephesians 1:3–14, election is a pastoral theme, spelled out for believers' encouragement, reassurance, support, and worship. That is exactly how Article 17 treats it, by drawing out in direct echoes of Scripture the comfort of election, by bypassing debates about reprobation, and by directing unbelievers, seekers, and saints alike to the "whosoever will" promises and mandates of the gospel, which chart the way of life. Because methodologically the article is such a good example of observing biblical parameters, and also because its contents bear directly on what we must deal with next, it is here reproduced in full, in hope that the quaintness of the wording will not obscure the quality of the thinking.

17 *Of Predestination and Election*

Predestination to Life is the everlasting purpose of God, whereby (before the foundations of the world were laid) he hath constantly [firmly] decreed by his counsel secret to us, to deliver from curse and damnation those whom he hath chosen in Christ out of mankind, and to bring them by Christ to everlasting salvation, as vessels made to honour. Wherefore, they which be endued with so excellent a benefit of God be called according to God's purpose by his Spirit working in due season: they through Grace obey the calling: they be justified freely: they be made sons of God by adoption: they be made like the image of his only-begotten Son Jesus Christ: they walk religiously in good works, and at length, by God's mercy, they attain to everlasting felicity.

As the godly consideration of Predestination, and our Election in Christ, is full of sweet, pleasant, and unspeakable comfort to godly persons, and such as feel in themselves the working of the Spirit of Christ, mortifying the works of the flesh, and their earthly members, and drawing up their mind to high and heavenly things, as well because it doth greatly establish and confirm their faith of eternal Salvation to be enjoyed through Christ, as because it doth fervently kindle their love towards God: So, for curious and carnal persons, lacking the Spirit of Christ, to have continually before their eyes the sentence of God's predestination [i.e., the thought of it] is a most dangerous downfall, whereby the Devil doth thrust them either into desperation, or into wretchlessness [recklessness] of most unclean living, no less perilous than desperation.

Furthermore, we must receive God's promises in such wise, as they be generally set forth to us in holy Scripture: and, in our doings, that Will of God is to be followed, which we have expressly declared unto us in the Word of God.

Calvinism, like Arminianism, is a word that means somewhat different things to different people. The present chapter has its place in an anti-Arminian symposium to which writers from various Christian traditions have contributed. I should like to observe here that the essence of my Calvinism, so-called (I do not refuse the label), is found in Anglican Article 17.

Knowing God's Love: The Biblical Witness

The love of God is a great and wide-ranging biblical theme on which one could dilate at length, but for our purposes the scriptural testimony may be summarized as follows.

God's love is spoken of by means of a varied and overlapping vocabulary. Goodness (glorious generosity), love itself (generous goodness in active expression), mercy (generous goodness relieving the needy), grace (mercy contrary to merit and despite demerit), and loving-kindness (KJV) or steadfast love (RSV) (generous goodness in covenantal faithfulness), are the main terms used. The often-echoed self-description whereby God expounds his name (Yahweh, the LORD) to Moses on Sinai crystallizes these ideas: "The LORD, the LORD, the compassionate and gracious God, slow to anger, abounding in love and faithfulness, maintaining love to thousands, and forgiving wickedness, rebellion and sin. . ." (Exod. 34:6–7). The New Testament gauges divine *agape* by the staggering gift of God's Son to suffer for mankind's salvation (see Rom. 5:7–8), and thus deepens all these ideas beyond what Old Testament minds could conceive.

God's love is revealed in his providential care for the creatures he made. "The LORD is good to all; he has compassion on all he has made. . . . The eyes of all look to you, and you give them their food at the proper time. You open your hand and satisfy the desires of every living thing" (Ps. 145:9, 15–16; and see also Ps. 104:21; Matt. 5:45; 6:26; Acts 14:17).

God's love is revealed in the universal invitations of the gospel, whereby sinful humans are invited to turn in faith and repentance to the living Christ who died for sins and are promised pardon and life if they do. "God so loved the world that he gave his one and only Son, that whoever believes in him shall not perish but have eternal life" (John 3:16; see also Rom. 10:11–13; Rev. 22:17). "God is love (*agape*). This is how God showed his love among us: He sent his one and only Son into the world that we might live through him. This is love: not that we loved God, but that he loved us and sent his Son as an atoning sacrifice for our sins" (1 John 4:8–10). And God in the gospel expresses a bona fide wish that all may hear, and that all who hear may believe and be saved (1 Tim. 2:3–6; cf. 4:9–10). This is love in active expression.

God's love is revealed when "because of his great love for us" (1 John 4:8) he brings the spiritually dead to life in Christ and with Christ under the ministry of the gospel (Eph. 2:1, 4–5), uniting us to Christ in co-resurrection for everlasting life and joy (vv. 6–7). "Dead" evidently signifies total unresponsiveness to God, total unawareness of his love, and total lack of the life he gives: no metaphor for spiritual inability and destitution could be stronger. What Paul speaks of here is the work of grace that elsewhere he describes as God "calling"—that is, actually bringing unbelievers to faith by his Spirit so that they respond to the invitation given and trust in Christ to save them. "Those he called, he also justified" (Rom. 8:30)—and no one is justified who has not come to faith. (For further instances of this Pauline usage see Rom. 9:24; 1 Cor. 1:9, 26; Gal. 1:15; 1 Thess. 2:12; 2 Thess. 2:14; 2 Tim. 1:9.) Other New Testament passages designate this same work of grace, whereby God makes us Christians, as new creation (2 Cor. 5:17; Gal. 6:15), and as regeneration or new birth (John 1:12–13; 3:3–8; Tit. 3:5; James 1:18; 1 Pet. 1:23; 1 John 2:28; 3:9; 4:7; 5:1, 4). No declarations that we do not become Christians without creative prevenient grace could be clearer. Passages like John 6:37–39; 17:2, 6, 9, 24; Romans 8:29; Ephesians 1:3–12; 2 Thessalonians 2:13 show that this grace is given according to a pretemporal divine plan, whereby its present recipients were chosen as sinners to be saved.

So it appears, first, that God loves all in some ways (everyone whom he creates, sinners though they are, receives many undeserved good gifts in daily providence), and, second, that he loves some in all ways (that is, in addition to the gifts of daily providence he brings them to faith, to new life, and to glory according to his predestinating purpose). This is the clear witness of the entire Bible.

Knowing God's Love: The Theological Models

The Reformation was an Augustinian revival. Its great discovery, the doctrine of justification by faith, was fitted into a robust Augustinian and Pauline doctrine of grace, according to which fallen humans are totally unable to respond in repentance, faith, and love to God, until prevenient grace—that is, the regenerating Holy Spirit—inwardly renews them. That is, God "calls" them in Paul's special sense of the word. The doctrine that the God who calls thereby shows love to the called that goes beyond the love he shows to others, and that this love is gratuitous and as such amazing, being the opposite of what they deserved, was taken in stride. But such teaching is strong meat, too strong for some stomachs, and as in Augustine's day it produced the reaction of semi-Pelagianism, so in the late sixteenth century it produced the reaction of Arminianism, an adjustment of the Calvinist thesis about God's saving love and man's moral responsibility. Our next task is to compare these two models of the saving love of God.

Historically, Arminianism has affirmed, in the words of W. R. Bagnall, "conditional in opposition to absolute predestination, and general in opposition to particular redemption."[2] This verbal antithesis is not in fact as simple or as clear as it sounds, for changing the adjective involves redefining the noun. What Bagnall should have said is that Calvinism affirms a predestination from which conditionality is excluded and a redemption to which particularity is essential, and Arminianism denies both. To Calvinism predestination is essentially God's unconditional decision about the destiny of individual sinners; to Arminianism it is essentially God's unconditional decision to provide means of grace to sinners, decisions about individuals' destiny being secondary and consequent upon foresight (or as Clark H. Pinnock, who denies God's foresight, would presumably say, discovery) of what use they make of those means of grace. To mainstream Calvinism, predestination of persons means the foreordaining of both their doings, including their response to the gospel, and their consequent destinies; to mainstream Arminianism, it means a foreordaining of destinies based on doings foreseen or discerned but not foreordained. Arminianism affirms that God predestined Christ to be the world's Savior, and repentance and faith to be the way of salvation, and the gift of universal sufficient grace to make saving response

2. W. R. Bagnall, in *Writings of Arminius,* trans. James Nichols and W. R. Bagnall (Grand Rapids: Baker, 1956), 1.3.

to Christ possible for everyone everywhere, but denies that any person is pre-destined to believe.

On the generic Calvinist view, election, which is a predestinating act on God's part, means the sovereign choice of particular sinners to be saved by Jesus Christ through faith, and redemption, the first step in working out God's predestining purpose, is an achievement that actually guarantees sal-vation—calling, pardon, adoption, preservation, final glory—for all the elect. In the generic Arminian view, however, what the death of Christ se-cured was a possibility of salvation for sinners generally, a possibility that, so far as God is concerned, might never have been actualized in a single case; and the electing of individuals to salvation is God noting in advance who will believe and so qualify for glory, as a matter of contingent (not foreordained) fact. Whereas to Calvinism election is God's resolve to save, for Arminianism salvation rests neither on God's election nor on Christ's cross, but on each person's own cooperation with grace, which is something that God does not himself guarantee.

Biblically, the difference between these two conceptions of how God in love relates to fallen human beings may be pinpointed thus. Arminianism characteristically treats our Lord's parable of the supper to which further guests were invited in place of those who never came (Luke 14:16–24; cf. Matt. 22:1–10) as picturing the whole truth about the love of God in the gos-pel. On this view, when you have compared God's relation to fallen humans with that of a dignitary who urges needy folk to come and enjoy his bounty, you have said it all. Calvinism, however, does not stop here, but characteris-tically links the picture of the supper with that of the Shepherd (John 10:11–18, 24–29) who has his sheep given to him to care for (vv. 14, 16, 27; cf. 6:37–40), who lays down his life for them (10:15), and who guarantees that all of them will hear his voice, follow him (vv. 16, 27), and be kept by him from perishing forever (v. 28). In other words, Calvinism holds that divine love does not stop short at graciously inviting, but that the triune God takes gracious action to ensure that the elect respond. On this view, both the Christ who saves and the faith that embraces him as Savior are God's gifts, and the latter is as much a foreordained reality as is the former. Arminians praise God for his love in providing a Savior to whom all may come to find life; Cal-vinists do that too, and then go on to praise God for actually bringing them to the Savior's feet.

So the basic difference between the two positions is not, as is sometimes thought, that Arminianism follows Scripture while Calvinism follows logic, nor that Arminianism knows the compassionate love of God while Calvin-ists know only his sovereign power; nor that Arminianism affirms a con-nection between persevering in faith and obedience as a means and reach-ing heaven as an end that Calvinism's "once saved—always saved" slogan actually denies; nor that Arminianism discerns a bona fide free offer of

Christ in the gospel that Calvinism fails to discern and take seriously; nor that Arminianism acknowledges human moral responsibility before God while Calvinism reduces our race to robots. No, the difference is this: that Calvinism recognizes a dimension of the saving love of God against which Arminianism has reacted and which it now denies, namely, God's sovereignty in bringing to faith and keeping in faith all those who are actually saved. Arminianism gives Christians much to thank God for, but Calvinism gives them more.

Arminians appear in public as persons supremely concerned to do justice to the love of God, the glory of Christ, the moral responsibility of man, and the call to Christian holiness. The reason why they maintain universal redemption; human ability, whether by nature or by grace, for independent response to the gospel; and the conditional character of election is that they think these assertions necessary as means to their avowed end. What they rarely see is that in all this they are not affirming what Calvinism denies so much as denying what Calvinism affirms. Everyone in the Reformed mainstream will insist that Christ the Savior is freely offered—indeed, freely offers himself—to sinners in and through the gospel; and that since God gives us all free agency (that is, voluntary decision-making power) we are indeed answerable to him for what we do, first, about universal general revelation, and then about the law and the gospel when and as these are presented to us; and that only those who persevere in their Christian pilgrimage ever reach the heavenly city. But Calvinism at the same time affirms the total perversity, depravity, and inability of fallen human beings, which results in them naturally and continually using their free agency to say no to God, and the absolute sovereignty of the regenerating God who effectually calls and draws them into newness of life in Christ. Calvinism magnifies the Augustinian principle that God himself graciously gives all that in the gospel he requires and commands, and the reactive rationalism of Arminianism in all its forms denies this to a degree. The Arminian idea is simpler, for it does not involve so full or radical an acknowledgment of the mystery of God's ways, and it assimilates God more closely to the image of man, making him appear like a gentle giant who is also a great persuader and a resourceful maneuverer, although he is sometimes frustrated and disappointed. But if the measure of love is what it really gives to the really needy and undeserving, then the love of God as Calvinists know it is a much greater thing than the Arminians imagine, and is much diminished by the Arminian model of God and his ways with mankind.[3]

3. Some of the material in this paragraph is adapted from J. I. Packer, "Arminianisms," in *Through Christ's Word: A Festschrift for Dr. Philip E. Hughes,* ed. W. Robert Godfrey and Jesse L. Boyd III (Phillipsburg, N.J.: Presbyterian and Reformed, 1985), 121–48.

Knowing God's Love: The Nature and the Extent of the Atonement

That the atoning death of Jesus Christ is the supreme achievement and demonstration of God's love is Christian common ground, on which both Calvinists and Arminians take their stand. Disagreement begins, however, when the cross is fitted into the larger theological frame that each embraces. The Reformed way, as marked out by Luther and Calvin (who, be it said, not all Calvinists think spoke the last word about the cross), was to celebrate the atonement in an inclusive rhetoric that aimed to highlight the availability to all of pardon through Calvary, and the sufficiency of Christ's blood to cleanse the foulest from sin. The Reformers then highlighted the particularity of God's love to his elect in their treatment of the calling, justifying, preserving, and glorifying of Christians. As we have already seen that both the universal availability of Christ and his benefits and the particularity of effectual calling are set forth in Scripture as expressions of God's love, the Reformers cannot at this point be seriously faulted. Later, however, when Lutheran and Arminian revisionists began to turn the apparent universality of the atonement against the idea of personal salvation as a fruit of God's sovereign election, Reformed theologians searched the Scriptures again; and, facing the view that Christ died for everyone equally, thus making salvation possible for all though guaranteeing it for none, they focused the question that Louis Berkhof with his unfailing pedestrian clarity states in the following way:

> The question . . . is not (a) whether the satisfaction rendered by Christ was in itself sufficient for the salvation of all men, since this is admitted by all; (b) whether the saving benefits are actually applied to every man, for the great majority of those who teach a universal atonement do not believe that all are actually saved; (c) whether the *bona fide* offer of salvation is made to all who hear the gospel, on the condition of repentance and faith, since the Reformed Church does not call this in question; nor (d) whether any of the fruits of the death of Christ accrue to the benefit of the non-elect in virtue of their close association with the people of God, since this is explicitly taught by many Reformed scholars. On the other hand, the question does relate to the design of the atonement. Did the Father in sending Christ, and did Christ in coming into the world, to make atonement for sin, *do this with the design or for the purpose of saving only the elect or all men?*[4]

And their answer, in brief, was that Scripture, when searched, shows clearly enough that Christ died at the Father's will with a specific purpose of saving the elect.

---

4. Louis Berkhof, *Systematic Theology*, 4th ed. (Grand Rapids: Eerdmans, 1949), 393–94.

John Owen's *The Death of Death in the Death of Christ* (Latin title, *Sanguis Jesu Salus Electorum*, the blood of Jesus the salvation of the elect), a polemical work published in 1648,[5] seems to show conclusively that biblical statements about the cross, viewed in context, are characteristically particularist. Christ is said to have died for his sheep (John 10:11, 15), his church (Eph. 5:25), God's elect (Rom. 8:32–35), "many" (Matt. 20:28), his own people (Matt. 1:21), "us" who now believe (Tit. 2:14, etc.), and among them "me" (Gal. 2:20); and the language of Christ "dying for" others (*hyper* or *anti* in the Greek) proves on examination regularly to imply that those others are or will be saved. The atonement thus appears as an effective propitiatory transaction that actually redeemed—that is, secured redemption for—those particular persons for whom Jesus on the cross became the God-appointed substitute (see Gal. 3:13; Eph. 1:7; Col. 2:14). Since the Bible rules out all thought of universal salvation, yet depicts the cross as effective for the salvation of those for whom it was endured, "particular" or "definite" redemption must be the true concept. Sometimes, for the sake of the T-U-L-I-P acronym,[6] Calvinists have spoken of limited atonement, but Roger Nicole counsels against this.

> The language of limited atonement describes inadequately and unfairly the view which is held by Reformed people. The problem is that it seems to place emphasis upon limits. It seems to take away from the beauty, glory and fullness of the work of Christ. We seem to say that it does not go quite as far as it could or should go . . . what we need to say is that the atonement is definite, that it is related to a particular people whom God has chosen. This helps us psychologically. Because if you say, "I believe in limited atonement," the one who disagrees with you will say, "I believe in *unlimited* atonement." He appears to be the one who exalts the greatness of the grace of Christ . . . Why put ourselves at a disadvantage? On that account, I will gladly send the tulips flying! You see, I am not Dutch; I am Swiss, and I do not care so much about the tulips. I do not care about acronyms. I care about the precious faith of the Reformed church . . . and I do not think that "limited atonement" represents me. I want to say "definite atonement" or "particular redemption," and I would encourage other people to do so also.[7]

Surely this is wise advice. I wish I had taken it earlier in life.

In 1959 I wrote a longish introduction to a reprint of Owen's treatise, as a kind of hors d'oeuvres to the study of the work itself. Though the essay was not originally intended to be read apart from Owen, I let it be reprinted as a

---

5. John Owen, *Works* (Edinburgh: Banner of Truth, 1967), 10.193–428.

6. T(otal Depravity)—U(nconditional election)—L(imited atonement)—I(rresistible grace)—P(erseverance of the saints). It works only in English.

7. Roger Nicole, "Particular Redemption," in *Our Savior God*, ed. James Montgomery Boice (Grand Rapids: Baker, 1980), 168–69.

separate pamphlet, and eventually reprinted it separately myself as a chapter in *A Quest for Godliness.*[8] (When you can't beat 'em, join 'em.) Terry Miethe, discussing it,[9] evidently did not think it necessary to read Owen's treatise, where the actual argumentation is contained, and faulted me for outlining in my introduction assertions about Calvinism that it would take a book or two to make good.[10] Miethe's whole discussion is unsatisfying; he regularly confuses his readers by not distinguishing his own idea of divine sovereignty and election, and of human freedom, from that of Calvinists generally and myself in particular; he fails to engage with the best exponents of the position he controverts; he presents arguments inexactly; he writes constantly as if what is at issue is the availability of Christ to all who turn to him, something that was never in dispute; he treats echoes of biblical phraseology in sixteenth-century Anglican formularies as the Church of England taking sides in a seventeenth-century debate; and he claims to be defending the view that "the redemptive events in the life of Jesus provided a salvation so extensive and so broad as to potentially include the whole of humanity past, present and future!"[11] But he never tells us how this salvation might reach humanity past, or persons who do not encounter the gospel in the present. Again, he writes: "Man's natural inability to believe, (it has been shown) is not taught, at least in Ephesians 2:8 [who ever thought it was?], and (I would argue) not in the rest of Scripture either"[12]—which makes one wonder how he would handle John 6:43–44; Romans 8:7–8; and 1 Corinthians 2:14. Understanding is not advanced by such discussions.

Knowing God's Love: Gratitude and Joy

We have seen that the measure of *agape* is its giving, and that our holy sovereign triune self-revealed Creator-God shows *agape* to all his rational creatures in some ways and to some in all ways; that is, not only in providential

8. (Wheaton: Crossway, 1990), 125–48.

9. Terry Miethe, "The Universal Power of the Atonement," in *The Grace of God, the Will of Man: A Case for Arminianism,* ed. Clark H. Pinnock (Grand Rapids: Zondervan, 1989), 71–96. "I was asked by my editor and publisher to 'address' Packer's introduction," 95 n. 44.

10. Ibid., 87–88. "This is a clear example of a simple assertion, which in logic amounts to nothing more than the fallacy of *petitio principii* (begging the question)." The same might with equal justice, or injustice, be said of Miethe's own statement. Miethe adduces a professional logician, Irving M. Copi, to explain what begging the question means (see 95 n. 43). From the Copi quote it is clear that when no inferential argument is being attempted, as in the Packer passage that Miethe is discussing, no question is or can be begged.

11. Ibid., 72; quoting from Donald Lake, "He Died for All: The Universal Dimensions of the Atonement," in *Grace Unlimited,* ed. Clark H. Pinnock (Minneapolis: Bethany Fellowship, 1975), 31.

12. Ibid., 86.

provision but also in saving them from sin for eternal glory. We have seen that there is a gospel addressed to all, which the church is charged to take to all, that proclaims a Savior who is there for all in the power of his atoning death and risen life; and we have seen that through this gospel a pattern of sovereign grace in effectual calling, justification, sanctification, and glorification is being worked out in life after life. We may now say that to know that nothing ever "will be able to separate us from the love of God that is in Christ Jesus our Lord" (Rom. 8:39) is the height of Christian assurance, and to that "to know this love that surpasses knowledge—that you may be filled to the measure of all the fullness of God" (Eph. 3:18–19) is the acme of Christian progress, and that these are the twin peaks of true Christian living in this world.

In all the Christian's knowledge of God's gracious giving Luther's *pro me*—the "for me" of Galatians 2:20—is central. To know that from eternity my Maker, foreseeing my sin, foreloved me and resolved to save me, though it would be at the cost of Cavalry; to know that the divine Son was appointed from eternity to be my Savior, and that in love he became man for me and died for me and now lives to intercede for me and will one day come in person to take me home; to know that the Lord "who loved me and gave himself for me" (Gal. 2:20) and who "came and preached peace" to me through his messengers (Eph. 2:17) has by his Spirit raised me from spiritual death to life-giving union and communion with himself, and has promised to hold me fast and never let me go—this is knowledge that brings overwhelming gratitude and joy. As Luther himself put it in his answer to Erasmus, "now that God has taken my salvation out of the control of my own will, and put it under the control of His, and promised to save me, not according to my working or running, but according to his own grace and mercy, I have the comfortable certainty that he is faithful and will not lie to me, and that He is also great and powerful, so that no devils or opposition can break Him or pluck me from Him. 'No one', He says, 'shall pluck them out of my hand, because my Father which gave them to me is greater than all' (John 10:28–29). Thus it is that, if not all, yet some, indeed many, are saved . . . Furthermore, I have the comfortable certainty that I please God, not by reason of the merit of my works, but by reason of His merciful favour promised to me; so that, if I work too little, or badly, He does not impute it to me, but with fatherly compassion pardons me and makes me better. This is the glorying of all the saints in their God."[13] Such glorying is in truth mainstream biblical Christianity—an immeasurably richer reality than can ever emerge from any account of the love of God that stops short at general goodwill and that drops the personal, individualizing *pro me* of sovereign grace.

13. Martin Luther, *The Bondage of the Will*, trans. J. I. Packer and O. R. Johnston (London: James Clarke; Old Tappan, N.J.: Revell, 1957), 314.

"Thank God for his gift that is too wonderful for words!" (2 Cor. 9:15 CEV). May all God's people come to appreciate it! In heaven we all most certainly will, and it is a sad thing that any in this world should take up with a theology that in any measure deprives them of this cognitive foretaste of heaven here and now. I pray that our loving God will show the full glory of his love, in its particularity as well as its universality, to us all.

19

Does Middle Knowledge Solve the Problem of Divine Sovereignty?

J. A. CRABTREE

In "Middle Knowledge: A Calvinist-Arminian Rapprochement?" William Lane Craig suggests that the views of the medieval Spanish Jesuit, Luis de Molina (1535–1600), amount to a reconciliation of the views of Calvinists and Arminians.[1] Accordingly, he recommends that we give fresh consideration to Molina's views, especially to his notion of divine middle knowledge. Craig is confident that if modern participants in the Calvinist-Arminian debate were to adopt Molina's notion of divine middle knowledge, we would see a closing of the gap that now divides them.

My purpose in this chapter is to offer a personal reaction to this particular call for reconciliation. Craig maintains that Molina has shown us how divine sovereignty and the absolute autonomy of the human will are compatible concepts. Accordingly, if I, a Calvinist with respect to my views on divine sovereignty, would adopt Molina's views on the matter, I could concede to my Arminian brother the reality of absolute human autonomy without compromising my commitment to divine sovereignty. And by doing so, I would greatly reduce the gap that divides us. Here then is the question I wish to address in this chapter: Can I, a Calvinistic divine determinist,[2] embrace Mo-

---

1. Published in *The Grace of God, the Will of Man: A Case for Arminianism*, ed. Clark H. Pinnock (Grand Rapids: Zondervan, 1989), 141–64.
2. By "divine determinist" I mean to denote one who believes that every aspect of everything that occurs in the whole of reality is ultimately caused and determined by God.

lina's conception of middle knowledge and thereby see my way clear to affirm the absolute autonomy of the human will?

My discussion, in four major sections, will explain Molina's theory of divine foreknowledge and middle knowledge in the context of the problem he was attempting to solve; assess whether Molina's theory of divine foreknowledge and his conception of middle knowledge are philosophically and biblically viable concepts and whether they reconcile divine sovereignty and human autonomy in the way that Craig and Molina claim that they do; address an underlying assumption in Craig's and Molina's appeal—namely, that Calvinism cannot give an adequate account of human freedom; and summarize the reasons why I am unmoved by Craig's appeal to embrace Molina's distinctive solution to the divine sovereignty/human freedom question.

Molina's Theory of Divine Middle Knowledge

To understand Molina's concept of divine foreknowledge and the concept of middle knowledge that accompanies it, we need to understand it as the solution to a problem he thought it solved.

Molina's Problem

In Molina's day, as today, the prevailing philosophical assumptions forced one to choose between two opposing theological positions, Calvinism and Arminianism. But, as Molina saw it, both positions are deficient when judged strictly from the standpoint of biblical teaching. Each holds some things that are right and some things that are wrong. The truth revealed in biblical teaching upholds some aspects of each of these opposing systems. It repudiates aspects of each as well.

To be specific, Molina believed that these four doctrinal positions capture the Scripture's teaching with respect to the points at issue:

1. The free-will choices of a human being are such that they always could have been other than they were. If person P freely does X at time T under the set of circumstances C, it is always true that P could have done not-X at exactly the same time and under exactly the same set of circumstances. Nothing necessitated that P do X at time T. Other than the resolution of P's own will at the time of his choice, nothing made it necessary that P do X at that time. Hence, there was no predetermination of P's choice of X by any cause. The human will is autonomous and functions independently of every other reality, including the will

of God. I will refer to this first doctrine as a belief in the *absolute autonomy of the human will,* or as a belief in *absolute human autonomy.*

2. At the same time, God knows infallibly every detail of every event that will occur in the history of the cosmos. He knows all this before anything has transpired in time. I will refer to this second doctrine as a belief in the *de fide*[3] *doctrine of divine foreknowledge* (where *de fide* means, literally, "of the faith").

3. God is the ultimate and final cause of every detail of every event that will occur in the history of the cosmos. I will refer to this third doctrine as a belief in the *de fide doctrine of divine providence.*

4. God's choice ultimately determines who will be saved and who will not be saved. I will refer to this fourth doctrine as a belief in the *de fide doctrine of divine election.*

We can summarize his views by saying that Molina believes in *the absolute autonomy of the human will* at the same time that he believes in the *de fide doctrines of divine sovereignty.* (By the *de fide doctrines of divine sovereignty* I mean to denote the *de fide* doctrines of divine foreknowledge, divine providence, and divine election. Throughout this chapter, when I refer to the de fide doctrines of divine sovereignty I mean to denote strictly the preceding definitions.)

Calvinism, by way of contrast to Molina, willingly embraces the de fide doctrines of divine sovereignty but rejects the absolute autonomy of the human will. Conversely, Arminianism embraces the absolute autonomy of the human will but rejects the de fide doctrines of divine sovereignty.

The problem, as Molina saw it, is that both Arminians and Calvinists are stuck in their respective systems. Their philosophical and theological commitments force them to embrace the doctrines that are entailed by their respective systems rather than the doctrines advanced by biblical teaching. Molina attempted to find a way for both Arminians and Calvinists to break out of their respective systems.

---

3. In Molina, *Concordia* 4.52.10, we read, "And this last point is surely demanded by the freedom of the created will, a freedom that is no less *de fide* than are that same foreknowledge and predestination, as was shown at length in Disputation 23." Translation is from Luis de Molina, *On Divine Foreknowledge* (Part 4 of the *Concordia*), trans. with an introduction and notes by Alfredo J. Freddoso (Ithaca, N.Y.: Cornell University Press, 1988). All subsequent citations from Molina are taken from this translation by Freddoso. In a footnote Freddoso writes, "A doctrine that is *de fide* (literally, of the faith) is one explicitly affirmed by the Church in a solemn manner (for example, in a creed of conciliar decree)." Molina, *On Divine Foreknowledge,* 169 n. 14. Molina's commitment to the doctrines of foreknowledge, providence, and election was based on his conviction that these doctrines were the established doctrines of the church. My use of the title *de fide* to describe these doctrines is intended to reflect Molina's conviction that these were officially established church doctrines. See also Molina, *Concordia* 4.53.21.

The Key to Solving the Problem

Why do Calvinists feel compelled to reject the absolute autonomy of the human will? Because they understand the absolute autonomy of the human will to be incompatible with the de fide doctrines of divine sovereignty. If the human will is autonomous, then it would be impossible even for an all-knowing God to have the foreknowledge that de fide theology says he has, to exercise the providential control it says he has, and to choose the saved in the way it says he does. In view of their commitment to the de fide doctrines of divine sovereignty, Calvinists are forced to reject the absolute autonomy of the human will.

And why do Arminians feel compelled to reject the de fide doctrines of divine sovereignty? Like Calvinists, Arminians believe that the absolute autonomy of the human will and the de fide views of divine sovereignty are incompatible. If the human will is autonomous, then God cannot have the foreknowledge, providential control, and power to elect that the de fide doctrines say he has. So, in view of their commitment to the absolute autonomy of the human will, Arminians are forced to reject the de fide doctrines of divine sovereignty.

Calvinists and Arminians agree fundamentally on an important point: the autonomy of the human will can in no way be reconciled to the de fide views on divine sovereignty. Where they disagree is at which pole of the contradiction the truth lies. So the two positions are at an impasse; there is no third way so long as the terms of the discussion remain here. If divine sovereignty and human freedom are incompatible, then there are only two choices: either Calvinism (which accepts divine sovereignty at the expense of human autonomy) or Arminianism (which accepts human autonomy at the expense of divine sovereignty).

Clearly, the assumed incompatibility of divine sovereignty and human autonomy channels Calvinists and Arminians into their respective systems. If Molina is to accomplish his agenda—if he is successfully to clear the way for both divine sovereignty and human autonomy to be embraced simultaneously—he must refute the prevailing dogma that divine sovereignty and human autonomy are incompatible. In other words, he must achieve their philosophical reconciliation.

Molina's Concept of Middle Knowledge

Middle knowledge is the key to Molina's reconciliation of divine sovereignty and human autonomy. To understand the concept of middle knowledge, let us engage in a bit of science fiction.

Imagine a genius human inventor named Egbert who created a whole world. (Call it Robo-world.) First, he created a huge building with thick, totally impenetrable walls, floor, and ceiling. Then he invented a computer and other equipment capable of counteracting every effect of the outside world within this building. Gravity, magnetism—all were canceled. As a consequence, the inside of the building was completely devoid of any physical laws; all had been nullified. More computers and machines were then invented to create an entirely new physical environment exactly to the specifications of Egbert. Inside the building, everything, down to the least physical law, was totally controlled by Egbert's computers.

Next Egbert invented scores of robots and programmed them all to move, act, communicate, and learn. He programmed each so that it had extremely detailed instructions as to how to respond and to act in any specific set of circumstances. Furthermore, he equipped each robot so that he could control its movements and actions by remote control. Therefore, each robot would be controlled either by its own internal programming or directly by the inventor when he might override the robot's programming.

Finally, Egbert set all the robots and a variety of inert props in exactly that initial state he wanted. And with the push of a button, he started Robo-world in motion.

Before programming his various computers, Egbert had carefully mapped out all of the various possibilities for what Robo-world could look like. He mapped out in exact detail every world that he could possibly achieve. Once he had defined the physical laws that would obtain, the programming that he would give to each of his robots and ruling computers, and the initial state of Robo-world, he was able to predict, moment by moment, exactly what would occur throughout the entire history of each of the possible Robo-worlds.

After he had predicted the exact history of every possible Robo-world, Egbert then selected the possible Robo-world that he decided he wanted to bring into being. He programmed all the computers and set up the initial state necessary to bring exactly that possible world about; then he pushed the button and set it in motion. The result was precisely the Robo-world that he had wanted to bring into being.

Our genius, Egbert, already knows, before he pushes the button, exactly what will transpire at every moment of this Robo-world that he is about to bring into being. He had already mapped out its entire history before he even decided to create it. So, with respect to the actual Robo-world, Egbert has *absolute foreknowledge*. Furthermore, he has providential-like control over this actual Robo-world, for everything that transpires in it has ultimately been brought about by his design, his act, and his choice.

As Molina understands it, God's creation of the actual world we live in is very much like Egbert's creation of Robo-world. Before he created anything, God had mapped out every detail of every event of every possible world. He considered each possible world (given his utterly detailed and exhaustive knowledge of each one) and chose the one he wanted to bring into existence. He then created the world that he had decided he wanted to bring into existence.

But there is a significant difference between Robo-world and our world. Robo-world is peopled by nothing but robots. Every creature in Robo-world has its every move totally determined by the programming and the engineering of Egbert. But our world is different. Alongside the biological and physical "machines" in our world are free moral agents, human beings. Human choices and actions are not determined by programmed instructions that God wrote for each human will. On the contrary, human choices are "free." They are autonomous, independent of any determining reality.

It is easy to see how Egbert could have mapped out every moment of every possible Robo-world; every move that is made in that world is determined by him and his choices. Given his exhaustive knowledge of the laws and the principles that would obtain in any possible Robo-world, he could understandably predict exactly what would happen. Similarly, it is easy to see how God could predict the entire history of any possible world he might create—if we ignore free-will creatures. Apart from them, everything else would be governed by physical laws and principles of which God had a complete and infallible understanding.

But what happens when you bring free-will creatures into the picture? According to Molina, nothing changes. God, unlike Egbert, is capable of knowing what choices a particular free-will creature will make in a specific set of circumstances. God is as capable of predicting the choice of one of his free-will creatures as Egbert is of predicting the choice of one of his robots. That God could have such knowledge is a mysterious and marvelous feat, of course. But God is more than a genius; he is God. And God can do such a thing. *This special and marvelous knowledge of what a particular free-will creature will do in a specific set of circumstances is what Molina calls middle knowledge.*[4]

Because of God's middle knowledge, God is capable of doing with respect to the actual cosmos what Egbert could do with respect to Robo-world. Before creating anything, he could map out the entire history of each and every possible world ahead of time and then, on the basis of an exhaustive knowledge of every detail of the history of each possible world, choose which possible world he wanted to bring into being.[5] Because of his ability to have middle knowledge, the free choices of the free-will creatures he would create in any possible world presented no obstacles to his mapping out the history of that world. He knew what each particular creature would choose in each and

4. For the purposes of this chapter, I will not discuss why it is called middle knowledge. For a helpful discussion of that question, see William Lane Craig, "Middle Knowledge: A Calvinist-Arminian Rapprochement?" in *The Grace of God, the Will of Man,* 141–64, esp. 144–51. See also Molina, *On Divine Foreknowledge,* 23 and 47.

5. Strictly speaking, Molina believes that the priority of God's foreknowledge of every possible world, his choice of a possible world to create, and his decision to do so constitute not a temporal priority, but a logical one. He sees all three of these events as temporally simultaneous. I have, for the sake of simplifying my discussion, chosen not to introduce this subtle complication into my exposition of Molina's views; it does not in any way affect my understanding or critique of them. See Craig, "Middle Knowledge," 145, for a discussion of this issue.

every situation. Hence, he could predict exactly the outcome of every event in every possible world.

As Molina understands it, this is how our world is situated with respect to God. The world that now exists is a world that God created, having freely chosen to do so. Of all the possible worlds he could have created, this is the one he wanted to bring into existence. And when he made his choice, he did so with an exhaustive knowledge of every detail of every event that would transpire within it throughout the full extent of its history.

The Reconciliation of Divine Sovereignty and Human Autonomy

It should be clear that Molina's understanding of God's foreknowledge is compatible with the de fide doctrine of divine foreknowledge. Under Molina's view, God foreknows every aspect of every event that will occur in our world.

Furthermore, under Molina's views, everything that occurs in our world is ultimately the result of God's free choice to create this world in particular. Hence, he is the ultimate cause of every aspect of every event in our world. This includes his being the ultimate cause of everything that occurs due to the choices of free-will creatures. In creating the possible world that he did, he was causing to come into existence every free-will decision that every free-will creature in that world would ever make. So Molina's God exercises a divine providence that is just as extensive as that which he exercises in the de fide view of divine providence.

Finally, no less than in the de fide doctrine of election, Molina's God elects those particular individuals who will be saved. That set of particular individuals who will come to salvation in this world is ultimately determined by the free choice of God. God created this particular world in which exactly this set of people, and not some other set, will (as a result of their own autonomous choice) choose to believe and to be saved. By his choice to create this particular world, God is the one who determines who will be saved and who will not.

But what is especially interesting to Molina is this: although his conception of divine foreknowledge (which is based on divine middle knowledge of the choices of free-will creatures) upholds the de fide doctrines of divine sovereignty, it also upholds a belief in the absolute autonomy of the human will. The free-will creatures who people this world are truly free. God does not cause them to choose what they choose. Nothing makes them choose what they choose. Their choice is nothing more than the resolution of their own will. Under Molina's view, therefore, we can acknowledge divine foreknowledge, divine providence, and divine election without in any way redefining or compromising our concept of human freedom.

So Molina thinks that, by means of middle knowledge, he has discovered a way to preserve a full-bodied commitment to the reality of human autonomy while accepting the de fide doctrines of divine sovereignty. In other words, he has found a way to embrace the truth lying at the core of Calvinism without rejecting the truth lying at the core of Arminianism, and vice versa.

The Viability of Middle Knowledge

Molina's views, as we have seen, depend upon his concept of middle knowledge. They therefore assume that middle knowledge is a viable and coherent concept. But is it?

The Surface Problem with Middle Knowledge

On the face of it, middle knowledge presents a problem: is it possible for God to know that X is true when nothing determines or necessitates that X be true? It is difficult to see how.

Take Peter as an example. Jesus predicted that Peter would deny him three times during the night of his arrest, before the dawning of the next day. How did Jesus—or, more importantly, God—know this about Peter? If Molina is right, God had middle knowledge of Peter's denials. He knew Peter so thoroughly that, knowing all the circumstances Peter would find himself in, he knew exactly how Peter would respond in each of those circumstances.

But how could God know that? If Peter's will is what Molina says it is—utterly autonomous—then nothing at the time of Jesus' prediction necessitates that Peter deny Jesus. In fact, Molina's view requires that Peter could have done otherwise. If Peter had chosen to do so, he could have been courageously loyal to Jesus instead of denying him. He acted the coward because he chose to, not because he had to. But if nothing whatsoever necessitated the choices that he made, up to the time that he made them, how could God have known what those choices would be? Peter's choices were not determined ahead of time. So, if they had not yet been decided, how could God know the outcome of those decisions? No one, not even God, can know the outcome of an autonomous decision that has not yet been made, can he? To assert the possibility of such knowledge is problematic.

Molina's Response to This Problem

In spite of this surface problem, Molina nonetheless thinks that middle knowledge is possible. Craig explains Molina's defense:

Now it might be asked how it is that by knowing his own essence alone God is able to have middle knowledge concerning what free creatures would do in any situation. Molina and his compatriot and fellow Jesuit, Francisco Suarez, differed in their responses to this question. Molina's answer is alluded to in the words of the initial citation above: "because of the depth of his knowledge." According to Molina, God not only knows in his own essence all possible creatures, but his intellect infinitely surpasses the capabilities of finite wills so that he understands them so thoroughly that he knows not only what they could choose under any set of circumstances, but what they would choose. In another place Molina speaks of "his immense and altogether unlimited knowledge, by which he comprehends in the deepest and most eminent way whatever falls under his omnipotence, to penetrate created free choice in such a way as to discern and intuit with certainty which part it is going to turn itself to by its own innate freedom." Because his intellect is infinite, whereas a free creature is finite, God's insight into the will of a free creature is of such a surpassing quality that God knows exactly what the free creature would do were God to place him in a certain set of circumstances.[6]

Molina's Dual Account of Middle Knowledge

Molina's explanation of the possibility of middle knowledge seems to incorporate two significantly different accounts of middle knowledge. On the one hand, his official account of middle knowledge is to describe it as a direct, noninferential, intuitive knowledge that God has. God knows immediately (and noninferentially) that person P will do X at time T. On the other hand, there are intimations of a very different account.[7] He subtly implies that middle knowledge is God's ability to infer infallibly that person P will do X at time T on the basis of his infinitely thorough knowledge of the will of P.[8] This implicit, covert account of middle knowledge plays an important role in Molina's presentation of his doctrine. It helps to make an otherwise problematic account of divine middle knowledge seem less problematic.

6. Ibid., 150. See also Molina, *Concordia* 4.52.11.
7. This is a central claim of this chapter; it is crucial to my argument. It is potentially controversial. Some defenders of Molina would want to dispute the existence of this different, second account of middle knowledge. Ideally, of course, my chapter should go on to present a thorough defense of the existence of this second account. I do cite, in the following pages of text and footnotes, what I think is the most important evidence that a second account influences Molina's thought and the formation of his doctrine. But finally demonstrate this claim would require a much more detailed and technical discussion than I can present here. I am confident that such a defense could be made.
8. To my knowledge, Molina never makes clear exactly what he understands the will of a person to be. Neither is it made clear, therefore, of what the knowledge of a person's will would consist. Molina's vagueness on the nature of the will leads to considerable confusion as to exactly what God's knowledge of an individual's will is. Precisely because of this confusion, Molina can operate according to two very different accounts of middle knowledge at the same time without being adequately aware of the logical tension that results.

The Official Account: Noninferential Knowledge

In his official account of middle knowledge, Molina appeals to the magnificence of God and his abilities.[9] The possibility of middle knowledge finds its explanation in the fact that God's knowledge is deep, immense, and unlimited. If God's knowledge of a particular finite will is infinitely thorough, how could it help but include a complete knowledge of everything that that particular person will choose in any and every situation? This account assumes that God's knowledge of what a particular person will do is a kind of immediate, intuitive knowledge. God does not infer or deduce what P will do from other things that he knows about P. Rather, he knows what P will do directly, immediately, and noninferentially.

This account of middle knowledge does not answer the question as to how middle knowledge is possible. It tells us instead why an answer will not be forthcoming. In effect, Molina's response is this: "How is God able to have middle knowledge of what person P will do, when P has not yet decided himself what he will do? Because he's God; that's how!" This is an appeal to divine "mystery." It is as if Molina were to say: "I shouldn't dismiss the concept of middle knowledge just because I can't make any sense of it. God 'works in mysterious ways,' 'his ways are not our ways' . . . ."

An appeal to divine "mystery" is a common but suspicious move. At times the mysteries we embrace are incomprehensible to us not because they are mysteries, but rather because they are nonsense. Nonsense masquerading in the respectable dress of mystery is still nonsense. So, before we settle for an appeal to divine mystery, we can reasonably ask for assurance that Molina's concept of middle knowledge is a coherent concept. Perhaps it is incomprehensible because it is an incoherent notion, not because, for lack of being God, we are incapable of imagining such a lofty feat. Consequently, if Molina wants us to embrace his views, he must offer a more compelling answer than "he's God; he can do it." The problematic question remains: If the human will is absolutely autonomous, how can we reasonably assert that God is able to foreknow what persons with autonomous freedom will choose?

In my judgment Molina, throughout all his discussions of this subject, implicitly suggests an answer to this latter question by means of an unofficial account of middle knowledge. At the same time that he officially disallows

---

9. Molina appeals to the magnificence of God's knowledge in a variety of ways. Among them, he appeals to God's "most profound and inscrutable comprehension" (Molina, *Concordia* 4.52.9), to his "absolutely profound and absolutely preeminent comprehension" (4.52.11), to his being able to comprehend free-will creatures with "infinite excess" (4.52.12), to "the infinite and wholly unlimited perfection and acumen of His intellect" (4.52.29), to "the acumen and absolute perfection of His intellect" (4.52.33), and to the "perspicacity and depth of the knower over and beyond the things known" (4.52.35).

it, he subtly and covertly relies on a fundamentally different account of middle knowledge to render his doctrine plausible.

The Covert Account: Inferential Knowledge

Molina's official account of divine middle knowledge is marked by some curious features. To focus on the most important one: Molina predominantly presents divine middle knowledge as a deep and profound knowledge of the faculty of choice and only rarely as a knowledge of the choice itself, that is, the outcome of a particular event of choosing.

> Finally, the third type is *middle* knowledge, by which, in virtue of the most profound and inscrutable comprehension of each *faculty* [emphasis added] of free choice, He saw in His own essence what each such *faculty* [emphasis added] would do with its innate freedom were it to be placed in this or in that or, indeed, in infinitely many orders of things—even though it would really be able, if it so willed, to do the opposite, as is clear from what was said in Disputations 49 and 50.[10]

> But God knows the determination of a created faculty of choice before it exists because of the infinite and unlimited perfection of His intellect and because of the preeminent comprehension by which He comprehends *that faculty* [emphasis added] in His essence in a way far deeper than that in which it exists in itself; and thus . . . He knows which part it will in its freedom turn itself toward.[11]

Molina's characteristic description of middle knowledge is curious; and it is significantly problematic in the light of what he officially claims middle knowledge to be. If middle knowledge is what Molina's official account says it is, the most apt description of it would be an intuitive, noninferential knowledge of the actual choice itself, that is, of the outcome of a particular event of choosing. Why, then, does Molina explain it in terms of a profound knowledge of the faculty that will make the choice? By Molina's own official account, it would seem that the nature of a person's faculty of choice does not determine, cause, or otherwise necessitate the precise choice he will make. How, then, is a knowledge of Peter's faculty of choice relevant to the issue of what Peter will choose? If his faculty of choice does not determine or necessitate what choices Peter will make, a thorough and deep knowledge of his faculty of choice will not provide God with any knowledge of what choices he will actually make. (Nothing is gained by stressing that God's knowledge of Peter's faculty of choice is infinitely deep.) Yet this is Molina's official account: God knows what choices Peter will make in a particular sit-

---

10. Ibid., 4.52.9.
11. Ibid., 4.53.1.14. See also 4.52.10, 4.52.11, 4.52.33, and 4.53.2.31. These citations reflect how Molina most frequently portrays divine middle knowledge.

uation precisely because, due to the "infinite and wholly unlimited perfection and acumen of His intellect," God has "the most profound and inscrutable comprehension" of Peter's "faculty of free choice."[12]

Molina's characteristic explanation of middle knowledge is at odds with his own official account of it because Molina has unwittingly imported a different account of middle knowledge into his own conception of it. According to this second, covert account, middle knowledge is possible because it is based on an inference from God's infinitely thorough knowledge of the particular will itself. God could know that Peter would deny Jesus because he thoroughly understood Peter's will. Peter has not yet made any decision. He has not yet even confronted the choice in question. But that is no obstacle to God's being able to know what Peter will do. God's in-depth knowledge of Peter himself, the one who will be making the decision, allows him to infer what Peter will decide from the thorough knowledge he has of who Peter is.[13]

This inferential account of middle knowledge has a distinct advantage over Molina's official account: it is comprehensible and rationally plausible. It does not simply appeal to the mystery of God and dogmatically assert that middle knowledge is possible because of the unfathomable immensity of God.

Even we mere human beings are capable of certain forms of middle knowledge of the inferential sort. My wife knows that, were she to offer me a piece of pie tonight, I will accept it. My wife knows that I will drink a cup of coffee when I arise in the morning. She knows that, out of a sense of duty, I will go teach my class tonight whether I feel like it or not. These are all forms of middle knowledge. My wife knows what I will choose, of my own free will, in specific situations in the future. And she is not guessing. She knows what I will do. This is exactly the sort of middle knowledge that Molina wants to ascribe to God.

But the middle knowledge we possess is significantly limited. My wife does not and cannot foreknow what future circumstances I will confront. Consequently, no matter how well she knows me, she cannot predict with unfailing accuracy all that I will eventually do. Even more importantly, even if she has a thorough grasp of the situation and knows me as well as any human being can know another, she still could be wrong. I could surprise her. I could, for some inexplicable reason, refuse the pie or the coffee. I could decide to be utterly irresponsible and not show up for class. However unlikely, I may act out of character in a way that my wife could never predict.

---

12. Ibid., 4.52.9 and 4.52.29.

13. See ibid., 4.52.10, 4.52.11, 4.52.12, 4.52.13, and 4.52.30. These passages all strongly suggest an account of middle knowledge that relies heavily on the notion that a person's choice results from the operations of his own will and that, as a consequence, to have a profound knowledge of the person himself and of his will shall necessarily give one a knowledge of what choices he will make. The citations in note 11 reflect this same conception of middle knowledge.

Here is where Molina's insistence that God's knowledge is deep and infinitely thorough is important. Whereas my wife could be surprised and find me choosing what she never would have predicted, God cannot and will not be similarly surprised. My wife's knowledge of me is finite; God's is infinite. My wife is surprised because there will always be subtle aspects of who I am and how I think that she does not understand. But not God; his understanding is infinitely thorough. No aspect of my will and being is beyond his understanding. God, therefore, can have utterly certain and totally infallible middle knowledge; his grasp of who I am is perfect.

It seems undeniable that this is Molina's real, working conception of middle knowledge, and it is utterly incompatible with his official account.

The Logical Tension in Molina's Account of Middle Knowledge

As we have seen, there are two important aspects to Molina's project. He wants to affirm the absolute autonomy of human choice. (For Molina, true autonomy would mean that human choice is not caused, not determined, and not necessitated by anything whatsoever.) Molina also wants to affirm that divine middle knowledge is a rationally coherent doctrine.

In order to achieve the former goal, Molina must affirm that nothing whatsoever determines in advance of a person's choice what that choice will be. He must affirm that no external causes necessitate the choices a person will make. But if he is committed to espousing this sort of human autonomy, then he cannot explain middle knowledge as a sort of divine inference. For, on the assumption that nothing whatsoever determines or necessitates Peter's choices, how could God infer what Peter will do? There is nothing to serve as the basis for such an inference. Peter's choice is not caused by anything; it is not determined or necessitated by anything. Hence, there is absolutely no basis from which God could infer the choice that Peter will make. Consequently, the only account of divine middle knowledge that is logically available to Molina is one wherein God has direct, immediate, intuitive knowledge of a yet unformed and undetermined choice that Peter shall make. Logically, therefore, if Molina is to successfully espouse true human autonomy, he has no choice but to conceive of middle knowledge as an intuitive, noninferential knowledge of voluntary choices. Officially, this is the account he wants to give,[14] for it succeeds at reconciling human autonomy with divine middle knowledge. But, as I have been suggesting, it is not that simple;

14. See ibid., 4.53.1.10–14. Molina appears to consider and explicitly reject something much like what I am calling his covert account of middle knowledge. Although he officially rejects it, he covertly relies upon it.

the other aspect of Molina's project is not satisfied by this official account of middle knowledge.

Molina's official account of middle knowledge does nothing to demonstrate the rational coherence of the doctrine (unless one is satisfied with a dogmatic declaration of the possibility of divine middle knowledge backed by an appeal to mystery). To understand middle knowledge as rationally compelling, therefore, Molina is constantly drawn to a radically different conception of middle knowledge—to a conception of middle knowledge as a sort of inferential knowledge.

The concept of middle knowledge is rendered plausible when it is viewed as an inference based on God's thorough knowledge of the forces at work within each person—the forces that determine and necessitate his choices. We have a kind of middle knowledge of one another's future choices. If divine middle knowledge is to be comprehensible to us, it will be by analogy to the sort of middle knowledge we possess. So, if divine middle knowledge is understood to be inferential in nature, it becomes analogous to our own and is thereby made comprehensible to us. Accordingly, over and over Molina is seduced into describing middle knowledge in a way that suggests just such an account. Middle knowledge as a form of divine inference is the implicit, covert account of middle knowledge that underlies everything that Molina argues.

But, as we have just seen, an account of middle knowledge as a form of inference is utterly incompatible with Molina's official account. It presupposes that God could have prior knowledge of some reality that will somehow cause, determine, or necessitate the voluntary choice that an individual will make in the future. If God is going to infer what Peter will choose, he must infer Peter's future choice on the basis of something he knows about Peter now. In other words, if something about Peter now necessitates that Peter will deny Jesus at a particular time in the future, then if God knows that relevant thing about Peter, he can know (infer) that Peter will deny Jesus. But if, as Molina maintains in his official account, nothing whatsoever necessitates or determines any of Peter's free choices,[15] then there exists nothing from which God could infer Peter's choices. So, if human choice is absolutely

---

15. An important question can be raised about this. Is Molina's position that nothing whatsoever causes, determines, or necessitates the voluntary choices of a human being? Or, is Molina's position that nothing other than the person's will itself causes, determines, or necessitates the voluntary choices of a human being? It seems that Molina is not clear on this point. When he is intent on pressing his official account in order to maintain human autonomy, he seems to emphasize explicitly the notion that nothing causes or necessitates human choice. But when he slips into reasoning in accordance with his covert account (in order to render the notion of divine middle knowledge as plausible as possible), he clearly seems to think that a person's actions arise from and are determined by the will of that individual. His double-mindedness on this issue seems to be an exact reflection of his double-mindedness on the nature of middle knowledge; for the two issues are intimately related to one another. Furthermore, as I suggested (n. 8), all of Molina's confusion is exacerbated by the vagueness of his concept of the human will.

undetermined and uncaused in the way that Molina officially maintains, then Molina's covert account of middle knowledge is logically incompatible with that official account. There can be no divine inference from God's knowledge of a person's faculty of choice to the choices he will make if, officially, the choices a person makes are in no way necessitated by that person's faculty of choice. Nonetheless, Molina's writings are fraught with this tension. He officially espouses middle knowledge according to one conception of it (as direct, intuitive knowledge), but he attempts to render it plausible with language informed by a very different conception of it (as inferential knowledge). The two conceptions are incompatible. Middle knowledge must be viewed either as a sort of mysterious noninferential knowledge or as a sort of inferential knowledge; but logically we cannot have it both ways. Yet this is exactly what Molina attempts to do.

We can summarize the tension in Molina's account this way: what is required for Molina to succeed at making middle knowledge comprehensible (and therefore plausible and beyond suspicion) is in fatal tension with what is required for Molina to succeed at coherently maintaining the absolute autonomy of the human will. To reconcile divine sovereignty and human autonomy, Molina offers an official account of middle knowledge wherein human autonomy is assumed at the outset. But to convince us that this official account of middle knowledge involves a viable and plausible concept, he resorts to descriptions of middle knowledge wherein the predetermination of human choice is logically assumed—thereby nullifying and denying human autonomy. Hence, he takes back with one hand what he has given us with the other.

Can Molina's Covert Account Reconcile Middle Knowledge with Human Autonomy?

But perhaps the equivocation we have discussed is sloppiness on the part of Molina. His equivocation on the nature of middle knowledge aside, is Molina not right? Do we not have in middle knowledge the key to reconciling divine sovereignty and human autonomy? If we were to hold Molina to an inferential account of middle knowledge (the account that is more rationally compelling), would he not be able to thereby reconcile human autonomy and divine foreknowledge?

Under my view as a divine determinist, it is clear how God's infinitely thorough knowledge of Peter's will could explain how God can foreknow what Peter will choose. God, the creator of Peter's will, determines the character and workings of that will. The character of Peter's will shall in turn determine what choices he will make. Therefore, if God understands the character and workings of Peter's will with infinite thoroughness—which is to understand his own design and purpose in the creation of Peter's will—then he will certainly be able to predict what Peter will choose. But all this assumes that there is a chain of causes leading up to the choices that Peter makes and that God, the creator, is the ultimate author and determiner of that chain of causes and the choices that ultimately result. But what if we assume human autonomy instead? Can inferential middle knowledge still adequately account for divine foreknowledge?

According to his (covert) inferential account of middle knowledge, Molina attempts to offer the same explanation of divine foreknowledge as does the divine determinist: namely, Peter's choices are determined by the nature and workings of Peter's will. Consequently, if God has an infinite knowledge of that will (its nature and its mode of working) he will be able to predict its output—Peter's choices. One's choices are the necessary reflection of who one is. So, if God knows Peter perfectly, then from whom he is he should be able to infer what he will choose.

But how can this account be available to Molina? Molina's whole project is to affirm divine sovereignty without compromising human autonomy. If he acknowledges that Peter's choices are necessitated by the nature of Peter's will, that is tantamount to acknowledging that Peter's choices are necessitated by God; for God is the creator and designer of Peter's will.[16] Molina cannot consistently offer such an answer. In order to be consistent, Molina must insist that whom God has created Peter to be does not dictate what Peter will choose in any given situation. Otherwise, Peter's choices are not truly autonomous; they have been determined by the character of his will which was, in turn, designed and determined by God. For Molina, then, Peter's choices cannot be necessitated by the God-given nature of Peter's will.

Consequently, Molina must affirm one of two things: either who Peter is does not ultimately dictate what he will choose, or whom God created and determined Peter to be is not the whole of who Peter is, that is, who Peter is

---

16. Some scholars would object that Peter's choices being necessitated by the nature of Peter's will is not tantamount to their being necessitated by God. They would agree that Peter's will is designed and created by God. They would argue, however, that God is responsible for and determines the existence of Peter's will but is not responsible for and does not cause the dynamic workings of Peter's will. In other words, God creates Peter's will without in any way determining how it will function and what it will choose. He creates it to be free from everything, even from his own determinative control. It is outside the scope of this chapter to explore this issue at length. But such a claim is fraught with philosophical confusion. How can God bring X into existence without thereby defining the nature of X, which will be determinative of how it will function and behave? If God has not defined its controlling nature, in what sense is it X that God has brought into existence (rather than not-X)? Suffice it to say that my argument assumes that there is an inextricable link between God's creating something and God's determining the nature of its being and functioning in reality. Hence, to create Peter's will is to create the nature, essence, and mode of working of Peter's will. If not—if God does not determine its nature, essence, and mode of working—then in what sense is it distinctively Peter's will that God has created, and how do we explain the origin of its nature, essence, and mode of working?

at any given time is in part determined by the free, autonomous choices Peter has already made over the course of his life (choices that were not determined by whom God created him to be). In other words, who Peter is, is in significant measure, self-determined.

If Molina affirms the latter—that is, who Peter is, is ultimately determined by Peter, not by God—then how can he appeal to God's infinitely thorough knowledge of Peter's will to explain how middle knowledge is possible? He replaces one question with another—namely, how it is possible for God to have an infinitely thorough knowledge of Peter's will? If at any given time, who Peter is has not yet been fully decided, then how is it reasonable to think that at any given time God can know Peter with infinite thoroughness? Who Peter is depends upon the outcome of his next autonomous choice.

If Molina affirms the former proposition—that is, who Peter is does not determine what he will choose—then knowing who Peter is, is of no help toward knowing what he will choose. In that case, an infinite knowledge of Peter's will cannot explain God's middle knowledge. From God's infinitely thorough knowledge of Peter's will, no conclusion can be drawn as to what Peter will choose, for the nature of Peter's will does not determine his choices.

Hence, to be consistent with the position that humans are autonomous beings, inference from God's infinite knowledge of Peter's will cannot satisfactorily explain the possibility of divine middle knowledge. His infinite knowledge of Peter's will is either irrelevant with respect to middle knowledge or it is as mysterious and problematic as middle knowledge itself (and hence has no explanatory value). In his covert, inferential account, therefore, Molina has produced no explanation of divine middle knowledge that is consistent with his assumption of human autonomy. (His explanation works only to the extent that human choices are assumed to be ultimately predetermined by God.) We are left with our original problem unanswered and unresolved: if the human will is absolutely autonomous, then how can we reasonably assert that God can know (infer) what it will choose in a given set of circumstances?

Middle knowledge based on inference (Molina's covert account of middle knowledge) gains its plausibility only under the assumption that human choice is not autonomous but is ultimately predetermined by the will of God. If our choices are not the result of a causal chain of which God could have knowledge, then God cannot infer what choices we will make from the nature of their causes. The sort of human autonomy upon which Molina insists precludes the sort of antecedent causation of our choices from which our choices could be inferred. Since human autonomy, as Molina conceives it, does not allow for human choice to have any antecedent causes, it would be impossible for God to infer a human choice from its antecedent causes. Hence, on the assumption of human autonomy, Molina is unable to make the possibility of inferential middle knowledge plausible.

Summary: An Assessment of Molina's Doctrine

Molina's exposition of middle knowledge involves a subtle confusion of two incompatible accounts of middle knowledge. He shifts which account of middle knowledge he wants us to consider, depending upon the question at issue.

When the question at issue is whether human autonomy and divine sovereignty are compatible, Molina would have us focus on his official account of middle knowledge: middle knowledge as God's mysterious ability to know directly and immediately what a particular person, acting in absolute autonomy, will do in a particular situation in the future. This official account of middle knowledge, if it can be shown to be a coherent and intelligible concept, successfully reconciles divine sovereignty and human freedom. It assumes the reality of human autonomy and by means of middle knowledge accounts for the attributes of divine sovereignty without compromising that autonomy. Insofar as we are satisfied to leave it at that, Molina has given us a believable account of how divine sovereignty and absolute human autonomy are compatible.

But if we are not satisfied to leave it in the realm of mystery, if we ask how divine middle knowledge is possible—given that it is supposedly a knowledge of choices that are as yet undecided by those who will make them—then Molina would have us shift our focus to his covert account of middle knowledge: God's ability to infallibly infer from the character of a person's own will what that person shall choose in a particular situation in the future. By means of this account, Molina does succeed in making middle knowledge comprehensible and plausible. Even we who are finite creatures have this sort of middle knowledge of one another. We infer what another person will do from the knowledge we have gained of his character. If we can have middle knowledge of this sort, certainly God can have it even more so, for he knows us with an infinite thoroughness.

Middle knowledge makes sense if it is a sort of inferential knowledge. But, in conceding this to Molina, we fail to keep his original project in view: to reconcile divine sovereignty and absolute human autonomy. Hence we fail to notice that, under Molina's plausible, covert account, human autonomy is not reconciled with divine sovereignty; rather, human autonomy is denied. As we saw, middle knowledge based on inference gains its plausibility only under the assumption that human choice is not autonomous but is ultimately predetermined by the will of God.

The force of Molina's defense of middle knowledge depends upon our failure to notice how very different his covert account of middle knowledge is from his official account and, more importantly, upon our failure to notice the contradictory ramifications of these two different accounts. If we do notice, then we realize that he has failed in his attempt to give us a compelling account of middle knowledge that does not compromise human autonomy. It is easy not to notice, for Molina's discussions involve a sort of philosophical sleight-of-hand wherein he gives us different, conflicting accounts of middle knowledge depending upon the philosophical needs of the moment. But once we have noticed, Molina's doctrine loses its appeal.

In the end, we cannot accept Molina's exposition as it stands. It depends on an equivocation in his account of what middle knowledge is. And we cannot accept Molina's unofficial, covert, inferential account of middle knowledge, for it does not successfully reconcile divine foreknowledge with absolute human autonomy. We are left, then, with Molina's official account. His doctrine, therefore, reduces to nothing more than a dogmatic assertion that divine middle knowledge is a reality and that its possibility is a divine mystery. I am not motivated to embrace Molina's views, given that this is what they amount to. I am not much attracted to what is no more than a dogmatic assertion that divine foreknowledge is possible even though human choices are absolutely autonomous.

Only on the assumption of divine determinism is the divine foreknowledge of free-will choices a rationally plausible doctrine. (This is one of the primary reasons that I embrace divine determinism.) Implicitly, therefore, Molina is urging me to abandon my rationally satisfying understanding of divine foreknowledge (based on the assumption of divine determinism) and join him in a dogmatic commitment to an incomprehensible mystery. Why should I do that? What assurance has Molina given me that middle knowledge under his conception of it—that is, middle knowledge of *autonomous* human choices—is a coherent concept? Until I am persuaded that the simultaneous affirmation of both divine middle knowledge and the absolute autonomy of human choice is not a blatant contradiction, Molina's attempt to bring Calvinism and Arminianism together is unpersuasive.

Human Freedom: Can Calvinism Do It Justice?

In the article to which I am responding, Craig invites us to join together in embracing Molina's views. If Molina's views are as unpersuasive as I have suggested, why would Craig venture to make such an appeal? Obviously, Craig considers Molina's views to be more compelling than I do. What accounts for the difference in our assessment?

Craig makes an unwarranted assumption, one that leads him to see Molina's arguments as more compelling than they really are. Craig assumes, with Molina, that Calvinistic divine determinism cannot do justice to the reality of human freedom. If doing justice to the reality of human freedom is genuinely a shortcoming of divine determinism, and if Molina's views have successfully preserved the truth of genuine human freedom where divine determinism has failed, and if he has done so without discarding or compromising the de fide doctrines of divine sovereignty, then surely his views would be attractive to

447

even the most obdurate Calvinist. To gain such a rich philosophical payoff, even a hard-headed divine determinist might be willing to tolerate an appeal to the realm of divine mystery and accept as dogma the possibility of middle knowledge. Surely, whatever risk of incoherence it entails is a small price to pay for the benefit of simultaneously embracing a de fide notion of divine sovereignty and an uncompromised notion of human freedom.

The Underlying Reasoning Behind Craig's Appeal

We can formalize the underlying reasoning behind Craig's appeal:

Given the following three convictions, it is utterly reasonable to embrace Molina's doctrines:

1. absolute human autonomy is a vital biblical notion that is required to provide a foundation for human freedom and responsibility;
2. the de fide doctrines of divine sovereignty are thoroughly biblical notions; and
3. Molina's views of middle knowledge and divine foreknowledge are the only way to reconcile beliefs in divine sovereignty and human autonomy.

Craig would maintain, I think, that the risk that middle knowledge may not be a coherent concept is not a sufficient deterrent to embracing Molina's views in the light of 1–3.[17] I think Craig is right about this. If I were committed to 1–3, I too would find it reasonable to follow Molina.

But this is exactly why Craig's appeal is not compelling to someone like me. The Calvinistic divine determinist does not share Craig's commitment to 1–3. Most notably, the divine determinist does not accept 1; correspondingly, he does not accept 3. Even though he does not affirm the absolute autonomy of the human will, he feels no inadequacy in his concepts of human freedom and responsibility; and he feels no lack of compatibility between human freedom and divine sovereignty—at least, not to the degree that Craig thinks he should.

To conclude my discussion, therefore, I shall explore this important issue: does the divine determinist's concept of human freedom fail to do justice to the reality of human freedom (as Craig and Molina assume)? If so, then Craig can reasonably argue that he should welcome Molina's solution. But if not, it makes no sense for the divine determinist to trade in his theory of divine determinism,

---

17. Craig and I undoubtedly assess the risks of middle knowledge being an incoherent notion quite differently. Craig, it would seem, is satisfied that middle knowledge is a coherent notion and sees little or no risk that he is embracing nonsense. I am certain that it is an utterly incoherent notion and am virtually certain that, were I to embrace it, I would be embracing nonsense. Craig fails to understand why the Calvinist will not embrace Molina's doctrines in part because he fails to see how certain the divine determinist is that divine middle knowledge makes no sense.

whatever problems its critics may think it has, for the theories of Molina; for, to the divine determinist, these theories are more clearly problematic than his own.

The Alleged Inadequacy in the Calvinist's View of Human Freedom

What inadequacy does Craig see in the divine determinist's concept of human freedom? Why does Craig think that nothing short of the absolute autonomy of the human will can adequately capture the true nature of human freedom?

For a human choice to be truly free, Craig thinks, it must be possible for that choice to have been other than it was. The divine determinist, by the very nature of his position, must say that at any given time no one can ever choose or act contrary to what God has willed. Clearly, then, the divine determinist does not believe that a human is free to do differently from what he did; he is constrained by the governing will of God. If the divine determinist espouses human freedom, it must be freedom in a qualified and limited sense (specifically, in the weaker sense known as the "liberty of spontaneity"). The divine determinist, so long as he sees one's actions constrained by the will of God, cannot espouse human freedom in an unqualified sense (specifically, not in the strong sense known as the "liberty of indifference").[18]

The essence of Craig's sentiments can be seen in the following:

> Here it must be admitted that Molina's perception of their [the Reformers'] teaching was clear-sighted: the principal Reformers did deny to man significant freedom, at least in his dealings with God. Luther and Calvin were prepared to grant to man only spontaneity of choice and voluntariness of will, not the ability to choose otherwise in the circumstances in which an agent finds himself.[19]

18. Craig alludes to these two specialized terms: "the liberty of spontaneity" and "the liberty of indifference." I first encountered these terms in the philosophy of David Hume. One exercises the liberty of spontaneity when what he does is done in accordance with his own will and desires. One exercises the liberty of indifference when what he does is such that he could have done otherwise. Hence, a person passing time in a room reading and enjoying himself and fully wanting to be there because of the pleasantness of his surroundings is exercising the freedom or liberty of spontaneity. He is exercising the liberty of spontaneity even if, unbeknownst to him, the room is locked from the outside and he would be unable to leave the room even if he wanted to. His being in this same room would involve the liberty of indifference only if the room is unlocked and he is free to leave it whenever he should so choose. In the Reformers' view of sovereignty, argues Craig, a person does not exercise the liberty of indifference because he cannot do other than God wills. He does however exercise the liberty of spontaneity insofar as what he chooses, determined though it is by God, is nonetheless a result of his own voluntary choice and is fully in accord with his own wants and desires.

19. Craig, "Middle Knowledge," 142.

And again,

> His [Calvin's] view of freedom is in the end the same as Luther's: the liberty of spontaneity. God's complete sovereignty excludes any genuine possibility of man's choosing in any circumstances other than as he does choose.
>
> Thus, according to the Protestant Reformers, in virtue of God's prescience [foreknowledge] and providence, everything that occurs in the world does so necessarily. Human choice is voluntary and spontaneous, but the will is not free to choose other than as it does. Now to Molina, such a doctrine was quite simply heretical. He could not see how mere spontaneity of choice sufficed to make a human being a responsible moral agent nor how the Reformers' view would not lead to making God the cause of man's sinful acts and, hence, the author of evil. He was therefore deeply exercised to formulate a strong doctrine of divine prescience [foreknowledge], providence, and predestination that would be wholly compatible with genuine human freedom, and he believed that in *scientia media* [middle knowledge] he had found the key.[20]

But there is something entirely disingenuous about Molina's charge against Calvin and Luther that, under their view of human freedom, "the will is not free to choose other than as it does." The same thing is clearly true under Molina's covert account of middle knowledge—the account upon which he ultimately relies to bring credibility to his doctrinal position (as we saw).[21]

Molina argued that middle knowledge is possible because, given the depth and infinite thoroughness of God's knowledge of a particular will, he knows what that will shall choose in any particular set of circumstances. That makes it possible for God to have an accurate and detailed picture of every possible world. But does this not entail (if his doctrine is to be coherent) that the particular choice one makes in situation S was made necessary by the will of the human person who made it? If not, then God, his knowledge of the person's will notwithstanding, cannot foreknow what that choice will be. According to Molina, if he is to be consistent, Peter's own will *necessitated* that he deny Jesus when he did. That being so, what complaint does Molina have against Calvin and Luther? Calvin and Luther assert that the human will is free, but then acknowledge a constraint on it—the outcome of its choices are necessitated by the will of God. Molina asserts that the human will is free, but then

---

20. Ibid., 144.

21. It is true that Molina's official account would allow him in good faith to contend that his position, unlike that of Luther and Calvin, gives an account of freedom wherein a person is free to do other than he does. But Molina's official account, as we have seen, is nothing more than a dogmatic assertion that God, in the mystery of his greatness, can have foreknowledge of an autonomous choice that could be other than it will be. But the problem with this official account, as we have seen, is that there is no basis upon which to accept such a notion of divine foreknowledge as a coherent and plausible doctrine.

he too must logically acknowledge a constraint on it—the outcome of its choices are necessitated by its own nature or character.

It is clearly not just, then, to condemn Luther's and Calvin's views of human freedom as inadequate on the grounds that, under their views, the human "will is not free to choose other than as it does." The same charge could be leveled against Molina.[22] If not being able to choose otherwise makes the Reformers' view of human freedom inadequate, then it renders Molina's view inadequate as well. Conversely, if Molina's view of human freedom is adequate even while acknowledging the reality of a necessitating constraint, then the Reformers' view is no less adequate. My point is this: whereas Craig, Molina, and other nondeterminists seem to argue that any sort of constraint on the human will whatsoever is completely incompatible with genuine human freedom, yet they too must acknowledge some kind of constraint on the human will. It is disingenuous, therefore, to argue that the Reformers' view of human freedom is inadequate because it posits a constraint on that freedom. If they are going to reject the Reformers' views while maintaining their own, they must produce a more compelling reason why their view portrays the realities of human freedom more accurately than does the Reformers'.

Undoubtedly, Molina would want to say that the constraint imposed by a particular will's own inherent nature and character is a radically different sort of constraint than that imposed externally, as it were, by God. It is reasonable to see the latter (God's external constraint) as inconsistent with human freedom while the former (the internal constraint of the character of one's own will) is not.

I offer two responses to this objection.

First Response

On Molina's view, how does he propose to have Peter's actions necessitated by the intrinsic nature of Peter's own will without having them ultimately necessitated (and imposed on him externally) by the divine will? God is ultimately the author and the designer of Peter's will. It functions in accordance with an intrinsic nature that God himself determined; hence, ultimately, Peter's actions have been directly determined by the God who created him.

We confront once again the philosophical schizophrenia of Molina's view. On the one hand, Molina wants to insist that Peter and Peter alone (through the spontaneous resolution of his own will), apart from any divine determination, determines his choice to deny Jesus. But, on the other hand,

---

22. With reference to his unofficial view, not his official one. In his official view, he clearly and explicitly asserts that the human will is capable of choosing other than it does.

in order to explain how God can foreknow what Peter is going to do, he must implicitly suggest that something other than the spontaneous resolution of Peter's will determines that Peter will deny Jesus. A definitive and knowable something determines how the spontaneous resolution of Peter's will shall come out. Namely, it is the intrinsic nature or character of Peter's will. But once Molina has allowed for that, one of two things must follow:

the very problematic suggestion that Peter's will is not created by God (i.e., it is either uncreated or self-creating), or

it is ultimately created and designed by God.

From the standpoint of a serious biblical philosophy, the first case (Peter's will is not created by God) is altogether unacceptable. In the latter case (if Peter's will is created by God), then Molina must acknowledge that Peter's choice to deny Jesus was ultimately determined by God. This is the very thing he has set out to deny.

Second Response

I will concede that Molina's hypothetical objection is indeed understandable. It is plausible for one to think that the external constraints imposed by the divine will are inconsistent with human freedom while the internal constraints imposed by the inherent nature of one's own will are not. But while I concede that this is plausible and understandable, whether it is ultimately "reasonable" is the crux of the debate between the divine determinist and the human autonomist.

To the divine determinist, the constraints imposed on our voluntary choices by the will of the transcendent creator God are ultimately of no more consequence than those imposed by the inherent natures of our own wills. Both are universal and necessary principles that, because of their universality and necessity, fail to have any import for questions of freedom, responsibility, and the character and nature of evil.

God is, to the divine determinist, the transcendent author of all that is. He is the one "in whom we live, and move, and have our being."[23] He is the one who wills all that exists into existence. Apart from him, nothing that exists could exist. Nothing—good or bad, evil or righteous, voluntary or involuntary, coerced or uncoerced, free or not—could exist were its existence not willed by the divine author of all things. That being so, then the fact that God has willed something to occur cannot in any way be relevant or meaningful to the important distinctions we make between what is freely chosen and

---

23. Acts 17:28. In this passage, Paul quotes with approval the words of Epimenides, a Cretan poet.

what is not, or between what is evil and what is good, or between what involves my culpability and what does not. It is not as if God wills what is not free and does not will what is free. That cannot be right, for God wills everything whatsoever. It is not as if God wills what is good and not what is evil; for, again, God wills everything whatsoever. In other words, to say that God has willed X (no matter what X is) is, for the purposes of defining human freedom, utterly trivial and philosophically useless.

Meaningful differences between them must define the difference between choices that are free and those that are not. It will be some important difference between a voluntary and involuntary action that will be philosophically useful and will distinguish the voluntary action as free. Being "willed by God," therefore, is philosophically useless with respect to defining human freedom, for it does not describe a difference between different kinds of human action. "Being determined by God" can neither make an action free nor preclude it from being free, for all actions, voluntary and involuntary, are determined by God.

What if, in a fit of absurdity, I were to suggest that the difference between voluntary and involuntary actions lay in part in the fact that voluntary actions do not really exist while involuntary actions do. Under such a suggestion, any adequate notion of true freedom would hold that voluntary actions are those that do not truly exist! (Remember, I'm being absurd.) Could I then reasonably charge the Reformers with having an inadequate notion of true freedom—by analogy to Molina's charge—in that the Reformers' concept of voluntary actions requires that such actions do exist? This, of course, would be ridiculous. How can something that must of necessity be universally true of all human actions in order for them to be human actions at all (namely, existence) be something that distinguishes between two kinds of human action? That makes no sense.

From the Reformers' point of view, Molina's charge against them is equally absurd. The Reformers, following the biblical authors, view the divine determinism of real human actions as a universal and necessary feature of any human action whatsoever. It cannot therefore serve to distinguish between two different kinds of action, voluntary and involuntary. How could it? Whatever it means for an action to be free, it cannot mean that it is free from the determinative will of God any more than it can mean that it is free from existence in the real world. Nothing can be free from what must necessarily and universally be true of every thing that is in order for it to even be a thing.

So the fact that my actions and choices are ultimately determined by the will of him who is the author of everything cannot reasonably be understood to nullify human freedom any more than the fact that my actions are ultimately determined by the intrinsic nature or character of my own will nullifies human freedom. My choices are determined by the intrinsic nature of my own will, for everything whatsoever is determined by the intrinsic character of what it is. That goes without saying. Likewise, my choices are determined by the divine will, for everything whatsoever is determined by the divine will. That too goes without saying. Therefore, to charge that divine determinism does not allow for truly free human actions because it will not assert that they are free from the determining will of God is a hollow condemnation. It has about as much substance as charging that the Reformers' view of freedom is not compatible with genuine freedom because it does not allow for human actions to be truly free from existence. Or, because it does not allow for human actions to be truly free from the will of the person performing them. These latter two criticisms would not likely have caused the Reformers to lose any sleep. And neither, I submit, would the former.

Whereas all actions whatsoever are consistent with the nature of that which produces them, and whereas all whatsoever are consistent with the will of the divine being who brings all things to pass, nevertheless, some we know to be free, voluntary actions while others are not. The crucial question is this: what is the difference? If the difference cannot lie in whether it has been determined by God, where then? What is the divine determinist's concept of a free choice?

Divine determinism holds that a free human choice is a choice that has in no way been determined by any other created reality. A free choice is one that has not been necessitated by any other thing, event, or cause that exists in and as a part of the created cosmos. Under this definition, being determined or caused by the transcendent Creator does not disqualify a choice as free. Only being determined or caused by some other *created* reality will do so. This is a completely adequate representation of genuine human freedom. Indeed, it is adequate in a way in which Molina's view is not!

Molina (at least in his covert account) replaces the determining will of God with the determining nature of a person's own will. In doing so, Molina has made human choice dependent upon another part of created reality. I choose what I do because something about the nature of me makes me do what I do. What exactly makes me do what I do? "The nature of my will," says Molina. But what is that? My genes? Then we have genetic determinism. The impact of my environment? Then we have a Skinnerian determinism. What is it about me (my will) that causes me to choose what I do? No matter what Molina answers, we appear to have some sort of natural determinism— some aspect of created nature is the necessitating cause of human choice and action. But is this not the sort of inadequate view of human freedom that Molina and Craig insist we must avoid? How can we be responsible for our actions if all our actions are necessitated by something in the created order?

The only way to avoid natural determinism and still have some sort of reasonable theory of human action is to embrace divine determinism. God can only foreknow what has been predetermined. What has been predetermined has either been predetermined by God (divine determinism) or has been predetermined by some other aspect of the cosmos (natural determinism). If it is the latter, then all of our intuitions tell us that our actions are not truly free.[24] My choices have been caused by something outside of me and my control. But if it is the former, then (unless we draw a faulty analogy to the case of natural determinism) our intuitions tell us no such thing. No intuition tells me that a divinely determined action cannot be a free action.[25] As we noted, what else is an action supposed to be—free or not—if not divinely determined?

Conclusion: Calvinism's Inadequate View of Human Freedom Is an Illusion

From the divine determinist's perspective, he has no problem with the compatibility of divine sovereignty and human freedom. Contrary to Craig's expectations, he is not itching for a solution to this problem. Hence, he is not eager to accept Molina's solution, heedless of the philosophical problems it entails. Craig is confident that divine determinism is fraught with philosophical problems of its own—namely, that it cannot adequately account for human freedom. But this is a problem the divine determinist does not feel or acknowledge. Human freedom is no real difficulty to his theory. It looks like a problem only to one who has created an artificial, arbitrary, and unrealistic criterion by which to judge true freedom—namely, that a truly free act will not be determined by anything whatsoever, including God. The divine determinist sees no

24. Not everyone would concur with this, but I am committed to a concept of human freedom that precludes natural necessity. If our actions are necessitated by brain states, brain chemistry, genes, or even more vaguely, the impact of our environment on us, then I have to agree with B. F. Skinner: the freedom and dignity of our actions is but an illusion. Since it is utterly unbiblical to view the freedom of our actions as illusory, I am forced by my own assumptions to reject natural determinism. If one could successfully argue for a naturally determined action being a truly free action for which the agent is fully responsible, however, then I would have no further reason to dismiss natural determinism as a possibility. The possibility that even natural determinism may not preclude human freedom and responsibility does not affect the argument of this chapter, however. Surely one can have no problem with divine determinism coexisting with human freedom if he is willing to concede that natural determinism can coexist with human freedom.

25. Many people would try to maintain that it is intuitively obvious that a divinely determined action is thereby not a free action. It is outside the scope of this chapter to defend my contention—specifically, that it is not intuitively obvious that a divinely determined action is not free. I have tried to argue elsewhere, in a series of lectures delivered at McKenzie Study Center in Eugene, Oregon, in 1987, that we have no such rational intuitions. Two things combine to leave us with the impression that divinely determined actions cannot be truly free: a cultural assumption that we rarely if ever examine, and an unexamined argument by analogy to a naturally determined action. The latter involves something like this fallacious argument to support it: Naturally determined actions are not free actions. It follows therefore that no determined action is a free action. Divinely determined actions are determined actions. Therefore, divinely determined actions are not free actions.

reason to accept such an arbitrary and naive criterion. An act can be a truly free act only if it has not been determined by him who determines all that is? That would be absurd! It is not the Calvinist who holds the inadequate view of human freedom! It is the Arminian whose view is inadequate.

Summary

Molina's attempt to reconcile the de fide doctrines of divine sovereignty with a belief in the absolute autonomy of the human will has an initial appeal, an initial plausibility. On closer scrutiny, we find that it contains a fatal tension that undermines it. The fatal tension—indeed, contradiction—lies between two conflicting conceptions of divine middle knowledge to which Molina alternatingly appeals. When we fail to notice the shift from one conception of middle knowledge to the other, Molina's reconciliation seems plausible. Its plausibility disappears when, recognizing the equivocation in his concept of middle knowledge, we see that his two different accounts of middle knowledge lead to contradictory results. If Molina's official conception of middle knowledge is right, then absolute human autonomy is salvaged. But if Molina's covert conception of middle knowledge is right, then absolute human autonomy is refuted. And yet, as we saw, the only way for him to render the notion of divine middle knowledge intelligible is by conceiving of it along the lines of his covert account—that is, by conceiving of it in a way that refutes absolute human autonomy.

Like a master illusionist, Molina prompts me to keep my eyes fixed on his first, official conception of divine middle knowledge when he wants to convince me that his views fully and uncompromisingly embrace absolute human autonomy. Then he prompts me to keep my eyes fixed on his second, covert conception of divine middle knowledge when he wants to convince me that divine middle knowledge is a viable concept. What he never prompts me to do is to notice that the second, covert account of divine middle knowledge entails the denial of the concept of absolute human autonomy that is assumed and advanced by the first.

Molina's views fail to persuade a divine determinist like me. If I ignore Molina's covert conception of middle knowledge and consider only his official account, then, although it is true that I could embrace the de fide doctrines of divine sovereignty at the same time that I affirm absolute human autonomy, Molina asks me to affirm a doctrine that is philosophically problematic to me (namely, direct and intuitive middle knowledge in the context of absolute human autonomy). At the same time, he asks me to reject the doctrine of divine determinism, which is not philosophically problematic to me. If I ignore his official account of middle knowledge and consider his covert account, then Molina asks me to leave one theory of divine determinism for a different theory of divine determinism. The one he wants me to leave is a countertheory to natural determinism and as such is biblically and philosophically viable. The one he wants me to embrace is biblically and philosophically problematic, for it entails a form of natural determinism. Molina's views do not solve any problems; they simply create new and greater ones.

20

God, Freedom, and Evil in Calvinist Thinking

JOHN S. FEINBERG

Sometimes it would be easier not to be a Calvinist. An intellectual price tag comes with any conceptual scheme, but the one that comes with Calvinism seems beyond the resources of human intelligence to pay. Calvinists hold views that appear at very least counterintuitive. This is especially so with respect to Calvinist accounts of God's sovereign control in relation to human freedom and moral responsibility for evil.

If Calvinists are right about divine sovereignty, there seems to be little room for human freedom. If freedom goes, so does human moral responsibility for sin. Worst of all, if Calvinists are right, it appears that God decides that there will be sin and evil in our world, maybe even brings it about that there is such evil, and yet, according to Calvinists, is not morally responsible for any of it. We are.

If this is Calvinism's God, Calvinism seems not only intellectually but also religiously bankrupt. Who would worship this God? Moreover, if atheists understand this portrait of God as paradigmatic of traditional Christianity, no wonder they are repulsed by Christianity. Although committed atheists will not likely abandon their atheism for any concept of God, at least the Arminian portrayal of God seems more attractive than the Calvinist portrayal.

Despite appearances, I believe it is possible to hold a strong view of divine sovereignty and still make room for genuine human freedom and resolve the problem of evil. Since all of this is admittedly counterintuitive, I have a lot of explaining to do. In what follows, I begin with a brief explanation of the Calvinist notion of divine sovereignty. I shall then address the question of freedom and sovereignty and the problem of evil from a Calvinist perspective to show how Calvinists might resolve these problems. In addressing the problem of evil, I shall confine myself only to the logical form of the problem. The basic responses to the evidential form of the problem are not peculiar to Calvinism, Arminianism, or any other brand of theism, so I shall forego addressing the evidential problem in this chapter.[1]

Calvinism on Divine Sovereignty

There are many varieties of Calvinism, just as there are different kinds of Arminianism. Despite differences, the starting point of most Calvinistic systems is a God who is absolutely sovereign. Calvinists typically define sovereignty the same way. Calvin was very clear about this divine attribute. For Calvin it did not mean that God is omnipotent but chooses not to act. Nor did it mean that God operates in a general way like a teacher who gives an assignment and watches while the class completes it. Nor did it mean that God watches us act and then intervenes to tidy up the mess we have made. Instead, God decides what will happen in our world and then sees that his decisions are carried out. As Calvin says:

> For he is deemed omnipotent, not because he can indeed act, yet sometimes ceases and sits in idleness, or continues by a general impulse that order of nature which he previously appointed; but because, governing heaven and earth by his providence, he so regulates all things that nothing takes place without his deliberation. For when, in the Psalms, it is said that "he does whatever he wills" (Ps 115:3; cf Ps 113(b):3, Vg.), a certain and deliberate will is meant. For it would be senseless to interpret the words of the prophet after the manner of the philosophers, that God is the first agent because he is the beginning and cause of all motion; for in times of adversity believers comfort themselves with the solace that they suffer nothing except by God's ordinance and command, for they are under his hand.[2]

1. In my book *The Many Faces of Evil* (Grand Rapids: Zondervan, 1994), I devote five chapters to the evidential problem, so the reader can consult that material for a description of and answer to the evidential problem. For other helpful explanations of the nature of this problem and answers to it see Alvin Plantinga, "The Probabilistic Argument From Evil," *Philosophical Studies* 35 (1979); Michael Peterson, *Evil and the Christian God* (Grand Rapids: Baker, 1982); Bruce Reichenbach, "The Inductive Argument from Evil," *American Philosophical Quarterly* 17, 3 (July 1980); and *Evil and a Good God* (New York: Fordham University Press, 1982).

2. John Calvin, *The Institutes of the Christian Religion*, vol. 20 of *The Library of Christian Classics*, ed. John T. McNeill, trans. Ford Lewis Battles (Philadelphia: Westminster, 1954), 200 (1.16.3). We also see this notion in Calvin's definition of providence. He writes, "By Providence, we mean, not an unconcerned sitting of God in heaven, from which He merely observes the things that are done in the world; but that all-active and all-concerned seatedness on his

For Calvin, then, God's sovereignty means he governs all things according to his will. This means God not only overrules in the affairs of men, but also determines what will happen in their lives. This providential determination extends to every area of our lives.[3] Because we cannot know what God has planned for our life ahead of time, Calvin says that events appear to happen by chance. But this is not so, because God sovereignly controls events as he works out what he has decreed.[4]

Calvin also related God's sovereignty to his foreknowledge. Calvin agreed that God's foreknowledge does not cause an event or an act, and he said that "foreknowledge alone imposes no necessity upon creatures."[5] However, he believed that God "foresees future events only by reason of the fact that he decreed that they take place."[6]

This is a robust view of God's control of the world. Within the Calvinist tradition it is standard fare. Consider as an example the Westminster Confession of 1647:

> God, from all eternity did, by the most wise and holy counsel of his own will, freely and unchangeably ordain whatsoever comes to pass; yet so as thereby neither is God the author of sin, nor is violence offered to the will of the creatures, nor is the liberty or contingency of second causes taken away, but rather established.[7]

According to this quote, God's sovereign control neither eliminates human freedom nor makes God the author of evil. Although not all Calvinists agree with this statement, many do. Those who do, of course, must explain how this can be so. If God decides what I shall do, it seems impossible for me to avoid it. How could I do other than what God decrees? If God controls things to the extent that Calvin and his followers claim, then God must see to it that there are sufficient conditions for each of my actions to guarantee that they will occur. But this is causal determinism, and causal determinism seems to rule out genuine freedom. Moreover, moral philosophers uniformly agree that one is morally responsible for one's actions only if they are done freely.

---

throne above, by which He governs the world which He himself hath made. So that God, as viewed in the glass of his Providence, is not only the Maker of all things in a moment, but the perpetual Ruler of all things which He hath created" (see John Calvin, "A Defense of the Secret Providence of God," in *Calvin's Calvinism*, trans. Henry Cole [London: Wertheim and Macintosh, 1857], 4).

3. Calvin, *Institutes*, 204–5 (1.16.6). Cf. John Calvin, "The Catechism of the Church of Geneva (1545)," in *Theological Treatises*, vol. 22, *The Library of Christian Classics*, ed. John T. McNeill and Henry Van Dusen (Philadelphia: Westminster, 1954), 125.

4. Calvin, *Institutes*, 205 (1.16.6).

5. Ibid., 954 (3.23.8).

6. Ibid.

7. Westminster Confession of 1647, 3.1.

Hence, if God's sovereign control rules out human freedom, it also eliminates human moral responsibility for action.

Common sense, let alone Scripture, suggests that we are free and morally responsible for our actions. Hence all of this sounds suspect. But, the apparent implications for God look even worse. If God controls all things and chooses whatever happens, how can he escape moral responsibility for all that occurs? Granted, he does not do my actions for me, but he decided what I would do, and he sees to it that conditions are such that I shall do what he has decided. In some significant sense, then, he seems to be the author of sin. Contrary to basic principles of Calvinist thinking, it appears that God's creatures are exonerated from moral blame while the majestic, holy sovereign to whose glory all things are said to redound is guilty of the sinful acts of his creatures.

In addition, if God has the kind of power the Calvinist says he has, he could have created a different world than ours, one without the evil ours has. If he created our world with its evil when he has the power to do otherwise (as Calvinism apparently holds), then he must be an evil God. If he is a good God, he must not have as much power as the Calvinist says. Either way, Calvinism seems in deep trouble.

Non-Calvinists are quick to point out these problems. One way to solve them is to deny that God is sovereign. Many Arminians are uncomfortable with saying God is not sovereign, but they are disinclined to agree with Calvinists lest human freedom goes by the board. Their resolution is to maintain that God has the power and control that the Calvinist says he has, but in order to make room for human freedom God has voluntarily chosen to limit his use of that power. Nobody forced God to do this, so relinquishing the exercise of his control in no way removes his sovereignty. God granted power to human beings, that is, he gave us free will, because he preferred that we do right and love him not because we have to, but because we freely choose to do so. If we love God because we are forced to do so, that is no bargain for God. For the Arminian, then, God must grant us true freedom, but God is still God. He has all the power that the Calvinist says; he just does not use it, so there is room for human freedom.

This resolution to the problems seems attractive to some, but Calvinists believe that God not only has absolute sovereignty, but also exercises it. But, then, the apparently intractable problems already mentioned confront Calvinism. Can Calvinism escape?

Calvinism on Divine Sovereignty and Freedom

When we move from the Calvinist doctrine of divine sovereignty to the implications of that doctrine for the rest of theology, we begin to see differences in Calvinistic systems. Some Calvinists hear the objections and see no way out. They dare not drop belief in God's sovereignty, but they agree that such divine control eliminates freedom. Others believe that Scripture teaches both sovereignty and human freedom and moral responsibility for our actions. Because Scripture teaches both, these Calvinists conclude that they must hold both. How this fits together without contradiction they do not know. God knows, but it is beyond our current knowledge. We must hold these views in tension.

But, what if you are uncomfortable with this? The approach that denies human freedom rules out moral responsibility, and that approach seems impossible to square with Scripture. If we are not guilty of sin, why have Christ die to remedy a nonexistent malady? Some scholars say we are not *free* but we are *responsible*, but they admit that it is a mystery as to how all of this can be true. That, of course, is just a roundabout way of admitting that they do not know how to remove the apparent contradiction. Of course, if one does not know how to resolve the apparent contradiction, and if one believes that a self-contradictory position collapses, it will be hard to accept this "mystery" view. Likewise, the view that says we are free and God is sovereign, but how this is so is a "mystery" will not seem convincing either.

My contention is that the best way out of this dilemma is for Calvinists to begin by reexamining what free will means. Scripture does not define free will, but philosophers discuss it. They speak of two main notions of free will. One is an indeterministic notion often called incompatibilism, contracausal or libertarian free will. The other is a deterministic view known as soft determinism or compatibilism.

According to indeterminism, an act is genuinely free if it is not causally determined. Indeterminists quickly add that this does not mean that our actions are random or arbitrary. Reasons and causes play upon the will as one chooses, but none of them is sufficient to incline the will decisively one way or another. Hence, an agent could have done otherwise than she did. Indeterminists admit that some actions are not free. Their point is that the basic condition of the will is to choose freely, that is, without the choice being causally determined.

The fundamental tenet of determinism (and the various forms of Calvinism are forms of determinism) is that for everything that happens, in light of the prevailing conditions, the agent could not have done other than he did.[8]

---

8. Richard Taylor, "Determinism," in *The Encyclopedia of Philosophy*, ed. Paul Edwards (New York: Macmillan, 1967), 2:359. Here I refer to determinism in the social sciences and in human action. One may also speak of determinism in the physical sciences, but even there the fundamental point is that whatever occurs is causally determined. For further elaboration of the different forms of determinism and indeterminism see my "God Ordains All Things," in *Predestination and Free Will*, ed. R. and D. Basinger (Downers Grove: InterVarsity, 1986).

For determinists, there are always sufficient conditions that decisively incline the agent's will to choose one option or another.

With this understanding of human action, determinists clearly cannot define free action as action that is not causally determined. Determinists who believe in free will define it in terms of lack of constraint. That is, genuine free human action is compatible with causal conditions that decisively incline the will without constraining it. By constraint compatibilists mean conditions that incline the will contrary to the agent's wishes. In other words, if conditions that surround my decision are sufficient to guarantee a specific choice, but that choice is contrary to what I really want to do, then I act under constraint. In that case, my action is not free. On the other hand, if conditions surrounding my decision move me to choose something I want to do, then I act without constraint. My act is causally determined but free, because I choose and act without constraint.

Elsewhere I have explained how this freedom works, especially when someone does not want to do what, for example, God wants her to do.[9] Suffice it to say here that God knows what it will take to convince her without constraining her to do what he has decided she will do. Hence, when he decides that she will do a given action, he also chooses whatever conditions are needed to bring her to change her wishes without constraining her to do so. And, after her wishes change, she does the act God decided she would do, but she does it in accord with her wishes. As with indeterminists, compatibilists believe some actions are not free. However, they believe the basic way in which the will functions is freely, that is, causally determined but not constrained contrary to one's wishes.

One further word of definition. For indeterminists, a person is free if he can do otherwise. There are various senses in which a person can do otherwise. For example, one can do otherwise if one has the opportunity to do so. One can do otherwise if one has the power to do so, that is, one has a will and it can make choices. Moreover, one can do otherwise if it would be rational to do so. In all of these senses of "could do otherwise," compatibilists can agree that the agent can do otherwise. In a way, the key ingredient in the basic notion of determinism is the idea that *given prevailing conditions*, the agent could not do otherwise. This does not mean that the agent has no power or opportunity to make a different choice. It means that in light of the conditions surrounding the choice, it is rational to do what he does. If prevailing conditions were different, it would be rational to make a different choice. Compatibilism does not rip reason and will out of us so that we no longer have a capacity to choose. With compatibilism the agent can do otherwise in every sense the indeterminist believes an agent can do otherwise ex-

9. "God Ordains All Things," 25–26.

cept in the contracausal or incompatibilist sense of "the agent could do otherwise."[10]

We have, then, two conceptions of free human action. They clearly contradict one another, but both are possible views of freedom. By saying that they are possible, I mean that neither is self-contradictory (like the notion of a round square or a married bachelor). Indeterminists typically refuse to acknowledge compatibilism as even a possible definition of freedom, because they say it is not what freedom means. Of course, this sort of defining one's opponent out of existence is illegitimate regardless of who does it. It begs the question. The question is what is the correct account of free human action. One cannot win that debate by defining freedom one's own way and refusing to admit that any other notion is possible. Some indeterminists see this point and argue their position on other grounds.[11]

Incompatibilism and compatibilism, then, are two mutually exclusive views of free human action. Both are possible, but which is most likely correct? Moreover, which view should a Calvinist hold? I believe Calvinists as determinists must either reject freedom altogether or accept compatibilism. Moreover, I believe there are good arguments in favor of compatibilism over against incompatibilism. Some are biblical and theological; others are philosophical. Space does not permit offering all arguments, but in what follows, I shall offer what seem the most significant. I begin with biblical and theological considerations.

I begin where Calvinists usually begin, divine sovereignty. Does Scripture teach the strong notion of divine sovereignty sketched earlier? I believe it does. Although many verses show God's control over various areas of life (Pss. 115:3; 135:6; Job 42:2; Dan. 4:35; Prov. 21:1; James 4:13–15), a verse that is as comprehensive as any is Ephesians 1:11. According to this verse, believers are predestined "according to the purpose of him who worketh all things after the counsel of his own will" (KJV). "Counsel" suggests that God's decisions are not arbitrary but are according to reason and deliberation. Moreover, the verse says that God has a purpose in what he does. It is safe to say that this purpose enters into his deliberation about what to do and guides the choice he makes (the will). Nothing in the verse suggests that his purposes, choices, or deliberations are governed by anything external to himself. I note also that the verse says God both chooses what will happen and also works it out according to his plan. Although the verse does not explicitly say this, God obviously must work some things immediately (totally by him-

---

10. Ibid., 26–28.
11. I am indebted for this point to Alan Donagan. He was a thoroughgoing indeterminist, but he recognized that compatibilism is a possible account of free human action. He rejected it, but not because "that's just not what we mean by freedom." He was too astute a philosopher to fall into that question-begging trap.

self) and others mediately (through the agency of his creatures). Finally, God's activities are said to cover all things, not just a few.

It should be clear that whoever holds a notion of divine sovereignty along the lines outlined in Ephesians 1:11 cannot be an incompatibilist. If incompatibilism operates in our world, no one can have the kind of control over our actions that this notion of sovereignty teaches. The sovereign God that this verse describes can guarantee that what he decrees will be done, but with incompatibilism there can be no guarantees. Some form of determinism is necessitated.

Is there any way to remain committed to biblical inerrancy and reject this notion of divine sovereignty? Arminians have tried to get around this verse and others like it, but I believe they have done so unsuccessfully. Some Arminians respond that they agree with this interpretation of Ephesians 1:11 and other verses that teach divine sovereignty. However, in light of verses that teach free will, God must have willingly decided to forego use of this power. God still has sovereign control; he does not always use it, so that we can have free will.

This view may sound attractive, but it encounters a major problem. No verse in Scripture says that God decided to relinquish use of his power or control to make room for our free will. Arminians typically point to verses that show there is human freedom as evidence that God did make this decision. However, these verses show that we are free, but they do not say whether the freedom is incompatibilistic or compatibilistic. Arminians assume that the verses must teach their notion of freedom, because they assume that is the only legitimate notion of freedom. But, that just begs the question.[12] As already said, one cannot win this debate by defining one's opponent out of existence or by saying that even though her notion of freedom is self-consistent, it is not a legitimate notion. Hence, this attempt to avoid the Calvinist's understanding of sovereignty fails.

Another way to handle this issue is to claim that I have misinterpreted Ephesians 1:11 and to offer a different interpretation. However, even if this were true, other verses teach this concept of divine sovereignty. I do not rest my whole case on this one verse, but use it only as a clear expression of the doctrine.

But, still, perhaps my interpretation is wrong. Some may say I have overlooked the context of Ephesians 1:11. The topic of the context is salvation of the redeemed, not the arrangement of all things. Thus, this verse is not about all things whatsoever, but only about all things relating to salvation.[13]

---

12. Do Arminians really do this? See, for example, Clark H. Pinnock's handling of this matter of freedom and sovereignty in the Basinger and Basinger volume *Predestination and Free Will*. Bruce Reichenbach's essay in the same volume similarly begs the question on the meaning of freedom.

13. See, for example, Jack Cottrell's handling of this verse. He limits the clause to apply to all things "required for uniting Jews and Gentiles under one Head in one body." See Jack Cottrell, "The Nature of Divine Sovereignty," in *The Grace of God, the Will of Man: A Case for Arminianism*, ed. Clark H. Pinnock (Grand Rapids: Zondervan, 1989), 115–16.

I have two replies. First, I grant that the fundamental topic of the verse is predestination to salvation, but I note that the portion of the verse in question is a relative clause. Paul makes a point about God's control of salvation and then uses the relative clause to make the broader point that the way God handles salvation is how he handles everything. Anyone who understands how relative clauses function in Greek or English understands my point.

My other reply grants the objector, for sake of argument, that the verse is only about all things in regard to salvation. Even so, this does not help the Arminian, for it means he admits that Calvinists are right about God's sovereign control over salvation. But if that is so, then no one incompatibilistically freely chooses to accept Christ. If God controls salvation as Calvinists say, then people accept Christ either compatibilistically freely or without freedom at all. In either case, incompatibilism is ruled out of this most important decision, and that should make Arminians very uncomfortable. Moreover, if Arminians grant God the kind of sovereign control we are talking about in matters pertaining to salvation, what can be the reason for rejecting such control over other areas of life? This reinterpretation of Ephesians 1:11 is no bargain for the Arminian. The fundamental tenets of incompatibilism are that free action is not causally determined and that the will normally acts in this free way. Arminians dare not agree that God has such control over salvation that no one who has ever accepted Christ has done so freely, because no one has incompatibilistically chosen him.

Perhaps Bruce Reichenbach's suggestion fares better. He thinks that the phrase in question is ambiguous. It may mean either that "God works all things according to his will" or that "God works everything that he works according to his will." My interpretation adopts the former understanding; Reichenbach thinks the latter is more likely.[14] The latter reading does not require God's control over all things, but control only over things he does. What God does may be a rather small portion of everything that happens.

This is an ingenious but unsuccessful attempt to avoid a Calvinistic understanding of the verse. The problem is that the phrase *that he works* is nowhere to be found in the Greek, nor does anything about Greek in general or the syntax of this verse in particular allow this reading. The verse flatly says God works all things according to the counsel of his will. Why is that ambiguous? Reading into the verse words it does not contain generates the ambiguity Reichenbach suggests, but as the verse is written, its point is clear enough. It teaches divine control of all things.

Perhaps there is some other way to reinterpret this verse so as to escape the notion of absolute divine sovereignty. If so, Arminians should suggest it and let us all test it for accuracy. Heretofore none are forthcoming. In light

14. Bruce Reichenbach, "Bruce Reichenbach's Response," in *Predestination and Free Will*, 52–53.

of the evidence presented, I conclude that Scripture teaches in Ephesians 1:11 and other passages the concept of absolute divine control. This means incompatibilism must be rejected and some form of determinism adopted. But, perhaps one should adopt hard determinism and argue against free will altogether. That brings me to my second line of argument.

My second line of argument for a Calvinism that adopts compatibilism appeals to Scriptures that show that human beings are free and morally responsible. Without freedom there is no moral responsibility, so if Scripture (or any other evidence) shows that humans are morally responsible, they must be free. Here Calvinists cite many of the verses Arminians raise as evidence of freedom and responsibility. None of those verses defines freedom, but they do show that humans are free moral agents. Examples of passages that either explicitly or implicitly teach human freedom are Exodus 32–33; Joshua 24:15; 1 Kings 18:21; Matthew 23:37; Luke 7:30. Verses that show implicitly or explicitly that we are morally responsible for our actions are Psalm 1:6; Ezekiel 18:4; Romans 1:18–20; 2:5–8; 3:9–19; 6:23; Hebrews 9:27; and the Book of Leviticus.

In light of these verses that teach freedom and moral responsibility, it seems impossible to hold any form of hard determinism that rules out freedom altogether. But, if humans are free, what kind of freedom do they have? From the argument for divine sovereignty we saw that incompatibilism could not be correct. That leaves compatibilism, and it does fit biblical teaching about God's sovereign control and man's freedom and moral responsibility. God can guarantee that his decisions will be enacted, but he can do so by arranging things so that most of the time we choose in accord with our wishes and thereby freely.

If compatibilism and divine sovereignty harmonize as I am suggesting, there ought to be some evidence that one and the same act is both under God's control and freely (in the compatibilist's sense) done by the agent. My third line of argument offers some verses whose interpretation seems best understood this way. Let me cite some examples and leave study of the details of these passages to the reader. Proverbs 16:9 says "in his heart a man plans his course, but the LORD determines his steps." Proverbs 16:33 says the "lot is cast into the lap, but its every decision is from the LORD." Both verses show God's control and man's free activity. In regard to Christ's death, Peter says, "this man was handed over to you by God's set purpose and foreknowledge; and you, with the help of wicked men, put him to death by nailing him to the cross" (Acts 2:23). The accounts in the Gospels of Christ's death make it clear that those who put Christ to death did not do so under constraint. They did it freely. Peter's point (as well as the Gospels' portrayal) is that those who did this are morally responsible. In Philippians 2:12–13 Paul tells his readers to work out their own salvation, for it is God who works in them to will and to act according to his good purpose. Exodus 8:15, 32; 9:34 say Pharaoh hardened his heart against God's commands, but Scripture also says it was God who hardened Pharaoh's heart (Exod. 9:12; 10:1, 20; Rom. 9:17–18). Apart from a compatibilist understanding of free will, it is hard to see how both can be true or how God could hold Pharaoh accountable for defying him.

In addition to these passages, the verbal plenary inspiration of Scripture supports a compatibilist analysis. According to this notion of inspiration, the writing of Scripture involved people who were not stenographers taking dictation. Their personalities, styles of writing, and personal concerns are clearly evident in the text. On the other hand, the Holy Spirit so superintended their work that even the words they chose were directed by the Holy Spirit. The result is that the books they penned bear their genuine imprint and at the same time are God's Word (2 Pet. 1:20–21; 1 Cor. 2:13). It is hard to see how this superintendence, which guaranteed that the product is God's word (2 Tim. 3:16), is consistent with anything but determinism. No evidence suggests, however, that the writers were forced to write contrary to their wishes. They apparently wrote freely. But, it seems hard to reconcile this notion of the dual authorship of Scripture with anything other than some form of compatibilism. Again, we have evidence that one and the same action can be under God's control so that his will is done, and at the same time can be the act of the person who does it freely.

I conclude my discussion of sovereignty and freedom with a philosophical consideration. It is more an argument against indeterminism than an argument for compatibilism. Indeterminists say that reasons and causes surround an act of volition. But they deny that any conditions are strong enough to incline the will decisively in one direction or another. Instead, the will, despite its inclination, is neutral enough so that it can and sometimes does choose contrary to the direction the causes incline it.

The problem with this was raised pointedly by Jonathan Edwards.[15] To summarize, Edwards argued that in intentional acts, the will follows the dictates of reason. If reason finds no sufficient reason for choosing one option over the other (as Arminians must maintain to uphold their incompatibilism), then, Edwards believed, the person would not act. If nothing inclines the will decisively in one direction or another, it seems hard to explain why the agent did whatever she did. To say she did it because of x, y, or z is to point to sufficient conditions, but incompatibilism says there are none if the act is free. To say she did it without sufficient conditions seems to say the choice was random, but indeterminists agree that randomness is not freedom, and they deny that this is what they mean by freedom. But then there is a dilemma. How is it that someone comes to act? If there is no sufficient

---

15. Jonathan Edwards, *Freedom of the Will*, ed. Paul Ramsey, Yale ed. (New Haven, Conn.: Yale University Press, 1966), part 1, sec. 2; part 2, secs. 6 and 7, esp. sec. 7, p. 207.

condition, she will not act, or if she does, the act is random. If there is a sufficient condition, then she will act, but the act will be causally determined. Either way, indeterminism is in trouble. Indeterminists often say the agent just acts. However, this claim simply repeats their view; it does not explain how the agent comes to act without being causally determined or without making a random choice, neither of which is incompatibilistic freedom.

Divine Sovereignty and the Problem of Evil

There is a way, then, to harmonize a strong notion of divine sovereignty with human freedom. But, Calvinism is not out of the woods just yet. If God is in charge of things as Calvinists say, why are we guilty when we do his will? No one puts the problem more clearly than does the apostle Paul. In Romans 9 he discusses predestination. In the midst of his discussion, he imagines the following objection (9:19): "One of you will say to me: 'Then why does God still blame us? For who resists his will?'"

This objection raises both intellectual questions and attitudinal problems[16] on the part of the questioner. The explicit intellectual question is: Scripture says we are guilty for sin, but how is this just? Since we cannot escape doing what God decrees, why should we be morally responsible for our sin?

A second intellectual problem is implicit. It is the inverse of the explicit problem. If God decides whatever happens, including evil, why isn't *he* guilty? This is actually the problem of evil. The problem of evil asks if God has done something wrong in making our world with all of its evil. Since it stands to reason that God will create whatever world he decrees, it should be clear that the question about God's guilt in virtue of his *decree* of evil is the same as the question about his guilt in light of evil in the world he *created*, that is, both raise the problem of evil.

Although we might wish otherwise, in Romans 9:20–21 Paul addresses neither intellectual question. He does not say there are no answers, but turns instead to the objector's attitudinal problems. But, what about the intellectual problems? The first is easier to handle than the second (the problem of evil). After briefly answering the first, the rest of my chapter treats the second.

16. The imagined objection appears to put God on trial and demand that he prove he is just. There is an accusing tone, as though God has done wrong and must explain himself to us. Verses 20–21 clearly show that this attitude is wrong. In addition, the objection implicitly reveals an attitude of self-vindication against God. The intellectual question becomes a veiled assertion that we are not guilty. God may have done something wrong, but in following the decree, we have not. This evidences a problem of self-righteousness on the objector's part.

Sovereignty and Human Moral Responsibility

Compatibilists have a ready answer to why human beings are guilty when they do what God decrees. We are guilty because we do the evil deed freely, that is, without constraint. The decree of evil, like God's decree of everything, is God's blueprint for whatever happens. But, it is not the actual actions and events of history. History is the working out of God's decree. Nor does the decree *make* anything happen; it is not an agent that *exercises* causal power over anyone. It is the plan according to which all happens, but the plan and the doing of the plan are two separate things.

Since God's decreed plan included our evil deeds, are we not constrained to do them? Scripture teaches that we have a sin nature that inclines us toward evil. As a result, we are thoroughly able and willing to do what is wrong. But, then, we clearly do these evil acts in accord with our wishes. Compatibilists would say there are sufficient conditions for accomplishing these acts (part of that set of conditions is our sin nature), so they are causally determined. But, no one forces us kicking and screaming against our wishes to do evil. We do it in accord with our wishes, and hence, in the compatibilist sense, we do it freely. Of course, if we act freely, we are morally responsible. This is why we are guilty for doing evil, even though God decrees it.

Opponents may reject this explanation, but their objection probably amounts to a belief that these acts are not done freely, if God decides in advance what we shall do. But, this only means that the objector is saying that if something is causally determined, it cannot be free. This amounts to the typical indeterminist complaint that indeterministic freedom is the only freedom there is. As we have seen, this begs the question. Compatibilism is another possible notion of freedom. Given compatibilism, our sinful actions are freely done because we act in accord with our wishes. And, moral philosophers agree that if we act freely, we are morally responsible for our actions.

Sovereignty and the Problem of Evil

The real rub for the Calvinist comes on the other side of the question. That is, if we are guilty because we are involved, why isn't God guilty since he is also involved? He decided to make this world, a world with both moral and natural evil. Does not the existence of evil show that he is either not powerful enough, not good enough, or even not holy enough to get rid of it?

Elsewhere I have in great detail addressed the problem of evil, so I shall merely present the highlights.[17] I begin with the ground rules for this problem. An initial principle is that there is not just one problem of evil confront-

---

17. See *The Many Faces of Evil*. It is an update and an expansion of my earlier work *Theologies and Evil* (Washington, D.C.: University Press of America, 1979).

ing theism. There are many problems. There is a religious problem about one's personal struggles with evil. There are also abstract problems about the kinds of evil (moral and natural), the degree or amount of evil, the intensity of evil (why are specific instances of evil so bad?), and the apparent gratuitousness of evil. Each of these poses a separate problem for theism. In addition, the problem of moral evil is not just one problem. There are as many of these problems as there are systems committed to divine omnipotence, in some sense of "omnipotence," divine benevolence in that God wills the removal of evil, in some sense of "evil," and the existence of evil in the sense alluded to earlier in this sentence. In other words, not every theist has the same account of God and evil. Each different account generates a separate theology, and a distinct problem of moral evil (as well as a distinct problem of natural evil, quantity of evil, etc.) confronts each theology. In addition to these problems, philosophers have distinguished two forms in which problems of evil can be posed, a logical form and an evidential form.

There are important implications of the fact that there are many problems of evil. For theists, the point is that they must be sure they know which problem is under discussion and that they answer that specific problem. For atheists, the implication is that it is illegitimate to complain that a given defence is inadequate because it does not cover all evils and all problems of evil. No defence does, nor is it intended to. But, because a defence does not solve all problems of evil does not mean it solves none. Thinking a given defence must solve all problems of evil and account for all evils assumes that there is only one problem of evil when in fact there are many.

As for the logical form of the problem of evil, some further ground rules relate exclusively to it. According to this problem, theistic systems committed to divine omnipotence and benevolence and the existence of evil are internally inconsistent. This means the theist's own system contradicts itself. If the accusation is true for a given theology, that theology collapses.

The implication of this point for the theist is that she must be careful not to incorporate in her theology contradictory accounts of God, evil, and human free will. As for atheists, this ground rule means it is illegitimate for them to attribute their own views to theists and then tell theists they have a problem of *internal* inconsistency. Unless the theist holds the views in question, there may be a contradiction in the views under discussion, but it is not *internal* to the theist's system.

Since the logical problem of evil is about contradiction, it is important to understand what the charge of contradiction means. To say two propositions are contradictory is to say they affirm and deny at the same time the same thing. It does not mean there may be a way to reconcile propositions, but we do not know it yet. It does not even mean God knows how but we do not. It means there is no *possible* way the propositions can all be true. Since this is the charge, the defender of the propositions need only show a possible way to fit them together consistently. Hopefully, theists will propose plausible ways to fit theistic doctrines together, but the only requirement is that the explanation be possible.[18]

In light of these ground rules, how should Calvinists respond to the charge of contradiction in their system? Typically, Calvinists who offer a defence appeal to the free will defence.[19] The problem with this is that the free will defence incorporates incompatibilism, but Calvinists who believe in free will are compatibilists. Compatibilism and incompatibilism contradict one another. Hence, Calvinists should look elsewhere.[20]

I begin my answer by specifying the particulars of my system. Since the logical problem is about internal consistency of a theology, we must clarify the commitments of the system in question before we can test for internal problems. I hold a broad form of theism known as modified rationalism. According to this position, God does not need to create anything, for his own existence is the highest good. However, creating a world is a fitting thing for God to do, but not the only fitting thing he can do. There is an infinite number of finite, contingent possible worlds God could create. Some are intrinsically evil, so God had better not create any of them. But, at least more than one is a good possible world. There is no best possible world. And, God is free either to create one of the good possible worlds or not to create at all.

My system also has its account of evil. I am a nonconsequentialist, which means I believe acts are right or wrong on the basis of something other than their consequences. In particular, I hold a form of a modified divine command theory. That is, I believe moral norms are prescribed by God, but I do not believe God prescribes arbitrarily. Instead, his precepts reflect his character.[21]

18. As Alvin Plantinga explains, "Clearly it need be neither true, nor probable, nor plausible, nor believed by most theists, nor anything else of that sort. . . . The fact that a particular proffered *r* is implausible, or not congenial to 'modern man,' or a poor explanation of *q*, or whatever, is utterly beside the point" (Alvin Plantinga, "Reply to the Basingers on Divine Omnipotence," *Process Studies* 11, 1 [spring 1981]: 26–27).

19. Here I use the term *defence* as opposed to *theodicy*. In contemporary discussions philosophers distinguish between offering a possible reason for God allowing evil and explaining the actual reason for God doing so. The former explanation is referred to as a defence, while the latter is called a theodicy. Given the charge of contradiction, it should be clear that all a theist needs to do is offer a possible explanation (defence) of how evil fits with the existence of an omnipotent, all-loving God. A case can be made that my defence offers God's actual reason for allowing evil, but for purposes of solving the logical problem of evil, it is not necessary to prove that one has specified God's actual reason for allowing evil. Hence, I offer my explanation as a defence rather than a theodicy.

20. For detailed proof that the free will defence rests on incompatibilism and that this contradicts compatibilism, see my book on the problem of evil (chap. 4) and my article "And the Atheist Shall Lie Down with the Calvinist: Atheism, Calvinism, and the Free Will Defense," *Trin J* 1 n.s. (1980): 142–52.

21. For explanation of this and other ethical theories, see John S. Feinberg and Paul D. Feinberg, *Ethics for a Brave New World* (Wheaton: Crossway, 1993), chap. 1.

Given modified rationalism, how does a problem of evil arise? I can state it as a question: does the evil in our world, evil as the modified rationalist defines it, refute the modified rationalist's claim that our world is one of the good possible worlds God could have created? To answer this problem, the modified rationalist must point to some feature of our world that makes it one of the good possible worlds God could create, despite the evil in it.

My defence for my system has three stages.[22] I begin by asking what sort of beings God intended to create when he made human beings. Here I am referring to the basic abilities and capacities God gave us as human beings. At a minimum, I believe he intended to create beings with ability to reason (that ability varies for each person), beings with emotions, beings with wills that are compatibilistically free (although freedom is not the emphasis of my defence), beings with desires, beings with intentions (formed on the basis of desires), and beings with the capacity for bodily movement. Moreover, he intended us to use these capacities to live and function in a world suited to beings such as we are. Hence, he created our world, which is run according to the natural laws we observe, and he evidently did not intend to annihilate what he had created once he created it.

In addition, God did not intend each of us to be identical in respect to these capacities. For example, some might have certain desires to the same degree other humans do, but in no two people would all these qualities of humanness be conjoined so as to obliterate individuality. In other words, the qualities of personhood would not be so similar in any two people that they would be stereotypes of one another. Finally, God intended to make beings who are finite both metaphysically and morally (as to the moral aspect, our finitude does not necessitate doing evil, but only that we do not have God's infinite moral perfection). In other words, God intended to create human beings, not superhuman beings or even gods.

I do not believe any of these features were negated by the race's fall into sin. I do not mean sin had no effect on us or our world. I mean only that it did not result in the removal of desires, intentions, free will, bodily movement, and the like. Because of our fall into sin, these capacities do not function as well as they would have without sin, but that does not mean we no longer have them. Likewise, the fall did not overturn the basic laws of nature and physics according to which our world runs. The fundamental features of humanity and of our world are still as God created them.

22. Here I note that I am addressing the philosophical/theological problem of evil, which is really the problem of moral evil. This is not peculiar to my system, for most defences theists offer address that problem. Unfortunately, many theists and atheists do not see that there are other problems of evil that must also be addressed and that a defence against moral evil does not suffice for all problems of evil, nor need it do so.

How do I know this is what God intended? I know it by looking at the sort of being he created when he created us, and by noting also that the world in which we live is suited to our capacities. Someone might think this same line of thinking could be used to say God also intended to create moral evil, because we have it. However, that is not so. Moral evil is not something God created when he created other things. It is not a substance at all. God created substances, including the world and the people in it. God intended that we be able to act, for he made us capable of acting. But he neither created our actions, nor does he perform them. Hence, we cannot say God intended there to be moral evil because we have it in our world. God intended to create and did create agents who can act; he did not create their acts (good or evil).

How do we know, though, by looking at what God did that he really intended to do it? Don't others at times act without fully understanding their own intentions? While it is true that human beings do not always know what they intend to do, that cannot be true of an omniscient being's awareness of his intentions. By seeing what he did, we can be sure we know what he really intended to do.

If humans are the sort of creatures I have described, how do they come to do moral evil (sin)? This brings me to the second stage of my defence, a consideration of the ultimate source of evil actions. My answer is not free will, although I agree that free exercise of will is instrumental in bringing about moral evil. However, as a compatibilist, I dare not use the free will defence.

In accord with James 1:13–15, I hold that morally evil actions stem from human desires. Desires in and of themselves are not evil nor do they perform the evil. James says, however, that desires (*epithumia* is the word for desire, and it can refer to any desire) are carried away *(exelkomenos)* and enticed *(deleazomenos)* to the point where sin is actually committed (conceived).[23] Many moral philosophers would agree that the point of "conception" is when a person wills to do the act if she could. Once that choice is made, then it remains only for her to translate that choice into overt public action.[24]

Morally evil acts, then, ultimately begin with our desires. Desires in themselves are not evil, but when they are aroused to the point where they lead us to choose to disobey God's prescribed moral norms, then we have sinned. Desires are not the only culprit, for will, reason, and emotion, for example,

---

23. Joseph B. Mayor, *The Epistle of St. James*, in the *Classic Commentary Library* (Grand Rapids: Zondervan, 1954), 54–55.

24. This interpretation of the point of sin's conception certainly squares with the tenor of Jesus' teachings, when he claimed that sin is committed in a person's thoughts first and made public later. Think, for example, of Matthew 5:27–28, where we find Jesus' teaching that if a man desires a woman in his heart, he has already committed adultery with her before doing any overt act.

enter into the process. But, James says individual acts of sin ultimately stem from desires that go astray.

If humans are the sort of creatures described, and if moral evil arises as I have suggested, what would God have to do to get rid of moral evil? This brings me to the final stage of my defence. Here I ask if God can remove moral evil. Clearly, if this is his only goal, he certainly can accomplish it. However, I hold a view of divine omnipotence that does not allow God to actualize contradictions. Hence, if I can show that by removing evil God would contradict some other goal(s) he wants to accomplish, then I will have shown why God cannot remove evil. Of course, if he *cannot* create a utopia without producing further and greater problems, he is not obligated to do so.

It is my contention that if God did what is necessary to remove moral evil from our world, he would either contradict his intentions to create human beings and the world as he has, cause us to wonder if he has one or more of the attributes ascribed to him, and/or do something we would not expect or desire him to do, because it would produce greater evil than there already is. To see this, let us look at how God might get rid of moral evil.

Some may think all God needs to do to remove moral evil is merely arrange affairs so that his compatibilistically free creatures are causally determined to have desires only for the good and to choose only good without being constrained at all. With respect to each of us, God should know what it would take, and he should be powerful enough to do it.

However, this is not as simple as it sounds. If people are naturally inclined to do what God wants, God may need to do very little rearranging of our world to accomplish this goal. If people are stubborn and resist his will, it may take a great deal more rearranging than we think. God would have to do this for every one of us every time we resist his will. Moreover, changes in circumstances for one of us would affect circumstances for others. After all, we do not live in isolation. But, what might be necessary to get us to do good might disrupt others' lives, constrain them to do something that serves God's purposes in regard to us, and perhaps even turn them toward doing evil.

Consider, for example, what it might take for God to bring even one person to choose good freely. To convince one person to do right would probably require rearrangements in other peoples' lives, changes that would require them to do things they do not want to do. If God wants those other people to do what he wants unconstrainedly, he may need to rearrange even other peoples' lives. To get that third group of people to do what he wants unconstrainedly may require yet more people to do something they do not want to do. I could go on, but the picture is clear. To uphold everyone's freedom may be much more difficult than we suppose. It is more likely that the free will of many will be abridged as a result of God's attempts to convince certain people to do good.

There is further reason to think it may be harder for God to get us to do right than we think. God did not create us with an inclination toward sin, but even Adam in ideal surroundings and circumstances sinned. According to biblical teaching, the race inherited from Adam a sin nature that disposes us toward evil. In light of that sin nature, it is not at all clear that a minimal rearranging of events, actions, and circumstances would achieve the goal of getting us to do good without constraining us. It might turn out that God would have to constrain many people to do things he needed done in order to rearrange circumstances to convince a few of us to do the right thing without constraining us. Of course, that would contradict compatibilistic free will for many of us, and would likely do so more frequently than we might imagine. Moreover, one begins to wonder how wise this God is if he must do all of this just to bring it about that his human creatures do good. Why not make a different creature who would be unable to do evil? But, of course, this would contradict God's decision to make humans, not subhumans or superhumans.

There is yet a further problem with this method of getting rid of evil. This method also assumes that if God rearranged the world, all of us would draw the right conclusion from our circumstances and do right. Our desires, intentions, emotions, and will would all fall into place as they should without abridging freedom at all. This is most dubious, given our finite minds and wills as well as the sin nature within us that inclines us toward evil. Hence, it is not clear that we can coherently conceive all the changes God would have to make to ensure that we got the right message and acted rightly.

Perhaps there is a simpler, more direct way for God to get rid of evil. Although we might wonder what other avenue is open to God, there are at least eight other ways in which God might get rid of evil. However, none of them would be acceptable. First, he could remove moral evil by doing away with mankind. Not only is this a drastic solution none of us would think acceptable, but also it would contradict his intention to create humans who are not then annihilated by his further actions.

A second way to remove moral evil is for God to eliminate all objects of desire. Without objects of desire, it is hard to see how human desires could be led astray to do moral evil. However, to eradicate all objects of desire God would have to destroy the whole world and everything in it, including human bodies (obviously, they are often objects of desire). Minds alone would remain, unless minds could be objects of desire that might lead someone astray.

Objections to this option are obvious. Its implications for human life and well-being make it unacceptable. Moreover, the God I have described would have to reject it, because adopting it would contradict his intentions to create human beings and put them in our world which he did not intend to annihilate once he created it.

Since sin ultimately stems from desires, a third way for God to remove moral evil would be to remove human desires. Problems with this solution again are obvious. God intended to create creatures who have desires, but if he removes all human desires, that contradicts his intentions about the creature he wanted to create. Moreover, removing desires would also remove the ultimate basis of action so that people would not act. However, that would contradict God's intention to create beings who perform the various actions necessary to remain alive. Of course, if that happened, the ultimate demise of the race would result. Surely, that would be less desirable than our world is now.

A fourth possibility seems to be one of the more likely things God could do. He could allow us to have desires but never allow them to be aroused to the point where we would do moral evil (perhaps not even to the point where they would result in our forming intentions to do evil). Now, since any desire can lead to evil, this would mean we would retain all our desires, but God would eliminate or neutralize them once they approached or reached a degree of arousal that would result in intending or willing an act of moral evil. If God chose this option, he could accomplish it in one of two ways. He could make us with all the capacity for our desires to run rampant, but then perform a miracle to stop them whenever they start to do so. Or, God could make us with the capacity to have desires aroused only to a certain degree, a degree that would never be or lead to evil. I shall address the former option when I discuss more generally the option of God removing evil by performing a miracle. The latter option concerns me now.

As for that option, there are several problems. For one thing, it contradicts the idea that God intended to create people who are not stereotypes of one another. Let me explain. I am not saying people would always desire the same things. Rather, whenever someone's desires were allured in regard to something forbidden, those desires could be enticed only up to a point, a point that would not be or lead to evil. What would be true of one person would be true of all. This might appear to leave much room for individuality, but that is not necessarily so. Any desire can lead to evil, and God knows when a given desire, if pursued, would do so. In every such case, we would have to be preprogrammed to squelch the desire before it went too far. That would seem to make us stereotypes of one another more often than we might think.

There is another problem with God making us this way. Imagine what life would be like. Whenever a desire would start to run amuck, one would have to stop having the desire (or at least not follow it), change desires, and begin a new course of action. The picture that comes to mind is one where our daily routine of action is constantly interrupted (if not stopped altogether) and new courses of action are implemented only to be interrupted and new ones implemented and interrupted *ad infinitum*. Life as we know it would probably come to a standstill. The world envisioned would be a different world (perhaps radically different), but not necessarily better or even as good as our world. Moreover, it would apparently contradict God's intention to create us so as to function in this world.

478

Perhaps the greatest objection to this fourth option is that to make us this way God would have to make us superhuman both morally and intellectually. We would not necessarily have to be divine or angelic, but we would have to be much different morally and intellectually than we now are. In order to make us so that our desires would never get out of hand, God would have to make us willing to squelch them whenever they would lead to evil (a hard enough thing to do). To do this we would also need to *know* when desires would lead to evil, so that we could stop them from being overly enticed. Whatever God would have to do to make us this way, it seems it would involve making us more than human. Of course, if that is so, God would have to contradict his intention to make human beings, not superhuman beings.

Fifth, God could allow desires of any sort and could allow us to form intentions for actions based on those desires, unless the intentions would lead to evil. God could remove these intentions in either of the ways mentioned for handling evil producing desires (by miracles or by making us so we would never develop intentions that would lead to evil). However, removing evil by handling intentions this way faces the same problems raised with respect to desires.

Sixth, God might eliminate evil by removing any willing that would produce evil. We could will good things freely (compatibilistically), but whenever we might will evil, the willing would be eliminated. God could do this either by miraculous intervention (to be discussed later) or by making us so we would never will evil. However, removing evil this way faces the same kinds of objections that confront the desire and intention options.

Seventh, God could eliminate the public expression of moral evil by stopping our bodily movement whenever we try to carry out evil. He could do this either by miracle or by making us as needed to stop bodily movement when it would lead to evil. Bodily movement would probably be interrupted and stopped quite often. However, this option faces the same kinds of objections the desire, intention, and will options face.

If all of these ways are problematic, perhaps God could still remove evil by miraculous intervention at any point as we do an action. Several problems, however, beset this method of removing moral evil. First, if God did this, it would greatly change life as we know it. At any moment, God would miraculously stop desires, intentions, willing, or bodily movement if he knew they would lead to evil. Since we would not always know when our actions would lead to evil,[25] we would not always know when to expect God to interfere. We might become too afraid to do, try, or even think anything, realizing that at any moment, our movements or thoughts could be eliminated. Under those circumstances, life as we know it might come to a standstill, and that would contradict God's desire to create people who live and function in

25. In this case, people would not have to be capable of having such knowledge, since God would take care of any possible problems by means of miracles.

this world. Moreover, it is not at all clear that a world in which there is a constant threat of removing our thoughts, willing, or bodily movements would be a better world or even as good a world as the one we have.

Second, it is one thing to speak of God miraculously intervening to eradicate desires, intentions, willing, or bodily movements that lead to evil. It is another to specify exactly what that means. As for bodily movement, God would probably have to paralyze a person as long as necessary (perhaps indefinitely) to stop bodily movements that would carry out an evil act. Of course, stopping bodily movement this way even momentarily would alter the nature of life altogether. Every few moments series of people would be paralyzed while trying to carry out an action. Once they are ready to change their actions, they would begin to move again while yet other people would be paralyzed. It is not clear that this would be a better world than ours. And, such a world would apparently contradict God's intention to make creatures who can live and function in this world.

In addition, it is difficult to imagine what miracle God would have to do to remove a desire, an intention, or an act of willing that would lead to evil. It hardly makes sense to talk about paralysis of intention, desire, or will. God would probably have to knock us unconscious or cause us to lose our memory for as long and as often as needed in order to remove evil-producing thoughts. The picture one gets is of a whole world of people who fall in and out of consciousness and undergo periodic spells of amnesia. Wouldn't that virtually bring life to a standstill and thereby be inconsistent with God's intention to make us so that we can live and function in this world? Moreover, miraculous intervention of the sort imagined seems to involve manipulations that would produce more evil than we already have.

A final objection to removing evil miraculously is that it would give reason to question God's wisdom. If God goes to all the trouble he did to make human beings as he has, but then must perform these miracles to counteract them when they express that humanness in ways that would produce evil, there is reason to wonder if God was wise in making us as he did. Of course, had God made us differently so that he would not have to remove evil by miracles, that would contradict his intention to make the sort of beings he has made. So, either God must perform miracles and thereby cause us to question his wisdom, or he must change our nature as human beings. But that would contradict his goal of making humans rather than superhumans or subhumans.[26]

26. My defence focuses on evil that is voluntarily produced. If a world where God removes intentionally evil actions is problematic, there is even more reason for concern when one realizes that involuntary and reflex actions can also produce evil. If it would disrupt normal life to remove evil-intentioned acts, it would be even more disruptive to remove also our good-intentioned and reflex actions that wind up producing evil.

This discussion about what God would have to do to remove moral evil shows that God *cannot* remove it without contradicting his desires to make the kind of creature and world he has made, causing us to doubt the accuracy of ascribing to him attributes like wisdom, or making a world we would not want and would consider more evil than our present world. Someone may suggest that God could avoid all these problems if he made different creatures than human beings. In other words, why not make creatures without desires, intentions, will, and/or bodily movement?

I agree that God could do this, and if he did, it would likely remove moral evil. The problem is that it would also remove human beings as we know them. It is hard to know what to call the resultant creature since it would neither move nor think—even "robot" seems too complimentary. Anyone who thinks there is any worth in being human would find this unacceptable.

Someone else might object that God should not make us subhuman, but moral evil could be avoided if he made us superhuman. I agree that God could do this. However, my contention is that humans as we know them are a value of the first order. Scripture says humans are created in God's image (Gen. 1:26–27). When God finished his creative work, he saw that all of it, including human beings, was very good (Gen. 1:31). Psalm 8:5–8 speaks of God crowning us with glory and honor and giving us dominion over the other parts of his creation. In light of this evaluation by God, who are we to say that human beings as created by God are not valuable? And, remember that as a modified rationalist all I need to show is that our world is one of those good possible worlds God could have created. It seems clear that a world with human beings in it is a good world.

Another objection confronts not only my theology, but also many other orthodox Christian systems. Theists, including myself, often say our world is a good world because of some feature in it. However, those same theists believe in a future state (call it the kingdom of God or the eternal state) in which there will be no evil. It is agreed as well that morally speaking, this will be a better world than our present world. Since God not only can create this better world but will do so some day, why didn't he do so to begin with? Since it will be a better world and God could create it, the fact that he didn't suggests something is wrong with him.

I respond initially that this objection demonstrates no internal inconsistency in my theology or in any other orthodox Christian system. Critics of theism might reject all orthodox theologies on this ground, but it would not be a rejection on grounds of inability to solve a logical problem of evil, a problem of internal inconsistency.

More directly to the point, this is a significant objection, but it contains a confusion. The confusion centers around what is required of a modified rationalist theology to solve its logical problem of evil. Modified rationalists do not claim there is a best world, but they do claim there is more than one good

481

possible world. Moreover, modified rationalism does not demand that God create the best world or even a better world than some other good world. It only requires God to create a good possible world. The task for a modified rationalist, then, is to look at the world God *did* create and explain why it is good in spite of the evil in it.

Since this is the requirement, neither I nor any other modified rationalist need to show that our world is the best or even better than some other good world God might have created. We need only to show that ours is one of those good worlds God could have created. I have done that by pointing to human beings, and arguing that God cannot both create them and remove evil. Hence, I have solved my theology's logical problem of moral evil.[27]

Can God remove moral evil from our world? I believe he can, if he creates different creatures than human beings. He also can if he creates humans and then removes evil in any of the ways imagined. But, we have seen the problems that arise if God takes any of those options.

Has God done something wrong in creating human beings? Not at all, when we consider the great value human beings have and the great worth God places upon us. As an empirical fact, we can say that moral evil has come as a concomitant of a world populated with human beings. Still, it is one of those good possible worlds God could have created. God is a good God. Our world with human beings demonstrates his goodness. This explanation of why there is moral evil renders my theology internally consistent, and hence solves the logical problem of evil that confronts it.

Conclusion

A Calvinistic system as well as an Arminian system can solve its problem of moral evil in its logical form. There are other problems of evil, and other theists and I have addressed them elsewhere.[28] Someone may still reject a Calvinist system altogether, because he believes it has an inadequate account of God, man, sin, or salvation. Chapters in this volume offer reasons why Calvinism is not inadequate in those respects. How-

27. I agree that this other world would be better morally, because there would be no moral evil in it. But, God cannot make that world and also make the nonglorified human beings he has. Was God wrong in making nonglorified humans? Only if they are evil themselves, and they are not. Is God obligated to create this other world, anyway? According to modified rationalism, God is free either to create or not create at all. If he creates, he is free to create any good possible world available. He is not obligated to forego our world in favor of the eternal state, so long as our world is a good world. And, I have shown why ours is a good world.

28. See *The Many Faces of Evil* as well as the vast amount of literature on this topic in books and philosophical and theological journals.

ever, from what I have shown in this chapter, one cannot legitimately reject a Calvinistic system like mine on the ground that it cannot harmonize divine sovereignty with human freedom or that it cannot solve the problem of moral evil in its logical form. If one understands the ground rules of those problems, one recognizes that the preceding discussion handles those problems successfully.

21

The Philosophical Issue of Divine Foreknowledge

PAUL HELM

Threaded through the debate about free will and free grace are opposed views of human freedom. The upholders of free will maintain that human agents have libertarian power, the power to act and to refrain from acting only where causal determination is absent. The upholders of free grace are inclined to take the view that God's providential control and saving grace are incompatible with libertarian freedom and that the absence of compulsion, not the absence of causal determination, is necessary for free and responsible human agency.

One important reason offered for maintaining that human beings have libertarian, indeterministic freedom is the claim that only such freedom places the responsibility for human sin on human shoulders and exonerates God from the charge of being the author of sin. It is argued further that the divine foreordination of human actions must make God the author of sin, whereas a divine foreknowledge of human actions that is consistent with libertarian freedom does not.

As a small contribution to this controversy I shall in this chapter attempt to show that the main arguments of those Christian thinkers who seek to uphold human libertarian freedom as a way of protecting God, of exonerating him from the charge that he is responsible for human sin, have a similar fate to the arguments of those Christian thinkers who seek to uphold free grace. Thus the thesis is that whatever makes for human responsibility for actions is not canceled or diminished by divine foreordination any more

485

or less than it is by mere divine foreknowledge if that knowledge extends to those actions.

So if the arguments that attempt to reconcile divine foreknowledge with human responsibility for sin succeed, then so do arguments that attempt to reconcile divine foreordination and human responsibility. If the arguments for the first fail, then so do arguments for the second. If these claims can be supported convincingly then there is no need for the Christian theist to commit himself to human libertarian freedom, with all the metaphysical difficulties to which such a view is heir, in order to attempt to take the responsibility for human sin from God's shoulders. Such an attempt is unnecessary. Non-libertarian freedom is sufficient to take this responsibility from God (with the qualifications to be noted later) and to place it where Scripture says it belongs.

In this short chapter it is not possible to cover all the arguments used by Christian libertarians, even if I knew them. The most that can be done is to consider the main arguments and to argue that because these fail, there is a presumption that all such arguments will fail. Perhaps somewhere there is a libertarian argument that succeeds in its aim, but the failure of the main arguments at least places the onus firmly on the libertarian to show this.

When Christians set out to reflect upon the relation between God's knowledge and power and human responsibility, it is important to understand what sort of task they face. They are not reflecting in an abstract way on these concepts, but upon the biblical witness insofar as it employs them. Christians hold this witness as a set of fixed points and reflect upon the cogency or coherence of the several parts of that witness. It is possible that at the end of these reflections they will reluctantly have to conclude that they cannot see how the parts cohere, that they cannot demonstrate consistency. But what is not open to Christians is to amend or to modify that witness in any way in the interests of greater comprehensibility.

The Fixed Points

What is that witness? Other chapters in this book deal with the biblical data in extenso. But in brief, the scriptural world view is one in which all things are created by God and ordered and governed by him; he numbers the hairs of our heads, directs the fall of a sparrow and the flight of an arrow; he turns the hearts of men as he wishes; like a potter, he has power over human clay. God's providence extends over all; he takes no risks. It is true that God is said to forget, to express surprise, and to act and react toward his people in blessing and chastisement. These may be thought to be the actions of someone of limited knowledge and power, but it is usually recognized that scriptural language in such cases is metaphorical or symbolic. Nowhere in Scripture is it suggested, in nonmetaphorical statements about the nature and the character of God, that the divine ordering and control of his creation is qualified or attenuated. So this is one fixed point that our theorizing should not attempt to stray beyond.

Scripture also teaches that men and women are accountable to God for their actions; not for all their actions, because a distinction is drawn between matters that are outside a person's control and that cancel responsibility, and those which are under a person's control. For actions under his control a person may be more or less accountable, as Scripture teaches; responsibility may be partly canceled, for example, by partial ignorance (Luke 12:7–8).

In his book on free will, *Elbow Room,* Daniel Dennett has this to say:

> Why do we hold ourselves and others *morally* responsible? At first it may appear that this inquiry is parasitic on a metaphysical question about the conditions under which someone truly *is* responsible. . . . Surely, it seems, we can make a distinction between the question of why we *hold* people responsible, or *take* responsibility ourselves for various things, and the question of why or whether we actually *are* responsible. . . . .
>
> But whatever responsibility is, considered as a metaphysical state, unless we can tie it to some recognizable social desideratum, it will have no rational claim on our esteem.[1]

In other words, according to Dennett, ascribing responsibility to oneself or to others is a human, social activity having a certain social function. A sense of responsibility that is not rootable in such a setting is not the sort of responsibility we ought to want to have. But in considering responsibility Christians place the emphasis in a different place than does Dennett.

When, as in this chapter, Christians are exploring the relationship between divine knowledge and power and human responsibility they might be doing one of two different things. They might be exploring the implications of divine knowledge for human responsibility as it is exercised, say, in families, or between friends and colleagues. Let us call this "everyday responsibility." Such an idea of moral responsibility is a familiar one, and needs to be distinguished from legal responsibility, to which it is related. Both moral and legal responsibility need in turn to be distinguished from human responsibility before God. Let us call responsibility before God "pure responsibility."

Why may everyday and pure responsibility be different? In order to hold a person justly responsible for his action, some knowledge of his state of mind, and the circumstances of his action, are necessary. Social and legal imperatives may require the ascription of responsibility when full knowledge is

---

1. (Cambridge, Mass.: MIT Press, 1984), 163.

unattainable; indeed, perhaps full knowledge is never attainable by us. In such cases what we have is an ascription of everyday or legal responsibility, not of pure responsibility. Since we can never be sure that we know all the relevant facts, the best human assessment that we can ever hope for falls short of what is necessary for pure responsibility.

But in the case of responsibility before God it must be presumed that God himself has perfect knowledge of the state of mind and the circumstances of every agent and every action. Part of the "righteous judgment" of God (Rom. 2:5) is thus that it is a judgment that is "based on truth" (Rom. 2:2), based upon all and only the relevant facts.

It is important to stress that the basic biblical emphasis is not upon everyday responsibility, but upon accountability to God. Because the moral accountability of one person to another, or legal accountability to the state, depends upon fallible human knowledge of the motivations and circumstances of ourselves and others, each can be only pale and imperfect reflections of the accountability each person has to God. This is perhaps one of the reasons why Christ's followers are warned against carrying out summary justice, as in Christ's teaching about an eye for an eye (Matt. 5:38–42).

So it is possible to maintain the importance of pure responsibility while combining this with some skepticism about judgments of everyday responsibility. When the apostle Paul urges his readers to "judge nothing before the appointed time" (1 Cor. 4:5) he would appear to be adopting such a mildly skeptical position; not saying that everyday responsibility bears no relation to pure responsibility, but that the judgments of everyday responsibility, because of imperfections in knowledge, are only partial and provisional, open to revision at "the appointed time." Perhaps this should be the general Christian attitude to all human assessments of responsibility.

Divine sovereignty and human responsibility; these are two of the fixed points. When faced with problems about the consistency of these concepts, it is tempting to modify one or both of them. But we must make every effort to avoid such a course of action. The Scripture holds them together, even speaks of them in the same breath, and so must we.

Nowhere is this more noteworthy and striking than in Peter's sermon in Acts 2, where he says that Jesus "was handed over to you by God's set purpose and foreknowledge; and you, with the help of wicked men, put him to death by nailing him to the cross" (v. 23; see also Acts 4:27–28). From this text it is possible to conclude that there are at least some occasions when the action of a wicked man is the result of the set purpose and foreknowledge of God, and that one such occasion was the crucifixion of Christ, the paradigmatic event of the Christian faith.

It is tempting to say, about the crucifixion of Christ, that if the men who crucified him were wicked then they cannot have acted as a result of God's set purpose. It is equally tempting to say that if the crucifixion of Christ came about as a result of the set purpose of God the men who crucified him cannot have been wickedly responsible for what they did. But each of these temptations must be resisted, for Scripture teaches both human accountability and divine sovereignty.

There is a third fixed point, one that is perhaps less frequently reflected upon. God's relation to the universe that he has created and that he sustains and directs is a relation that is without parallel. It is unique, incomparable, sui generis. This is not surprising, or it ought not to be; after all, there can only be one God, and (as far as we know) there is only one universe. We cannot have experience of more than one God or of more than one universe. Those critics of the argument from design, such as David Hume, who argue that we do not, in the nature of things, have experience of more than one world, make an important point. It is one that can be turned to advantage against critics of the view that God is sovereign and human beings are responsible for their actions.

Emphasizing the sui generis character of the relation between God and his creation is another way of saying that God's relations with his creation are incomprehensible. But comprehensibility, like temperature, comes in degrees; for a state of affairs to be incomprehensible it is not necessary for it to be fully or totally incomprehensible, but rather to be not fully comprehended.

So it is a mistake to think that because God's relations with his creation are sui generis, we inevitably fall into paradox, self-contradiction, or gibberish whenever we attempt to think or to speak about them clearly. Nevertheless the uniqueness of the Creator-creature relationship should carry a warning against thinking of it as we do of relations between creatures. In what follows we shall try to comprehend aspects of the relation of divine sovereignty and human responsibility while recognizing that we can never, in the nature of things, fully comprehend it.

A Preliminary Point

We shall consider some of the main libertarian arguments intending to show that God is not responsible for human sin. Since divine knowledge is going to loom large in what follows it is necessary to make a preliminary point about it.

Philosophical theologians have tended to think of the knowledge that God has of the created universe in one of two ways: either as being an anticipation of what is to take place in that world[2] or as being the cause of what happens

---

2. Richard Swinburne, *The Coherence of Theism* (Oxford: Clarendon, 1977), chap. 10.

in that world.[3] It is possible to combine elements of each. Thus on the overall account of God's knowledge offered by Richard Swinburne, God is able to anticipate the course of the universe because he has unsurpassable degrees of evidence of how things will turn out based, for example, on his knowledge of the laws that he has ordained, and on how things have turned out in the past. Although the distinction between these two ways of knowing is obviously important, nothing rests on it in the arguments that follow.

For ease of exposition the arguments will be divided into two classes, which I shall label omniscience-affirming and omniscience-denying arguments, respectively. Let us begin by considering two libertarian arguments that are omniscience-affirming.

The Middle-Knowledge Solution

In work of unsurpassed elegance Alvin Plantinga has maintained that it is consistent to suppose that God is all-good and all-powerful and that there is moral evil.[4] The supposition depends upon God endowing human beings with libertarian freedom. Not even God can ensure that any human being that he creates thus empowered with libertarian free will is such that he only ever freely does what is right. Whether or not he always does what is right, Plantinga avers, is not up to God but up to the creation. There may be creatures who freely only do what is right, but if there are it is not because God has ensured that there are. It is because the creatures have freely chosen to do so. What such a creature does is, as Plantinga characteristically states, "up to him," and not up to God. And it is possible that each creature God created would freely choose to do evil.

But while God does not—because he cannot—determine what any of his free creatures will do, but only watchfully anticipate what they are going to do, God does know what each possible person would do if he were actualized and placed in such and such circumstances. That is, God has middle knowledge; knowledge not only of necessary truths, and of those truths that he has freely willed to come to pass, but also knowledge of an infinite number of "what if . . ." propositions. Thus he infallibly knows the truth of what a creature with a certain character, and possessing libertarian freedom, would do were he to be placed in a given set of circumstances.

Suppose we conclude that not even God can cause it to be the case that I freely refrain from A. Even so, he *can* cause me to be free with respect to A, and to be

3. Aquinas *Summa Theologiae* Ia 14.8.
4. Alvin Plantinga, *The Nature of Necessity* (Oxford: Clarendon, 1974), chap. 9; *God, Freedom and Evil* (London: Allen and Unwin, 1975), pt. 1.

in some set S of circumstances, including appropriate laws and antecedent conditions. He may also know, furthermore, that *if* he creates me and causes me to be free in these circumstances, I will refrain from A.[5]

> Further, God knows in advance what Curley would do if created and placed in these states of affairs.[6]

So when God creates indeterministically free persons he does so already knowing what they will do when they are placed in given circumstances. This knowledge is a consequence of God's omniscience, his knowledge of all truths.

In considering the appeal to middle knowledge, and Plantinga's elegant version of that appeal, it ought to be emphasized that the validity or the soundness of his reasoning is not in question here, though some have questioned it. In particular, it has been claimed that the counterfactuals of freedom are such that God could not know them, since they do not have a truth-value.[7]

The commitment to divine omniscience is particularly clear in the classical treatment of middle knowledge in Luis de Molina. In commenting on the background to this, Alfred J. Freddoso writes:

> Since God is the perfect artisan, not even the most trivial details escape His providential decrees. Thus, whatever occurs is properly said to be *specifically decreed* by God; more precisely, each effect produced in the created universe is either specifically and knowingly *intended* by Him or, in concession to creaturely defectiveness, specifically and knowingly *permitted* by Him only to be then ordered toward some appropriate good.[8]

The picture that Plantinga and all upholders of God's middle knowledge present is that God endorses with actuality some particular free conditionals. Knowing that if Jones were to be placed in such circumstances he would freely choose what is evil, God actualizes Jones and, by his free choice, Jones does evil. Because he is omniscient God not only knows that some of the free

---

5. Plantinga, *Nature of Necessity,* 172.
6. Ibid., 185–86.
7. For further discussion of these issues see, for example, R. M. Adams, "Middle Knowledge and the Problem of Evil" in *The Problem of Evil,* ed. Marilyn McCord Adams and Robert Merrihew Adams (Oxford: Oxford University Press, 1990); William Hasker, *God, Time, and Knowledge* (Ithaca, N.Y.: Cornell University Press, 1989), chap. 2; and Richard M. Gale, *On the Nature and Existence of God* (Cambridge: Cambridge University Press, 1991), chap. 4. Middle knowledge is defended by William Lane Craig, *The Only Wise God* (Grand Rapids: Baker, 1987).
8. Alfred J. Freddoso, "Introduction" to Luis de Molina, *On Divine Foreknowledge,* trans. Alfred J. Freddoso (Ithaca, N.Y.: Cornell University Press, 1988), 3. See also William Hasker, "Providence and Evil: Three Theories," *Rel S* (1992): 95–96.

actions thus actualized will be evil actions, but also knows precisely and infallibly the kind, intensity, and incidence of this evil.

On this account God is omniscient and, in particular, he knows not only all counterfactuals of freedom, but also those particular conditionals that are not contrary to fact but that are what happens as a matter of fact, because God chooses to actualize certain individuals to "weakly actualize" them, as Plantinga puts it,[9] by placing them in those conditions.

So since the Holocaust occurred, and (let us suppose) at least some free actions were involved in perpetrating it, we are entitled to conclude that, in actualizing those free actions, God knew perfectly well what would happen, and allowed it to happen, at least if an expression as weak as "allow" is compatible with the weak actualizing activity that Plantinga attributes to God.

In human situations in which one person watches another commit some evil knowing that he is going to commit that evil and supporting him in doing so (when he might have discouraged or prevented him), we are strongly inclined to say that the one who watches shares the responsibility for what happens. Thus if Jones watches while Smith gives an old lady a severe battering after throwing acid in her face, and was able to anticipate from what he knew of Smith that, in that situation, Smith would attack the old lady, and had the power to prevent the attack, then we are strongly inclined to say (in the absence of some factor that at present does not occur to me) that Jones was an accessory to the battering, that he shared responsibility for it. In the divine case matters are, if anything, worse, in that God's knowledge is infallible.

But perhaps we are incorrect to assume that, unlike Jones in our example, God could have prevented what happened. According to the upholders of middle knowledge God certainly could not have interfered with Smith in any way that flouted Smith's free choice. But he was able to act more radically than that, by choosing not to instantiate Smith, but rather to instantiate Smith*. Smith*, instead of freely battering the old lady, freely asked her if she had any letters she needed posting. On Plantinga's view it seems that God could have instantiated Smith*. That is, with full foreknowledge God could have weakly actualized Smith knowing that he would freely choose not to batter the old lady but to help her post some letters. Whether or not the battering of the old lady occurred was up to Smith, but it was also up to God, who chose to actualize Smith knowing what he would freely do. So since what happened was not logically necessary God could have prevented it.

It may be further objected that it is unfair or inaccurate or in some other way improper to think of the God of middle knowledge as sharing responsibility, as being an accessory, as standing back while the old lady is given a battering. It may be said that these expressions have their proper location in

---

9. On weak actualization see Plantinga, *Nature of Necessity*, 173–74.

relations between human beings and not at all in divine-human relations since God, as the Creator and actualizer of the world, is in a unique, incomparable position. I shall return to this objection later.

The Timeless Eternity Solution

I turn from attempts to meet the problem of divine responsibility for moral evil by an appeal to middle knowledge to the invocation of divine timeless eternity. These arguments are not exclusive of each other; there may be versions of the middle-knowledge argument that assume that God exists in time, others that assume that he exists timelessly, Plantinga is on record as inclining to believe that the idea of God's atemporal existence is incoherent.[10]

Proponents of divine timeless eternity such as Aquinas and Boethius offer timeless eternity as a solution to the problem of divine foreknowledge and human freedom. Thus Boethius argues that God's knowledge

embraces all the infinite recesses of past and future and views them in the immediacy of its knowing as though they are happening in the present . . . and if human and divine present may be compared, just as you see certain things in this your present time, so God sees all things in His eternal present. So that this divine foreknowledge does not change the nature and property of things; it simply sees things present to it exactly as they will happen at some time as future events.[11]

As we have noted, some philosophers are doubtful about the cogency of divine timeless eternity[12] just as there are those who argue that timeless eternity is not compatible with libertarian free will.[13]

But let us suppose, for our present purposes, that divine timeless eternity is a cogent concept and that it is compatible with libertarian free will, that it

10. "On Ockham's Way Out," in *The Concept of God*, ed. Thomas V. Morris (Oxford: Oxford University Press, 1987), 176. On the other hand, it is pretty clear that for Molina God's middle knowledge is something that he possesses atemporally. See Freddoso, "Introduction," 30–32.

11. *The Consolation of Philosophy*, trans. V. E. Watts (Hardmondsworth: Penguin, 1969), 165–66.

12. See, for example, Swinburne, *Coherence of Theism*, chap. 12; Anthony Kenny, *The God of the Philosophers* (Oxford: Clarendon, 1979), chap. 4. Defenses of the idea of divine timeless eternity can be found in Eleonore Stump and Norman Kretzmann, "Eternity," in *The Concept of God*; Paul Helm, *Eternal God* (Oxford: Clarendon, 1988), and Brian Leftow, *The Nature of Eternity* (Ithaca, N.Y.: Cornell University Press, 1991).

13. Helm, *Eternal God;* Plantinga, "On Ockham's Way Out." For further discussion see David Widerker, "A Problem for the Eternity Solution," *Int J Ph R* 29, 1 (1991): 87–95.

provides one solution to the vexed charge of that incompatibility. The inconsistency between divine foreknowledge and human libertarian freedom is only apparent, these upholders of timeless eternity argue, because the mode of God's knowledge is such that, being timeless, he does not foreknow anything at all. It is possible to foreknow only if the knower is in time, but God is timelessly eternal.

Then it will follow, among other things, that when Smith blinds and then batters the defenceless widow on 22 March 1885, God timelessly knows that Smith is blinding and battering the widow on that date. Of course, God is not on this view ordaining the battering, since we are assuming that timeless omniscience is compatible with libertarian choice; but God is complicit in the blinding and the battering. We can say, perhaps, that he permits this callous and cowardly attack, and that he could have intervened to prevent it, assuming that the idea of timeless eternity is compatible with God's intervening in time, as most proponents of that view allow.

Despite the appeal to timeless eternity we are once again faced with a whole range of charges that is possible to level against God; that he is an accessory, that he is coresponsible for what takes place, a bystander, and so on. Any epithets that it is possible to hurl at God in the case of middle knowledge it is also possible to hurl at him in the case of timeless knowledge.

Many years ago Jonathan Edwards wrote that

> God's viewing things so perfectly and unchangeably as that there is no succession in his ideas or judgment, don't hinder but that there is properly now, in the mind of God, a certain and perfect knowledge of the moral actions of men, which to us are an hundred years hence. . . . We know, that God knows the future voluntary actions of men in such a sense beforehand, as that he is able particularly to declare, and foretell them, and write them, or cause them to be written down in a book, which he often has done; and that therefore the necessary connection which there is between God's knowledge and the event known, does as much prove the event to be necessary beforehand, as if the divine knowledge were in the same sense before the event, as the prediction or writing is.[14]

We have looked at two important statements of the argument for the compatibility of the existence of an omnipotent, omniscient, and all-good God with human responsibility for sin. Our examination of them should lead us to concur with Edwards's verdict that true knowledge, whether temporal or

---

14. Jonathan Edwards, *The Freedom of the Will* (1754), pt. 2, sect. 12. For a modern discussion of the relation between prophecy and God's timeless eternity from a different perspective than that of Edwards, see Eleonore Stump and Norman Kretzmann, "Prophecy, Past Truth, and Eternity," in *Philosophical Perspectives* 5, ed. James E. Tomberlin (Atascadero, Calif.: Ridgeview, 1991).

eternal, has consequences for human freedom no more or less severe than does divine foreordination.[15]

Omniscience-Denying Arguments

One currently favored way of rebutting the charge that God is the author of evil is to deny that he foreknows the outcome of free human actions. Sometimes the argument is that the future is radically different from the present and the past; that until human actions actually occur that part of the future that depends upon the outcome of such actions cannot be known.[16] More often it is claimed that although God could know the future he has freely chosen not to. Thus Swinburne argues that God voluntarily limits his knowledge:

> In choosing to preserve his own freedom (and to give others freedom), he limits his own knowledge of what is to come. He continually limits himself in this way by not curtailing his or men's future freedom. As regards men, their choices are much influenced by circumstances and this makes it possible for a being who knows all circumstances to predict human behaviour correctly most of the time, but always with the possibility that men may falsify those predictions.[17]

So the picture is that in the interests of freedom, both human and divine freedom, God voluntarily limits his knowledge of the future; since he knows a great deal about the circumstances in which human beings live, he will be able to make many correct predictions of human actions on the basis of this knowledge, though never infallibly.

This ingenious proposal faces a number of difficulties. There is space to mention only three. The first question to be asked is whether it is consistent with what should be a fixed point for Christians, the biblical account of divine omniscience. Is the idea of God curtailing his knowledge biblical? Does not God know the end from the beginning? Is he not acquainted with all our ways? But even if it could be argued that such a view is consistent with the

---

15. In "God's Responsibility for Sin," in *Divine and Human Action,* ed. Thomas V. Morris (Ithaca, N.Y.: Cornell University Press, 1988). William E. Mann claims that, given a number of plausible theses regarding the nature of God's will (for example, that any actual situation that God knows he also wills), it follows that God is causally responsible for human sins (200) and argues that (as far as theodicy is concerned) such a view fares no worse than rival views that emphasize God's permission (206).

16. A. N. Prior, "The Formalities of Omnisciency," *Papers on Time and Tense* (Oxford: Clarendon, 1968).

17. Swinburne, *Coherence of Theism,* 176.

biblical fixed points, it faces difficulties that are parallel with those noted in discussing the earlier views.

According to Swinburne, God does not have infallible knowledge, but he predicts the future correctly for most of the time. But if this is true, then God knows for most of the time what evil his free creatures will get up to, and permits it. It is hard to see how God can in these circumstances be freed from some responsibility for that evil. But what is even more serious, think of the enormity of the responsibility that God bears in freely choosing ignorance. If, knowing that Smith is about to attack the old lady, Jones freely chooses to look the other way, is he not a heartless accessory to what happens?

We have surveyed a number of arguments, some of which have been and all of which could be used to show, that, given libertarian freedom, human beings are responsible for evil and God is not. Perhaps we should conclude that on any arrangement in which God has omniscience he is going to be responsible in some sense for all that takes place within it; and postulating middle knowledge, as Plantinga does, or timeless eternity, or voluntary ignorance hardly lessens this. Indeed perhaps such stratagems increase it, for on Plantinga's hypothesis God is actualizing possible individuals whom he foreknows will do evil, and yet chooses to go ahead. And if, with Swinburne, we think of God as not being omniscient, but instead limiting his knowledge of the future, this hardly helps in removing responsibility from God.

But maybe we are mistaken in drawing this conclusion. Perhaps there is reason to think that God is nonetheless exonerated from responsibility. But if this is so, then he is also exonerated from responsibility even when he foreordains whatever comes to pass. So the issue is not a black-and-white one, with the advocate of divine foreordination being Mr. Black and the advocate of libertarian freedom being Mr. White.

In closing this chapter, I shall consider one objection to the claim that there is a significant parallel between the appeal to divine foreknowledge and the appeal to divine foreordination as regards human evil.

It might be said that the denial of human libertarian freedom makes matters worse, for on such a view God is not merely knowingly allowing some morally evil state of affairs, but is positively ordaining it.

But it is surely a plain matter of fact that there is a significant difference between ordaining evil and doing evil. To begin with, it is clear that the ordaining of the Holocaust and the perpetrating of it are two distinct acts. So that in ordaining that Hitler bring about the Holocaust, God did not do what Hitler did, and necessarily did not do it, because Hitler planned the Holocaust in his own evil mind and for his own evil ends.[18] Surely God's

18. For brief discussion of this see Hasker, "Providence and Evil: Three Theories," 93–94. Cf. Mann, "God's Responsibility for Sin," 207–9, who argues that while God brings about evil he does not do evil.

relation to Hitler is rather like his relation to the Assyrian as outlined in Isaiah 10:5–14.

Further, not only did God not directly bring about the Holocaust, he necessarily did not do so, because necessarily God is distinct from Hitler. So not only did God not directly bring about the Holocaust (although he ordained it), but he could not have directly brought it about.

There may be reasons for ordaining evil that are not reasons for doing evil. This also seems to be obvious, and to follow from the first point. Hitler's motives for ordering the Holocaust are in broad terms well-known; his desire to exterminate the Jews and to establish an Aryan master race by force. Not only is there absolutely no evidence that God had such reasons in ordaining the Holocaust, but God could not have had such reasons, since such reasons are necessarily evil and God cannot be tempted to do evil, much less do it.

What seems clear, if God ordained Hitler's evil Holocaust, is that in doing so God had other ends in view than Hitler did. And to those acquainted with the Bible this is a familiar idea. In sending Joseph into Egypt, his brothers performed an evil act. But God meant it for good (Gen. 45:5, 7). In sending the Assyrian, God was punishing his people, but the Assyrian was aiming at political domination (Isa. 10:11). In ordaining the crucifixion of Christ the authorities were performing an evil act, the punishing of the innocent, but in ordaining this by his own determinate counsel and foreknowledge, God had other ends in view.

But it might be claimed that this is too quick a solution. If God, in ordaining the evil acts of Hitler, did not have Hitler's evil ends, but necessarily had other, high, and holy ends, then if God is not directly implicated in the event, is he not indirectly implicated and guilty of ordaining evil that good may come? Is this not a case of the end justifying the means?

Let us suppose that it is. But then it will not have escaped notice that precisely the same accusation can be made in the case of those other views of divine and human responsibility that we considered earlier, views that depend upon human libertarian freedom. For these views say that in giving men and women libertarian free will God was permitting evil, or at least permitting the risk of evil, in order to produce a universe in which men and women made morally significant choices. And surely in these circumstances God would be indirectly implicated in the evil that occurs. He permitted evil for a good reason.

Is God, who ordains everything that comes to pass, tainted with evil, then? Yes, in a sense he is. But it needs to be remembered that as it is used here "taint" is a metaphor. God is not tainted with evil as some fish are tainted with mercury. And God is no more nor less tainted under these assumptions than he is tainted with evil by choosing not to know what his free creatures will do, or by choosing to actualize possible persons knowing that they will freely do evil, or by having timelessly eternal knowledge of human evil. Such, at least, is what I have tried to argue.

Index of Persons

Index of Subjects

Hell, 295
Holiness, 163, 167, 300, 394
Holocaust, 496–97
Holy Spirit, 54, 219, 246, 292, 347, 391, 469
    Arminius on, 260–61
    assurance and, 394–95
    inner witness, 411n
    partaking of, 147–48, 153
Hope, 157–58, 166
Humility, 408

Illumination, 373, 375–76
Image of God, 76, 81, 481
Imputation, 306–9
Incompatibilism, 463–70, 473
Indeterminism, 463–70
Indicative and imperative, 77, 247
Individuality, 474
Inferential knowledge, 439–40, 445, 446
Infralapsarianism, 253–54
Instrumental cause, 228
Introversion, 404
Intuitive knowledge, 441–43
Irresistible grace, 20, 280, 339–40, 346–47, 352n, 356. *See also* Effectual calling
Islam, 315
Israel
    covenant relationship with God, 193
    election, 27n
    hardening of heart, 115–16
    historical destiny, 90–98, 105
    salvation of, 90–98, 105
    wilderness wandering, 160–61, 172, 174

Jesus
    atonement, 423
    blood, 178
    as Bread of life, 348–51
    death, 52, 111–12, 358, 360–61, 377–78, 488–89
    election, 53, 102–3, 341–43
    as fulfillment of promises, 237–38
    natures, 102, 408, 412
    sovereignty, 239
    submission to the Father, 239–40
    teaching on election, 50–53, 54–55

    as wisdom of God, 239, 361
Judas Iscariot, 396
Justification, 70, 135–37, 153, 300, 306–9, 361–62, 385, 386, 420
    assurance and, 409

Kingdom of God, 77, 163

Law
    Calvin on, 288
    written on hearts, 162
Libertarian free will, 463
Liberty of indifference, 449
Liberty of spontaneity, 449
Logic, 103–4, 124n, 379
Lordship salvation, 389
Love, 166, 410, 413–14
    election and, 72n, 109
    foreknowledge and, 191–92, 319
    of God, 15, 412
Lutheranism, 191n, 255, 423

Manicheanism, 279
Maturity, 151–52
Mercy, 281
Middle knowledge, 19, 20, 184, 258, 265–69, 277, 429–57, 490–92, 493
Minutes Controversy, 309–10
Miracles, 212
Missions, 20, 323–26
Modified rationalism, 481–82
Moravians, 298, 300
Mystery, 81, 438, 463

Natural liberty, 190n
Natural theology, 371
Nature, and divine sovereignty, 210–12
Necessary knowledge, 264, 268
Necessitarianism, 271
Neo-Arminianism, 124n, 343n
Neo-Platonism, 279
Neo-Socinianism, 198
New covenant, 121, 162, 167, 168, 393–95, 398, 412
New Hampshire Confession of Faith, 334
Nihilism, 233
Noninferential knowledge, 437–38, 441–43

Obedience, 167, 171, 385, 388–89, 410

Index of Scripture

517